WITHDRAWN
University of
Reading Library

90 0818713 8

7 DAY

Memory and Nation Building

Memory and Nation Building

From Ancient Times to the Islamic State

Michael L. Galaty

ROWMAN & LITTLEFIELD
Lanham • Boulder • New York • London

Published by Rowman & Littlefield
An imprint of The Rowman & Littlefield Publishing Group, Inc.
4501 Forbes Boulevard, Suite 200, Lanham, Maryland 20706
www.rowman.com

Unit A, Whitacre Mews, 26-34 Stannary Street, London SE11 4AB

Copyright © 2018 by The Rowman & Littlefield Publishing Group, Inc.

All rights reserved. No part of this book may be reproduced in any form or by any electronic or mechanical means, including information storage and retrieval systems, without written permission from the publisher, except by a reviewer who may quote passages in a review.

British Library Cataloguing in Publication Information Available

Library of Congress Cataloging-in-Publication Data

Names: Galaty, Michael L., author.
Title: Memory and nation building : from ancient times to the Islamic state / Michael L. Galaty.
Description: Lanham, Maryland : Rowman & Littlefield, [2018] | Includes bibliographical references and index.
Identifiers: LCCN 2018011818 (print) | LCCN 2018029454 (ebook) | ISBN 9780759122628 (Electronic) | ISBN 9780759122604 (cloth : alk. paper)
Subjects: LCSH: Nationalism and collective memory—Case studies. | Collective memory—Political aspects—Case studies. | State, The—Case studies.
Classification: LCC JC311 (ebook) | LCC JC311 .G2225 2018 (print) | DDC 320.1—dc23
LC record available at https://lccn.loc.gov/2018011818

∞™ The paper used in this publication meets the minimum requirements of American National Standard for Information Sciences—Permanence of Paper for Printed Library Materials, ANSI/NISO Z39.48-1992.

Printed in the United States of America

In memory of Liam
I will never forget you

The actual past is brittle, ever-dimming + ever more problematic to access + reconstruct: in contrast, the virtual past is malleable, ever-brightening + ever more difficult to circumvent/expose as fraudulent.

The present presses the virtual past into its own service, to lend credence to its mythologies + legitimacy to the imposition of will. Power seeks + is the right to "landscape" the virtual past. (He who pays the historian calls the tune.)

Symmetry demands an actual + virtual future, *too. We imagine how next week, next year, or 2225 will shape up—a virtual future, constructed by wishes, prophecies, + daydreams. This virtual future may influence the actual future, as in a self-fulfilling prophecy, but the actual future will eclipse our virtual one as surely as tomorrow eclipses today.*

David Mitchell, *Cloud Atlas*, 2004: 392–93

Contents

Acknowledgments	ix
List of Figures and Tables	xi
Prologue: Bosnia	xiii
Preface: Memory: An Effort After Meaning	xix
1 Introduction: Collective Memory Defined	1
2 Egypt: Unification	33
3 Greece: Diversification	65
4 Albania: Adaptation	99
5 Conclusion: All These Memories Have Gone	133
Epilogue: Alabama	159
Bibliography	165
Index	197

Acknowledgments

This book was a long time coming. I would, therefore, like to thank, first and foremost, the various editors with whom I have worked. They showed real patience.

Various colleagues, including Sylvia Deskaj, Wayne Lee, and Robert Schon, read draft chapters. For their input and advice, I am grateful. Any mistakes are, of course, my own.

Many of the ideas developed in this book were presented to the faculty at the University of Arizona in a Distinguished Lecture in Archaeology and to the students in Schon's graduate seminar on statecraft. I would like to thank them for their spirited discussions regarding collective memory and the origins of states.

I would like to further acknowledge the financial support I have received from various institutions, including Millsaps College, Mississippi State University, and the University of Michigan, without which this writing project would not have begun, continued, and come to completion.

Finally, thanks to my Egyptian guides, Tarek Yahia and Ahmed "Friday" Gomaa. They inspired me with their dedication to Egypt's past despite difficult times.

List of Figures and Tables

FIGURES

Prologue, Image 1.	xiv
Prologue, Image 2.	xv
Prologue, Image 3.	xvii
Prologue, Image 4.	xviii
Figure 1.1. The cultural fields of doxa and opinion	20
Figure 1.2. Two models of collective memory production based on the changing input of six interacting cultural variables and their effect on the fields of doxa and opinion	24
Figure 1.3. Chart demonstrating the positive relationship between political control and collective memory	30
Figure 2.1. Cavafy's bedroom, Alexandria, Egypt	34
Figure 2.2. Map of Egypt with sites mentioned in the text	41
Figure 2.3. Chart depicting Egyptian religious structures and the decline in accessibility across space and through time	45
Figure 3.1. The Treasury of Atreus, Mycenae, Greece	66
Figure 3.2. Map of Greece with sites mentioned in the text	74

Figure 4.1.	Boundary Stone, Theth, Shala	100
Figure 4.2.	Map of Albania with sites mentioned in the text	106
Figure 4.3.	Ceremoni Vorrimi ne Dukagjin [Funeral Ceremony in the Dukagjin]	122
Figure 4.4.	Zoje Mustafa–Vajtojce nga Dukagjini [Lady Mustafa–Wailer from Dukagjin]	124
Figure 4.5.	Dorezimi Armeve (Kaipten Mark Raka dhe Bajraktari i Shales) [Surrendering Arms (Captain Mark Rapa and the Bajraktar of Shala)]	128
Figure 4.6.	Carved Hellenistic block from the destroyed Church of St. Ilias, Shtyllas, Albania	130
Figure 5.1.	Philae temple	138
Figure 5.2.	Destroyed village of Qurna, near Valley of the Kings, Egypt	140
Figure 5.3.	Luxor, Egypt	141
Figure 5.4.	Graph of nation-states and periods discussed, arranged along a political-mnemonic scale from weak to strong, depicting varying life spans, created with reference to figure 1.3, producing a "normal" distribution	156
Epilogue, Image 1.		160
Epilogue, Image 2.		161
Epilogue, Image 3.		162
Epilogue, Image 4.		163
Epilogue, Image 5.		164

TABLES

Table 2.1.	Egyptian Chronology	39
Table 3.1.	Greek Chronology	72
Table 4.1.	Albanian Chronology	105

Prologue
Bosnia

Slavonski Brod, Croatia. December 17, 2012. 8:00 a.m. Destination: Sarajevo. 34 degrees F. Memory: fog. Our French rental car slips through the gloom, out into the countryside, heading south. Cold, wet, muddy. Patches of stale snow. Buildings old and new float in and out of view. A broken-down barn. A cinder-block house. Bus by cart, truck by bicycle. Sylvia honks the horn and sheep scatter. An old woman dressed in black flips her switch and watches us go. Fog curls around her body, wraps her in gray. Fleeting, indistinct, hazy. I smell dust.

We rumble over a bridge. The Sava River. Ahead of us march mothers and children, holding hands; stout young women in tight jeans; old men in wool suits. Memory: the border. A Cold War relic, an insult to the new Europe. A symbol of bureaucracy, and state control. A Croatian guard leans from his booth: *Dobar dan*. Good day. He extends his hand, we surrender our passports—Bam! Bam!—and pull away. The line to get into Bosnia is long. We slow to a halt. Sylvia points. I look. A flag, but the wrong flag. Three stripes: red, blue, white. *"Welcome to the Republika Srpska."* The car idles and we watch pedestrians come and go, from one new? nation? to another? Horse's hooves: clip clop, clip clop, clip clop.

A large male guard. Gray hair, yellow teeth, tired eyes, bad breath. Gun in holster, hat on head, badge on hat. *Dobar dan*. Sylvia hands him our passports. He wants our car papers, too. He steps into his booth. Sylvia frowns. I frown. The guard frowns. Two Americans . . . a man and a woman . . . the woman is an Albanian from Kosovo, a Muslim . . . going to visit family in Sarajevo . . . in a French rental car. *Oprostite*. I'm sorry. . . . Is he? Sylvia doesn't think so. I'm not so sure. Fuck borders. Fuck bureaucracy. Fuck the

xiv *Prologue*

state. We turn the car around, and drive back toward Croatia. A Croatian guard looks up from his newspaper, nods and smiles. Sylvia shrugs her shoulders: *Republika Srpska*. Guard, in broken English: There is no *Republika Srpska*, only *Bosna*. Back across the Sava, back to the highway, running against the human stream. What happened to Yugoslavia? Where did it go?

Image 1.

Prologue

Županja, Croatia. December 17, 2012. 12:00 p.m. Destination: Sarajevo. 32 degrees F. Still foggy. Failed at Slavonski Brod, now driving east on the A3 to the next border crossing. A new town. Different guards. The Croatians stamp our passports and wave us through. We approach Bosnia, again. *Republika Srpska*, again. This time, the guard is a young woman. Same gun, same cap, same badge. Same frown. Our car papers are not in order. Sylvia: Please. Guard: *Ne*. No. It is not possible. (The rallying cry of all civil servants everywhere.) Sylvia: Please. We drove all the way from Paris. Guard: *Ne*. Sylvia: *Molim*. Please. Memory: her eyes. You are Bosnian! she exclaims. Sylvia: *Da*. Yes. I am going to Sarajevo to see my *dajdža*, my mother's brother. The guard stares at us for a moment, then leaves. She confers with her fellow guards, in whispers, with glances. She returns: You may go, but you must cross at this border crossing tomorrow after 7:00 p.m., after my shift begins. We will, we promise. Kinship trumps law. Tribe conquers state. Into the *Republika Srpska* we go.

Signs of war remain. Burned out buildings. Bullet holes in houses. Warning! This field is mined. The Dayton Accords ended the war, but could not put Bosnia back together again. We drive through small, forgotten towns. People stare as we pass. Ghosts in the fog. Sylvia is nervous; relatives of hers died in the war. We stop for coffee at a gas station. A woman looks up from a nap. The café is closed, but she'll make coffee for us anyway. Balkan hospitality. She is old beyond her years. Memory: a

Image 2.

wrinkled face. She brings our coffee in tiny cups, rimmed with gold. We invite her to join us. Sylvia offers her a cigarette. She accepts. We sit silently, in the cold, damp room, and sip our coffee. She coughs, a smoker's cough. Détente. We have made our peace with *Republika Srpska*.

Sarajevo, Bosnia. December 17, 2012. 5:00 p.m. 32 degrees F. Still foggy. We pass through the mountains beyond Tuzla and into the city. A city of mosques and cemeteries, saints and martyrs. A city groaning under its own historical weight. This is where the Great War began. Memory: an Olympic flame. Memory: gunshots. Sylvia's uncle lives in the hills to the west, so we cut straight through downtown. The roads narrow, the traffic growls, and we are spit out the other side, onto a grand boulevard. I imagine (remember?) tanks rolling through the streets.

Bosnia and Herzegovina has a problem. It is a nation in name only. A country composed of two, non-integrated political "entities": the Federation of Bosnia and Herzegovina and the Republika Srpska. Ethnic conflict runs deep and three religions—Catholicism, Orthodoxy, and Islam—vie for control. Despite a shared language and regional history, Bosnians have not forged a new national identity. The national psyche is yet dominated by traumatic memories of the war: Srebrenica and the siege of Sarajevo, detention camps, rape, ethnic cleansing.

Enter the Bosnian pyramids. They were "discovered" in the town of Visoko in 2005. Pyramids of the Sun and Moon, the Earth, the (Bosnian) Dragon, and Love. Archaeologists and geologists who have visited Visoko have roundly denounced the pyramids as "a cruel hoax, perpetrated on an unsuspecting public." Nevertheless, a national park was created and "excavations" commenced. The pyramids were said to be 14,000 years old, the oldest and largest monumental structures in the world. At over 200 meters in height, the Pyramid of the Sun would thus be "the mother of all pyramids" and Bosnia the font of civilization. Meanwhile, real archaeological sites in Visoko are being destroyed by the digging and the federal budget for archaeology, already paltry, has been directed to the Bosnian Pyramid of the Sun Foundation. On October 4, 2012, the National Museum of Bosnia and Herzegovina closed its doors after 125 years of operation.

We spent a relaxing evening with Sylvia's family. We ate dinner together. She dispersed presents. I slept soundly that night, straight through to morning, and awoke to find snow, lots of snow. Still falling. We would have to take a less direct, less mountainous, route back to Županja for our 7:00 p.m. appointment. Straight through Visoko. Right by the pyramids.

Visoko, Bosnia. December 18, 2012. 11:00 a.m. 32 degrees F. Still foggy. Snowing. Destination: Zagreb. The town is old, pretty, wrapped in white. A wild river runs through it.

Image 3.

We drive slowly down the main street and immediately spot signs for the pyramids. Official signs, for tourists. The Pyramid of the Sun, dead ahead. We park in a small lot and cross the street, through slush. A shape, a form, indistinct, looms above houses. Shrouded in cloud. A pyramid? A hill. We climb up to its base. The wind blows. Big flakes fall. Not much to see.

Across the road is the Pyramid of the Moon. A small visitor center has been constructed, but is closed for the winter. A large structure floats in the distance, on the horizon. A pyramid? A hill. We head into town for lunch, to the old bazaar. We want to eat pyramid-shaped ćevapi (sausages) at the Ramses Café, but can't find it. Maybe it has closed. We settle for normal ćevapi and they are excellent. All around us are bizarre images of Maya pyramids, but we can find no pyramid souvenirs. No T-shirts ("I Visited the Bosnian Pyramids!"), no paperweights. Perhaps pyramid fever has run its course. Memories: a medieval castle, a battle, a nation born. Tvrtko, the first Bosnian king, a charter, a crown. People go about their business, unaware.

The Bosnian Pyramid of the Sun, or something like it, was inevitable. Actual Bosnian history is insufficient, too charged, too divisive. A virtual

Image 4.

Bosnian history had to be created, one that is neutral, expansive, usable. Why think small? When you have experienced nothing but pain and loss, failure and heartbreak, why not go big? Be the font of civilization.

The main point. The idea of the pyramids, the idea of Bosnian primacy, came from the people. The recaptured "memories" of an exceptional Bosnian past challenge the orthodox understandings of the nation's history, both distant and recent. A new nostalgic cultural imaginary is born. Tapping ancestral memories that predate ethnic division, reclaiming a glorious "Illyrian" past. The narrative is good, it resonates. So good, in fact, that the Bosnian state had to co-opt it. But memories, like fog, like snow, melt away, leaving cold dead space. A nation cannot be built on air.

Županja, Croatia. December 18, 2012. 7:18 p.m. 32 degrees F. Clear skies. Destination: Zagreb. We have no problem leaving Bosnia. The guard stamps our passports and waves us through. The Croatians, on the other hand, search our car. We've crossed in and out of their country three times in two days. We claim to be archaeologists, but we might be smugglers. The customs agent finds nothing of interest, so we repack our bags and go.

Memory: headlights cut the dark.

Preface

Memory: An Effort After Meaning

> It is fitting to speak of every human cognitive reaction—perceiving, imaging, remembering, thinking and reasoning—as an *effort after meaning*.
> (Bartlett 1932: 44, italics in the original)

Memory matters. Human cultural behavior is impossible without it. As individuals, we depend on our ability to remember in all aspects of our daily lives. But memory facilitates social organization, as well. To form viable communities, we must be able to remember together, and thereby form collective visions of shared pasts and possible futures.

Despite decades of research, however, we still do not know exactly how individual humans create, preserve, and retrieve memories. Nor do we know exactly how human groups construct cultural memories. What we do know now, or at least suspect, is that these two processes are somehow linked: the cognitive act of individual remembering is culturally conditioned, and the cultural act of social remembering depends on cognition.

This book addresses the links between human cognition and group behavior. In some ways it constitutes a "positivist" response to Olivier (2012). In it, I demonstrate that the bridge connecting cognition to behavior is memory. My approach is diachronic and comparative, and it crosses cultures. I trace the practice of collective memory making through time in three different regions—Egypt, Greece, and Albania—and show that memory was deployed in similar ways in all three from prehistory to the present. Comparative analysis indicates that controlling the past was an important—perhaps the most important—strategy in the formation of early states, and that manipulation of the past remains central to modern nation building. And yet, it is unclear whether today's interconnected, digital world renders controlling and manipulating the past more or less difficult. Have its bonds been broken, or will the "tyranny of memory" be forever with us (Nora as quoted in Erll 2011: 25)?

THE ORGANIZATION OF THIS BOOK

In this book I explore five interconnected ideas related to memory.

Collective memory is necessary to human cultural behavior. It drives social history and creates social solidarity. From the family to empires, social groups demand shared understandings of a common past, whether real or fabricated. These "regimes of memory" (Hodgkin and Radstone 2006) help determine individual social roles—they help mold social-subjective selves—but also set social-structural limits. In chapter 1 I first define collective memory (*vis-à-vis* "culture" and cultural memory), and then present an explanatory model, which shows how societies generate collective memories, and why. The model is tested in subsequent chapters in three different contexts: in Egypt, Greece, and Albania. A diachronic, comparative approach demonstrates that collective memories function similarly through time in different places: that is, they are constructed (i.e., mediated, situational), imperfect representations of reality, but therefore malleable (and contestable), and if usable, retained. Those memories that are not usable, or that lack traction, are forgotten. They are let go. In this way, cultural remembering (and forgetting) is much like individual remembering (and forgetting). Indeed, I argue that the former is a manifestation of the latter, that collective memory is subject to biological limits imposed by human neurophysiology.

Collective memory is a product of individual memory. Individual human beings store and retrieve memories through various neurological processes, many of which are still poorly understood, despite the advent of powerful imaging tools, like MRIs. Experimental research indicates that we gather sensory data related to memory selectively and that storage of these data is distributed throughout the brain depending on type. Not everything we see, hear, smell, touch, or taste is committed to memory, short- or long-term. Additionally, sensory data that are committed to long-term memory may fade; they are not permanent. Individuals who cannot forget are in fact incapable of normal cognitive functioning. Recall is prompted by cues or triggers. Once triggered, a memory is assembled from its various constituent parts. This process is not perfect, and so memories may be imprecise. They are created to serve particular emotional or functional needs and are not necessarily faithful reconstructions of the past. In chapter 1, having defined and discussed collective memory, I explore in more detail collective versus individual memory making. A collective memory is very much like an individual human memory. The former is, however, a function of the latter, and is therefore subject to the same limits. This is not mere analogy or metaphor (see Erll 2011: 96–101); rather I assert that collective memories are identical in form and function to individual human memories precisely because they are products of individual human brains, working in concert. Like humans, social organisms have devised means to record, process, and elicit memories, which depend on similarly complex systems of "parallel processing" (Schacter 1996: 9).

Collective memories are made in simple societies via oral history, through veneration of the dead, and in response to various mnemonic devices. Prior to the appearance of writing, human groups recorded collective memories orally, in several different distributed, narrative forms (e.g., through the recitation of kinship lines; via the telling of stories and origin myths; and by invoking tradition, particularly at times of ritual importance). All of these so-called communicative memories (Assmann 2008), though increasingly rare in today's world, still take place, in some shape or form, in many family groups, as well as in larger communities, thereby providing a sense of group identity. Group identity is typically linked to shared ancestry, traced through common descent, often marked by the veneration of ancestors. In many cultures, ancestral memory is encoded in burial grounds and/or through mortuary practices. In some cultures, bodies of the dead, or body parts, are employed as memory cues, mnemonic devices that encourage (often nostalgic) recollection of important people and past events. Likewise, important landmarks may prompt cultural remembering, in particular when people move through the landscape and occupy important places. Finally, simple societies may employ ritual practices that help preserve collective memories and support tradition. Ritual behaviors in simple societies are typically performed and participatory; they are experienced and embodied. These multiple "simple," but ultimately powerful, memory regimes mitigated against changes in social complexity leading to state formation. They encoded group histories that often ran counter to official, state-sponsored histories. State officials could not integrate non-state human communities without dislodging and/or harnessing traditional forms of collective memory making, but these were distributed throughout and across various social subsystems, making them resilient, adaptive, and not easily changed.

In order to form and function, states must control collective "cultural" memories, which are used to create a shared sense of national identity. A state can be defined in general terms as a form of government that relies on internally specialized and hierarchically organized decision-making systems. States are large, integrating thousands, sometimes millions, of people, and they typically benefit a small upper class, who manage the economy. Order is maintained by force and legitimized through new, formal religious ideologies. The first states appeared about 5,000 years ago, in places like Mesopotamia and Egypt. State systems now dominate all other forms of political organization. One key question is why, after millions of years of egalitarian social organization, humans would allow institutionalized social inequalities to form. I contend that the transition to social inequality, and state systems of government, was facilitated in trans-egalitarian communities by destabilizing traditional, localized regimes of collective memory. The first step in this process involved changing the ways in which individuals related to each other, in extended kin groups, through lineage, and via ancestor worship. Domestic religious practices were relocated from house to temple, and formalized. Oral memory systems were replaced by written ones, made subject to divine law, and placed under the control of priests and scribes. Family and tribe were subsumed by nation, and this required building national identities. New forms of collective—in Assmann's (2008) terms, "cultural"—memory, based on written history, were turned to this purpose. Monumental works of propagandistic art were inserted into the landscape, and state-sponsored religious rituals and festivals were created. However, as I describe in more detail below, despite the success of the nation-state, traditional memory regimes survived, and provide alternatives to official, sanctioned memory regimes.

Resistance to the state was/is effected by creating counter memories. State-sponsored collective memories are typically taken as real or actual representations of the past. Because they are constructed and turned to a purpose—creating national identity—they are often exclusionary, designed to build national unity by identifying those groups that do not fit. Targeted, marginalized groups may resist official, national memories and histories by deploying "counter-memories" and "counter-histories" (Foucault 1980). Counter-memorial and -historical narratives often evolve along a nation's edges. They may appear and disappear, but sometimes they may work to challenge "orthodox" memory discourses and produce meaningful, even revolutionary, change. Mapping this dynamic process helps explain how collective memories form and evolve through time, and defines the roles individual agents may play in driving historical change. It highlights the importance of the state in maintaining formal, dogmatic memory regimes as well as the complicity of memory workers, such as archaeologists, who help construct national pasts. In recent years many countries have built heritage industries, which generate income, but also support and reinforce collective memory making and national identities (Anheier and Isar 2011; Benton 2010). Consequently, heritage resource management can be defined as "memory work" and is vital to modern nation-building projects.

Based on these five ideas, in chapter 1 of this book I devise a general explanatory model that addresses the connections between collective memory making and political control in nation-states. In chapters 2 through 4, I test the model against three cases, Egypt, Greece, and Albania, and compare their experiences of collective memory and counter-memory production from prehistoric to modern times. Egypt, Greece, and Albania each evince different historical trajectories and experiences of state formation through time, despite their common Mediterranean ancestry. Egypt is one of the world's primary states and so it may be used to discuss and demonstrate the effects of memory on primary state formation. The importance of religion and the cult of the dead in the transition from trans-egalitarian to state-level societies is particularly evident for ancient Egypt. In fact, as I will show, changing contexts of death and burial have affected memory systems in all three cases, right down to the present. Additionally, all three regions were connected as early as the Bronze Age via Mediterranean Sea trade, which facilitated the creation of "transcultural" memory systems (Erll 2011: 65–66). As a result, it should not be surprising that memory regimes in all three regions bear many, not insignificant, similarities. Furthermore, all three regions experienced Ottoman conquest and imperial incorporation. Consequently, variation in collective memory making in all three nations in modern times stems from their differential experiences of Ottoman administration. Generally speaking, the Ottoman Empire preferred to exercise mild forms of political control in conquered territories, making it somewhat of an outlier compared to other state-level political systems. Conquered peoples were allowed to maintain their traditional ethnic and religious identities, though they were often penalized for it. This opened up some space for counter-memory production, which spurred resistance movements in all three regions. Interestingly, Ottoman imperial practices induced different long-term responses in all three nations, each of which consequently deployed different memory-control strategies in modern times, post-independence. Understanding the reasons for these quite different, cross-regional responses to memory is an important goal of this book, and these will be summarized in chapter 5. Analysis of collective memory behavior in Egypt, Greece, and Albania provides the means to anticipate and explain the sometimes unexpected and confusing behaviors of various non-state actors, like the Islamic State, that currently work to become nation-states. In the end, then, this book is as much about the origins and past of states as it is about their continued existence and future, one that depends significantly on how collective memories are made, stored, and assigned meaning in a post-modern, digital age.

1

Introduction
Collective Memory Defined

The concept of collective memory has a short, and checkered, history in the social sciences (Misztal 2003). Its origins can be traced to the French sociologist Maurice Halbwachs, who was a student of Emile Durkheim, and died at Buchenwald in 1945. The book for which he is best known, *Les cadres sociaux de la mémoire*, was first published in 1925, and in English translation in 1992. Halbwachs (1992; see also 1980) believed that collective memories are generated, and preserved, through human interactions, and possess an existence that is separate from, yet dependent upon, individual human memories. In effect, there can be no individual memories without collective memory, and vice versa (Halbwachs 1980: 34, 44–49). Verbal conventions form the primary basis for shared memory (Halbwachs 1992: 45), but the main loci for "traditional" forms of collective memory making were families and their homes, within which children were socialized and ancestors worshiped (Halbwachs 1992: chapter 5). However, in Halbwach's (1992: chapter 6) estimation, collective memory had been slowly, perhaps inevitably, co-opted by other, more complex institutions, like organized religions. He described, for example, the shift in early Christianity from oral testimony, based on eye-witness accounts of the life and death of Jesus, to written history (Halbwachs 1941). But he also noted that for the Gospels to be accepted as true representations of the past, they had to be verifiable; the places associated with Jesus had to be located in the landscape (Halbwachs 1980: chapter 4, 1992: 198–99). Halbwachs (1941) tested these ideas by analyzing the construction, by pilgrims and crusaders, of the Holy Land as a Christian landscape, and a key source of medieval collective memories, necessary to the creation of European nations. His work was strongly influenced by the *annaliste* historians (Alcock 2002: 24; Coser 1992: 11), who subsequently adopted the idea of collective memory from him (e.g., Le Goff 1992). Thus, from the beginning, collective memory was tied by Halbwachs to space, across time.

Halbwach's concept of collective memory was, and is, controversial. Many scholars, including some sociologists, continue to deny its existence or consider it epiphenomenal, the ambiguous, secondary product of individual human memories. With some exceptions (e.g., Schacter 1996), the psychological approach to memory remains "materialist" and reductionist; memories are made by neurotransmitters and reside in the brain (Coleman 1992: 600–602). Some scholars, historians in particular, admit that something like collective memory must exist, but are unsure how "public" memory structures might be erected and maintained through the accretion of seemingly disconnected, "private" individual beliefs. As Funkenstein (1993: 6) has written, "Just as a nation cannot eat or dance, neither can it speak or remember" (see also Alcock 2002: 15).

For most anthropologists, including archaeologists, collective memories are thought to form just like any other cultural product. Simply put, individual human beliefs and actions produce separate and "real" social structures, which organize human behavior and persist, through enculturation and transmission, despite the death of individual humans. Following Geertz (e.g., 1973), most anthropologists now believe that human behavior, including memory, is biologically determined but individually variable, culturally constructed, and relative. Thus (*contra* Funkenstein 1993: 6), all humans have the anatomical capacity for dance, but how and why they dance depends on a suite of rules and conventions—structures—communicated from generation to generation. For Geertz and other "interpretive" anthropologists (e.g., Cohen 1985), the challenge is not merely to describe these structures, but to situate them symbolically, attach significance, and thereby understand them and their effects. Given this approach to human behavior, it is almost impossible to avoid the fundamental role played by memory in creating culture (Cohen 1985: 98–103). It defines what matters, what is possible and allowable, where to act and when. It socializes the individual, legitimizes the collective, and justifies continuity, linking now and then, here and there, the living and the dead, through chains of ancestral relationship. These connections to the past, to our ancestors, make us human and give life meaning.

Collective memory can thus be defined as: *a symbolic, social-structural system that situates cultural behaviors in space and time by linking them to a constructed past.* As such, collective memory making is but one cultural behavior among many, albeit an exceedingly important one. Collective memories are essential to the proper functioning of culture, but they are not the same as, or co-terminus with, "culture" writ large. My definition of collective memory is more expansive than that of Halbwachs (1992), and similar to Assmann's (2008) definition of "cultural" memory. Collective (i.e., cultural) memory systems function in *all* cultures, small and large, simple to complex, past and present. However, whereas cultural behaviors tend to be tacitly and unconsciously formed and transmitted, collective memories can be, and often are, overtly defined and promulgated. They provide individuals with powerful means to shape and direct culture to particular ends, with sometimes dramatic results.

My definition of collective memory emphasizes certain key characteristics. Collective memory is constructed: the "actual" historical past (the past that really happened) is truly past, and to a large extent, irrelevant. It is inaccessible, a "foreign country" (Lowenthal 1985). As such, collective memories may be turned to various political needs (Bradley 2003: 223). They are "virtual" and may be entirely false. For this reason, collective forgetting is just as important as collective remembering (Van Dyke and Alcock 2003: 2). Through selective forgetting, groups fashion a past for themselves. They create "memory communities" (Alcock 2002: 15), each associated with different memory regimes. These may sometimes clash, leading to memory conflicts. As a result, collective memories may change or be changed to meet the needs of the group.

Collective memory thus situates human behavior in space and time, thereby giving it meaning, and it was the *cadre matériel*—the "material framework"—that provided the stuff, the supporting lattice, upon which collective memories were built, as when Christians followed the Way of the Cross (the *Via Dolorosa*) in Jerusalem (Halbwachs 1941). Despite the fundamental importance of the *cadre matériel*, Halbwachs (1992) tended to deemphasize the lived experience of remembering. Rather, this issue has been addressed by phenomenologists (e.g., Casey 1987), who frequently evoke the power of "place" and "things" to provoke individual, and therefore collective, remembering (e.g., Casey 1987: 181–215). A place gains symbolic meaning when space and time intersect (Black et al. 1989), and important places are typically marked and memorialized with objects and monuments. A place is rendered sacred through continual use, across generations, or through its association with an important, memorialized event. Many anthropologists now emphasize the significance of human "embodiment" within particular places (e.g., Joyce 2003), such as in houses (Bahloul 1996), asserting that collective memory must be repeatedly performed to be "conveyed and sustained" (Connerton 1989: 1). Connerton (1989: 38) stresses the importance to collective memory of embodiment through ritual practice, which Halbwachs (1992) overlooked. The ritualized act of following the Way of the Cross, including prescribed ways of moving and reciting prayers, as practiced by thousands, if not millions, of people, over the course of hundreds of years, was (and is) just as important to the collective memory of Christianity as were the mnemonic cues strewn along the Way. In some cases, trips to sacred places could be memorialized by individuals and for groups through the return of objects—souvenirs and relics—that helped perpetuate and build shared memories (see, e.g., Maran and Stockhammer 2012 re. "materiality," that is the various effects that material objects, like heirlooms, have on humans and human behaviors). It is in performing the past within symbolically charged places, employing meaningful objects, a process Basso (1996: 55) calls "interanimation" (see also Casey 1996: 22), that human groups encode collective memories, and perpetuate them, thereby creating particular memory regimes and communities.

Nora (1996) refers to such places as *lieux de mémoire*, "sites of memory," loci of commemoration where collective memory is performed. War memorials (Borg 1991) provide good examples of *lieux de mémoire*, though Nora (1996) defines such sites very broadly. The example *par excellence* of a memory site is that of Masada in Israel, the modern collective memory of which is a complete fabrication, a "myth" in Ben-Yehuda's (1995) terms. Because *lieux de mémoire* are evocative of collective memories—are culturally constructed and symbolically charged—they may be contested by competing memory communities, which distort and politicize them, leading to conflict (Alcock 2002: 15). For this reason, *lieux de mémoire*, and collective memories generally, can be traumatic. They may memorialize dark periods in a nation's, or the world's, past. The Holocaust, for example, has been memorialized, and thereby committed to collective memory, in hundreds, if not thousands, of different ways (Young 1994). Tahrir Square in Cairo provides a good example of a *lieux de mémoire* in the making.

Collective memories are symbolically charged. They are active and rarely benign. They can be used by interest groups and factions to craft change, or impede it. They are a potential source of tremendous human agency. They can be built and destroyed. Understanding how they are made is therefore of critical importance.

MAKING COLLECTIVE MEMORIES

Psychologists recognize several different types of memory: episodic or autobiographical (personal, contextual: "I witnessed a robbery last night"); declarative or semantic (factual, non-contextual: $2 + 2 = 4$); cognitive (remembering and recall: as of the meaning of a word or phrase); procedural (skills: driving a car); and habit (performative, symbolic: e.g., how to shake someone's hand, and when and why it is appropriate to do so) (Connerton 1989: 22; Misztal 2003: 9–10; Schacter 1996: 17). Sociologists and historians have tended to focus on episodic memory and sought to demonstrate how individual episodic memories propagate and are encoded as collective memories. Halbwachs (1992) anticipated this focus on episodic memory in his analysis of how the personal recollections of the apostles were set down in the Gospels. This was clearly an imperfect process, given the large number of witnesses involved and the discrepancies in the various extant documents. But the constructability of collective memory, its fallibility even, is one of its key, salient characteristics, and in this, collective memory is very much like individual human memory. This is not a deficiency; the selectivity of human memory is an efficiency, a strength. It provides evolutionary advantages (Schacter 1996: 3–4) and humans exploit memory's subjectivity for personal and cultural reasons. It is for this reason that Schacter (1996: 11) refers to the "fragile power" of memory.

The process of collective memory making is determined by human neurophysiology in other ways, as well. We used to think that memories were like snapshots, or recordings, filed away in the brain in perpetuity—for Thomas Aquinas, following Aristotle, like the "imprint of a seal on wax" (quoted in Carruthers 1990: 55). Remembering was the process of retrieving a file; forgetting occurred with time, as files were lost or damaged. As it turns out, this model of memory is simplistic, and inaccurate. As first demonstrated by Bartlett (1932; following work done by Ebbinghaus 1885), memory is not an imprinting process (the recording of "traces"), but is subjective and strongly conditioned by social context (the formation of "schemata"). What one intends to do with a memory changes its content and perspective (Bartlett 1932: 307; Schacter 1996: 21–22). When a memory is made, a representative "engram" is produced based on an idealized schema, which includes, or integrates, all related sensual and emotional data. These may include sights ("It was large"), sounds ("It was barking"), and smells ("I smelled dirt"), but also the feelings ("I was terrified") and motor attitudes ("I was running") that accompanied the episode (a dog attack) being committed to memory. These disparate memory data are encoded and distributed in various places throughout the brain, a tactic called "parallel processing" (Schacter 1996: 9), which saves storage space and increases recall efficiency. When someone remembers, the engram's constituent parts are reassembled and the episode is recollected. Obviously, recollection does not produce a "true" representation of the event being remembered; it is idealized, and individually ("I hate dogs") and culturally ("But dogs are a man's best friend . . .") interpreted.

Very meaningful, exciting, or especially traumatic episodes tend to be remembered more easily than mundane or routine episodes. Such memories may be subject to "deep" processing; that is, they may be linked to other, similar memories, making recall easier (Schacter 1996: 43). The act of remembering depends on a trigger or "retrieval cue" (e.g., Proust's *madeleine*), which stimulates recall. Mnemonic cues were vital to medieval practitioners of the *ars memoriae* (the "art of memory"), which used complex mental images (e.g., houses with many rooms) to aid memory and the recitation of long, complicated passages (Carruthers 1990; Yates 1966). Likewise, various artistic media and objects can serve as powerful memory triggers (Küchler and Melion 1991), or impediments: "Objects are the enemy of memory, they are what tie it down and lead to forgetfulness" (Forty 1999: 7). Clearly, mnemonic cues are important. They can be employed to improve and encourage remembering, or to fabricate and distort, as when powerful suggested cues cause "false memory syndrome" (Schacter 1996: chapter 4). Memories can also be lost due to injury or as a response to trauma, leading to amnesia, which may be temporary or permanent, minor or catastrophic (Schacter 1996: chapter 8). Freud had a particular interest in forgetfulness (repression), and by 1900 he could declare that the aim of psychoanalysis was to "fill in the gaps in memory" (quoted in Casey 1987: 8). Freud is discussed in more detail in chapter 2, on Egypt.

This brief discussion of individual human memory and neuropsychology is instructive when it comes to explaining collective memory making (cf. Joyce 2003). I contend that the process of collective memory making is determined in large part by human biology, which defines the structure and limits of individual memory making. This is not an analogy or a metaphor (Erll 2011: 96–101). Collective memory is a product of individual memory; the former is created in ways that are conditioned by the latter.

The vast majority of events that occur in the life of a social group, be it a family or nation, are not preserved by its collective (episodic) memory system. This is true of individuals, as well. Memory is selective. Events that are highly important to a group (e.g., unique, transformative, or traumatic) may be memorialized by the collective. This requires, of course, that they are witnessed by one or more individuals. Cognitive, semantic, and procedural memories are also essential to individual and group functioning, and are culturally encoded in ways similar to episodic memories, but they do not tend to drive social change. They are instead conservative. They form the basis for *habitus* (Bourdieu 1977; cf. Papoulias 2003). Likewise, habit memory tends to maintain social solidarity and stability but can also be deployed to support social change (Connerton 1989), as discussed in more detail below. My focus here is episodic memory.

When a particularly exciting event occurs in a social (i.e., public) context (e.g., the construction of a new capital at Amarna by Akhenaten, or the modern protests in Tahrir Square), and is witnessed by a subset of individuals, they may commit the event to memory—they may construct a memory engram for the event—in ways discussed above. Depending on the situation, they may share their memories of that event with others in their community, in culturally appropriate ways, producing "communicative" memories (Assmann 2008). They may tell stories around the fire, commemorate the event through ritual, or memorialize it in art. Memory of the event is thereby distributed throughout the social organism, among many individuals, and symbolized: by storytellers, shamans, and artists. We can thus refer to a process of "cultural parallel processing" that duplicates the parallel processing of individual human memories. However, whereas individuals depend on large numbers of integrated schemata (and neurons) when they remember, groups depend on large numbers of integrated individuals (Bartlett 1932: 310–11; cf. Bastide's [1970: 24] concept of "memory networks"), who serve as "satellite memory stores" (Ostrom 1989: 213). The collective memory system is thus heterarchical, as opposed to hierarchical, in particular in "simple" societies. Memory work is distributed among many individuals, all of whom have equal, and equally important, roles to play in the functioning of what is essentially a self-organizing system. One memory worker does not tell any other memory worker what to do.

If the event witnessed is culturally meaningful—if it is of functional, symbolic use to the group—its memory will spread and take hold; it will percolate through society, down to the youngest members. If its meaning is limited or not "useful," or damaging, it will fade. As the memory of an event spreads through society, if it spreads, it is embellished, as individuals who were not there make mistakes or add information. As participant eye-witnesses die, they may be inserted into the evolving collective memory as characters. In this way, oral histories become linked to ancestral histories, tying family genealogies to wider socio-cultural narratives. Much of this process is implicit, just as when an individual embellishes a personal memory (Schacter 1996: 9–10). But sometimes, as a set of individual memories is transformed into a collective memory, it will be embellished in certain, patterned ways for social or political reasons (cf. Geary 1994), which leads to "goal interdependence" (Ostrom 1989: 213). The collective memory creates social cohesion and identity, and helps delimit social goals, moving forward. It is for this reason that collective (episodic) memories can act as powerful drivers of social and political change.

The end product of the collective memory making process is a "collective memory engram" (Schacter 1996: 58–59). When the group remembers, it assembles the relevant collective engram from its constituent individual parts, from its satellite memory stores. As is the case when an individual remembers, collective remembering does not generate a perfect, "flashbulb" image of an event. The collective memory is constructed, mediated, situational, and inter-subjective. This is not a deficiency in the collective memory making process. Distributed, parallel collective memory processing is a necessary, flexible, resilient, and efficient social-structural system.

Cultures, like brains, are not capable of remembering every event perfectly, in perfect detail. Such a solution to collective remembering would prove paralyzing.

Like individual memory engrams, collective memory engrams also depend on cues, which trigger recall. Repeated triggering helps to preserve memories, though this has little effect on overall accuracy. Groups employ various strategies to help record and cue collective memories. These cues can be "inscribed" or "incorporated" (see discussion in Connerton 1989: 72–79 and Rowlands 1993, based on Whitehouse 1992: 795–96). Inscribed memory practices depend on frequent, conventionalized, public presentation, whereas incorporated memory practices encourage symbolic or secret, exclusionary exegesis. Landscapes, for example, can serve as media for many different forms of memory cue (Schama 1995) and are robust sources of *cadre matériel*. Memory cues are sometimes "written into" (inscribed in) a particular landscape and can be read by group members like books, and the locations in the landscape where important events took place might themselves be memorialized, turning them from spaces into places (i.e., *lieux de mémoire*, see above). Such places may become sacred, ritual sites, at which community members "perform" memory, cueing recall. Through time, and with repetition, ritual cuing of collective episodic memory can stimulate the production of collective habit memory. A good example of this is the Christian Eucharist, which commemorates a particular event, but depends strongly on shared habit memories (Connerton 1989: 57). Because they are "embodied," rituals represent potentially powerful, incorporated memory practices.

Just as cultures need means to remember, they must also forget. Collective memories that have lost meaning or ceased to function properly may be let go. Whereas individual forgetting is largely involuntary, collective forgetting (i.e., "cultural amnesia;" Schacter 1996: 302) is often deliberate, purposeful, and regulated (Lowenthal 1999: xi). This is true for all groups, but is especially so for highly centralized states, such as modern dictatorships, which practice "organized forgetting" (Connerton 1989: 14) (e.g., the Roman practice of *damnatio memoriae*). When memory communities forget, conflict may ensue, since forgetting entails exclusion. Complex societies possess a remarkable facility for forgetting (Forty 1999: 7), despite access to complicated memory regimes, including writing. In fact, written history, it might be argued, encourages forgetfulness by relieving individuals of the need—the obligation—to remember (Pine et al. 2004: 13). This has led some scholars (e.g., Nora 1996) to describe the loss of "real" or "authentic" collective memory making as traditional practices disappear. We might ask, therefore, what distinguishes collective memory making in "simple," traditional societies from collective memory making in "complex," non-traditional ones.

COLLECTIVE MEMORY MAKING IN "SIMPLE" SOCIETIES

So-called traditional societies possess extremely sophisticated means, whether "inscribed" or "incorporated/embodied" (see above), of constructing collective memories, which provide a shared sense of identity and solidarity (Eber and Neal 2001: 169). These typically depend on face-to-face, oral systems of communication and transmission (e.g., through gossip, storytelling, myth-making, poems, tales, proverbs, songs, etc.) (Vansina 1985). In recent years, some scholars have drawn a sharp distinction between oral and literate cultures, associating the former with "memory" and the latter with "history" (see, e.g., Nora 1989, in particular). According to some historians (most notably Le Goff 1992), memory, based on orality (so-called ethnic memory), is limited in its ability to capture and preserve the past, whereas history, based on writing, is designed to "make time stand still," so that critical historical analysis becomes possible (Hutton 1993: 98). In a series of books on the topic, Goody (1968, 1977, 1986, 1987; see 1998 for an excellent summary related specifically to memory) has emphasized just how different fully oral cultures are when compared to literate ones. He asserts that memory in oral cultures is "vague" and that in the absence of books (or other *aide-mémoires*), proper performance of ceremonies, like funerals or initiation rites, depends on the input of many participating, remembering minds, so that "one person's recollection will help another" (Goody 1998: 74). Other scholars maintain that the line between oral and literate cultures has been too sharply drawn (e.g., Fentress and Wickham 1992). In fact, literate societies commonly employ oral systems of communication and transmission (Geary 1994)—how could they not?—and oral societies may devise or adopt record keeping systems that mimic writing (see Lillios 2008).

I will argue that the instruments (and regimes) of collective memory making fall along a continuum from more to less distributed (as defined above) and therefore are more or less open to manipulation and control. Through time, and with changes in technology, there has been a narrowing of distribution (which disrupts parallel processing) and a widening and deepening of control, though this depends on context. As discussed in detail by Halbwachs (1992), the primary social context for collective memory transmission is, and continues to be, the family. In traditional societies, individual identity is created within the home, through enculturation. Individual allegiance is owed to the family first, and to larger social collectives second. Small, egalitarian social groups, such as families and tribes, typically create and maintain collective memories in private, through oral exchanges (even in today's world), and these are of little interest to outsiders. However, for larger, more complex social systems to form, based on social inequalities, collective memory making had to be shifted out of the home, away from the tribe, and directed toward the creation of new, public identities and allegiances (thereby facilitating the shift, in Assmann's [2008] terms, from "communicative" to "cultural" memories). This happened in trans-egalitarian societies the world over, contributing to the formation of archaic states (a process described in the next section, below).

One of the most important oral activities performed in families is genealogical: the recitation and commemoration of ancestral lineages. Kinship plays a key role in collective memory and identity formation in traditional societies, by tracking relatedness, and thereby signaling who belongs and who does not. Kinship presents an excellent example of a widely distributed memory system. Genealogical knowledge is held by all members, but by elders in particular (as described by Bergson 2004 [1912], who was a major influence on Halbwachs [1980, 1992: 47–48]). It is transmitted in families, from old to young, and more and more complex kinship maps can be assembled through the cooperation, often public, of multiple elders, representing different lineages, from throughout the tribe (or village, or region, etc.). Importantly, kinship systems can be situated spatially, within landscapes, thereby defining who lived where and when, and confirming ownership of, or access to, land and resources. Ancestral claims to land are frequently made by burying the dead beneath the house, near the hearth, or on family or communal property (Halbwachs 1992: 63–65). Bodies, or body parts, may be conserved or exhumed for display, which reinforces property rights. All such ritualized mortuary practices affect group identity in powerful ways (see Küchler 2002), by cuing episodic collective memories linked to important people, and by embodying kinship through habit memories related to treatment of the dead by the living.

A beautiful example of this practice comes from the Neolithic Near East in the form of plastered skulls. Kuijt (2008: 172) argues that:

> social memory in Neolithic communities was linked to the construction and presentation of death. The definition and reiteration of the naturalized social order appear to have been linked to the manipulation and intergenerational use of bodily representation and recirculation of the dead with human skulls serving as ritual heirlooms.

I contend that this type of memory behavior was central to the formation of collective identities in most (maybe all) traditional societies beginning in the Neolithic, and perhaps earlier, and that it was this type of memory behavior—distributed, parallel-processed, symbolic, situational, inter-subjective, performed, participatory, and embodied—that mitigated against changes in social complexity.

In traditional, oral societies, and in the absence of writing, "mnemonic systems" (Goody 1998) function to connect episodic to habit memory regimes; they link the collective cognitive process of remembering to the performed, embodied act of memorializing—the knowing to the doing. In the Near East, during the Neolithic, a body was buried accompanied by various mortuary rites. These rites reinforced the social relationships of the living, the collective memory of kinship, land ownership, and therefore group identity. After some time (one to two generations), the skull was exhumed, plastered (one to two generations later), and the ancestor venerated and "symbolized" (Kuijt 2008: 178). For Neolithic societies, skulls served as mnemonic cues, helping to structure collective memory schemata, triggering the production of cultural engrams. Other mnemonic cues were/are employed by traditional peoples. These may be found embedded in landscapes (Feld and Basso 1996), built into monuments (various in Bradley 1990; Williams 2003), represented in art (various in Küchler and Melion 1991), and strewn throughout material culture generally (Jones 2007). However, as Williams (2003: 6–7) notes, mnemonic cues need not be large and/or aesthetically complex to prompt memory (see also Lillios 2012); in fact, they need not even be visible. Sometimes the destruction, disarticulation, or general absence of a thing, such as through the burning, dismemberment, or decay of a body, helps perpetuate memory (Forty 1999: 10). Holes in perception, signaling that which was once present but is now gone, can serve as incredibly powerful, and poignant, mnemonic cues.

These kinds of distributed memory regimes are not easily dislodged or appropriated, rendering social change leading to inequality difficult to effect. For this to happen, shared mnemonic cues, including those related to death and kinship, had to be turned to new, larger social collectives. I contend that this happened throughout the world, at various times and in various places, when states and state identities formed. Moreover, the process of appropriating traditional memory regimes has continued over the course of the last 5,000 years and is ongoing today, as nations work to incorporate traditional societies and build national identities and capitalist economic systems. The process of nation building is one of targeted memory work and requires state control of memory regimes, at all levels of society. This is accomplished through institutionalization of the enculturation process, through schooling, and by destabilizing family, community, and class memory structures. Having defined collective memory and discussed how it forms, generally and in traditional societies specifically, we are now in a position to explore collective memory making in states.

COLLECTIVE MEMORY MAKING AND THE STATE

Cities and states appeared throughout the world beginning about 5,000 years ago. Ancient cities, and therefore states, depended on populated agricultural hinterlands for their support. As a result, administrators of states had to control land and secure borders, which required controlling people and communities. Control, and extraction of goods and services, was maintained through coercion, which was costly and difficult, or via cooperation, which was relatively cheap, albeit not uncomplicated. In either case, ideological structures, including religion, were deployed in support of command and control systems, which rarely worked fully and smoothly; there was always room for dissent, even in the most centralized of state systems (as discussed below with regard to modern Albania). State social systems are usually hierarchically organized and administrators and members of the upper class always benefit through their control of state economies. One important anthropological and historical question, then, is why, when states formed, human beings ceded control over the means of production (and their independence) to others, and under what circumstances. States have engulfed the whole world, and all (or nearly all) human beings are now integrated, to some degree, into state economies. Explaining how we got to this point is thus of critical importance. I assert that the assimilation of local, traditional collective memory regimes by budding political elite in prehistoric middle-range societies was one key step on the way to state formation and the formation of state (and eventually national) identities.

When human beings began farming and village life appeared, social hierarchy became possible. Those who wanted to be in charge had to take charge, of land for example. One way to do this—though certainly not the only way—was to short circuit local, communicative mnemonic systems, which resided in families, connected people to their land, and were maintained by elders. Memories, whether collective or individual, tend to change gradually, through time; they do not typically change in revolutionary fashion. So the process whereby traditional collective memories changed was a slow one, and implicit, as is the process whereby individual human memories change, through substitution and embellishment. As described above, kinship and mortuary practices constitute two integrated, traditional collective memory sub-systems that serve to define membership in small social groups. These sub-systems reinforce episodic collective memories, through commemoration, and stimulate habit memory, through performance and participation. Day in and day out, elders instructed the young in the oral history of the group, including kinship, employing various mnemonic cues to encode shared memory schemata.

These schemata helped shape individual and group identities. When distributed ("parallel-processed"), individual (episodic) memories were assembled by elders, cultural engrams emerged, and collective memories were made or reaffirmed. Collective remembering (and forgetting) was particularly common on special occasions, such as when a member of the group was initiated or died. At such times, the oral history of the family or tribe might be recounted, and the roles of both the living and the dead defined. Similar memory practices made and remade societies through time, across the globe.

In some cases, ambitious individuals drove change in collective memory systems, often as one strategy among many meant to help garner social power. In most cases, though, such strategies were tacitly and inconsistently applied. Either way, for collective memory systems to change, or be changed, several things had to happen. First of all, oral histories, songs of praise and remembrance, and rituals performed in homes, among family and friends, at hearths and tombs, had to be relocated, socially and spatially, out of the family and away from the house. In trans-egalitarian societies, this meant building political structures, both vertical (e.g., moieties) and horizontal (e.g., sodalities), that reduced factionalism and (re)connected lineage segments (Bonanno et al. 1990). These new structures were led by "big men" or chiefs, who had the wherewithal to fund public ceremonies, like feasts and potlatches (Dillehay 1990). These were held at central locations, in so-called large-scale integrative facilities, like kivas and men's houses, and encouraged new forms of social solidarity (Adler and Wilshussen 1990; Flannery and Marcus 2013). This change in social organization is usually accompanied in the archaeological record by a shift from individualizing burial practices (focused on particular ancestors) to corporate, co-mingled burial (which symbolized the new body politic) (Schroeder 2001). Second of all, leaders had to create alternative memory regimes that modified or replaced those of the family and clan and legitimized new political behaviors. This was made possible through the malleability of memory, including collective memory, and the propensity for strategic forgetting. Aspiring chiefs created new ancestral memories, based on fictive kinship, which explained the importance (and origin) of chiefly lineages and reinforced their authority. These new collective memories were supported by constructed, or repurposed, mnemonic devices, whether objects or places. Object "biographies" in particular could be re-symbolized to fit new use contexts and realities (Jones 2007: 78–80). At the same time, memory workers—those who made memory devices and interpreted memory cues, such as bards, shamans, and artists—were attached to chiefs, and chiefly lineages, leading to functional specialization. This process took what had been distributed, heterarchical collective memory systems, and transformed them. The new "cultural" memory systems were centralized and hierarchical, and therefore more easily controlled by political authorities (Assmann 2008). Once this change had been effected, chiefs had means to justify the expropriation of resources, such as agricultural surpluses and land. Finally, as states emerged—that is, forms of government that rely on internally specialized and hierarchically organized decision-making systems—new memory regimes were formalized and linked to innovative ideological, legal, and economic systems. A key technological development was, of course, writing, which allowed oral memory systems to be displaced by written ones. Veneration of the dead became a primary function of religious officials, who wrote down and sang the songs once sung by elders. The old "kitchen" gods were replaced by new "sky" gods, who were all-powerful and remote, and whose laws, like the king's, could be displayed for all to see. Rules pertaining to land ownership, once symbolized by bodies and body parts, were codified and deeds to property were recorded and filed. Tax rolls were created. These, and many other literate memory regimes, replaced traditional, oral memory regimes, justifying the appearance of new behavioral structures, such as social hierarchies, by linking them to new constructed pasts.

Most of the changes described above can be implicated in the rise of the very first states, in Mesopotamia (and later, in Syria-Palestine; see Feldman 2012). Beginning about 3100 BC, Mesopotamian culture experienced a shift from oral to written memory regimes, associated with changes in religious practice (Jonker 1995: 72–73). Before 3100 BC, Mesopotamians had invoked the dead in the home or temple, by singing songs of praise and remembrance, and by leaving offerings of food and drink. Ancestors were represented by large, sometimes life-sized, statues, which represented deceased individuals and were similar in function to the aforementioned plastered skulls (Kuijt 2008: 102). Statues cued collective memories related to kinship and were central to the performance of various daily and seasonal, inter-generational mortuary rituals. After 3100 BC, and with increased urbanization, more and more of this commemorative behavior was shifted to temples and the ritual invocation of the dead was transferred to temple officials. Eventually, they were granted full control over the mortuary memory system and, in order to remember the requisite genealogical data, began writing names down, recording who had brought what offerings. In this way, many of the methods employed by state administrators find their origins in the temple. Eventually, commemoration of the dead in temples was reserved for the elite, including members of the royal lineage, and temples were transformed into sacred precincts where deities were kept and worshiped. Thus, by the time of state formation, traditional kinship systems, and the mnemonic cues that supported them, both inscribed and incorporated, had been destabilized and destroyed. Slowly but surely, families and villages lost title to their lands and free access to the canals that watered them. Allegiance was owed not to local communities, but, rather, to the king, the state, and its official deities. Works of monumental architecture became potent new mnemonic cues in early states (Sinopoli 2003), encoding cultural schemata that were symbolic of state power. Images and names of kings, like Ur-Nammu, who established the Third Dynasty of Ur, were carved into buildings, hillsides, and canals (Jonker 1995: 97). In fact, in all times and places, states, like those in Mesopotamia, developed long-term interests in the past and sought to construct it to their advantage (Yoffee 2007). Elamite kings, for example, acquired Akkadian and Babylonian royal stelae, such as those erected by Naram-Sin and Hammurabi, and re-inscribed and reused them hundreds of years after their ritual abandonment (Alcock 2002; Crawford 2007; Jonker 1995). In medieval times, in early European states, Christian monks sought to undermine the place and power of women in society, by specifically attacking their roles in rituals of death, mourning, and collective memory making (Geary 1994: 52–59). And in modern times, Saddam Hussein similarly sought to manipulate the past and remake collective memory in his image, by rebuilding Sumerian palaces, for example (Yoffee 2007: 4).

Each state, whether ancient, medieval, or modern, had to create a sense of shared identity for its people. This was particularly true of ancient territorial states, which conquered and incorporated various different ethnic groups. These disparate memory communities had to be stripped of their pasts and integrated into the state's historical narrative. Nation-states are peculiarly modern creations and have particular needs when it comes to identity formation. A nation can be defined as a state that depends on ethnic purity and a shared sense of history and heritage to build social cohesion and maintain territorial integrity. Because nations are entirely constructed political entities, they constitute "imagined communities" (Anderson 1983). Nations were (and are) almost entirely dependent on constructed collective memories, which often refer back to an idealized golden age. These memories may have little or no basis in fact and usually depend on a sense of nostalgia (Appadurai 1996; Bal 1999: xi), a feeling that the golden age was somehow better than the present age. As such, nations build numerous monuments to the mythical past, which serve as mnemonic cues to contrived cultural memories. This was especially the case during the 19th century in Europe, when nation building and nationalism were at their height (Hobsbawm and Ranger 1983). As discussed by Hutton (1993), the formation of new national cultures prompted a sense of loss (e.g., of traditional ways of life), which entailed forgetting. And forgetting often leads to dissonance and conflict. Consequently, marginalized memory communities not accommodated by national historical narratives may oppose them and fight for a place in the nation's collective, cultural memory.

COUNTER-MEMORY

Human memory is influenced by individual and social needs and wants. These needs and wants may be appetitive and instinctual, or political (Bartlett 1932: 307). Similarly, collective memory may meet the general functional needs of states, or be constructed by them to reach specific political ends. Consequently, collective memory may accommodate various forms of human agency. It can be used to build nations or resist them (Van Dyke and Alcock 2003: 3), and is employed by those with power not as a right or privilege, but as an instrument (Jonker 1995: 235). However, because it functions as an instrument, collective memory can also be taken and turned against the state, by those who have no power or aspire to power. Marginalized groups may deploy counter-discourses that challenge the narrow, exclusionary historical discourses upon which states depend. Foucault (1980) showed that these counter-discourses may be found scattered throughout both official (written) and traditional (oral) histories, which form the bases for national memorial and counter-memorial narratives. For Foucault, the presence of these counter-discourses demonstrates the active, continuous making and remaking of the past (Hutton 1993: 5–6), as agents of the nation battle agents of resistance over its content and shape. Contests over the past matter since the past is used to shape identities, both those of individuals and those of groups (Schacter 1996: 93). "Identity needs memory to give shape to itself" (Jonker 1995: 235), and this holds for both people and nations.

The centralized, hierarchical mnemonic systems of states are very difficult to challenge, let alone replace. Groups that resist the state often practice forms of "moral entrepreneurship," as described by Ben-Yehuda (1995: 23). They find weak points in a nation's social memory system, and exploit them, opening narrative gaps and raising questions. Filling these gaps and answering the questions often requires "do-it-yourself construction" of alternative mnemonic systems (Wachtel et al. 1990: 10). Traditional societies may attempt to re-establish distributed, heterarchical mnemonic systems, through processes of "retraditionalization," for example. This may require relearning dying languages, origin stories, and genealogies, which are necessary to the creation, or recapture, of group (episodic) memories and identity. Once elders have died, however, this is almost impossible to do, and so in many cases "retraditionalization" fails or lacks authenticity. Long abandoned or outlawed ceremonial practices may be reconstituted, but once the habit memories associated with those practices have been lost, they cannot be found again; even if recorded on film, the necessary motor skills will have atrophied. For these reasons, and others, most counter-memories and counter-memory systems founder and die. Some may survive and propagate, and can constitute real, meaningful challenges to established memory regimes, but this is rare.

The production of oppositional counter-memories, sometimes referred to as "public" or "unofficial" memories (Misztal 2003: 62), engenders discursive conflict between the state and those who would resist the state, but also within and between various memory communities, as individuals and groups seek to control and benefit from new memory narratives and systems. As described above, the process of collective memory production and evaluation is largely implicit, but individuals and groups can manufacture and launch explicit, targeted counter-memories meant to achieve particular goals. Modern media, digital media in particular, have made this tactic increasingly effective. Often, however, some kind of crisis must ensue before a particular counter-memory gains widespread recognition. In a crisis, those who resist the state may more freely question its authority and interrogate official collective memory systems, allowing open discussion of various alternative, counter-memories. Once accepted and promulgated, a counter-memory may destabilize systems of social solidarity upon which nations depend, by putting the lie to historical narratives of ethnic purity, for example. Such transformations in national collective memories and histories may cause or coincide with severe disruptions and trauma. It is for this reason that the collective memories and histories of many nations, including the United States, are built largely around various traumatic events, like the Civil War, which serve as touchstones in the construction of national pasts and identities.

In this book I track the effects of imperial conquest on collective memory and counter-memory production in three Mediterranean nations—Egypt, Greece, and Albania—each of which was incorporated by the Ottoman Empire. Their shared experiences of Ottoman subjugation have generated easily identifiable and comparable regional-historical collective-memory schemata. Ottoman-derived collective-memory schemata have been encoded in numerous ways by disparate Mediterranean peoples with different effects through time and across space. Importantly, unlike earlier episodes of imperial conquest and occupation, memories of the Ottoman period are accessible in both traditional oral and written sources. Wars of national liberation from the Ottomans, for example, serve as episodic collective-memory sources for numerous Mediterranean and Eurasian peoples, including various marginalized minority groups. It is in defending or contesting these particular historical narratives, and others like them, that various agents have staked claims in the on-going construction of the past in former Ottoman-held territories, the most extreme case being that of the Bosnian pyramids, described below and in the prologue to this book.

Systematic description of collective memory and counter-memory production in different regional and chronological contexts helps illustrate how memory regimes and systems change through time, which classical social theorists, like Durkheim and Halbwachs, who emphasized solidarity and stability, could not easily address (Misztal 2003: 69). I intend, however, to move beyond descriptions of collective-memory processes, and instead build a comparative explanatory model (cf. Assmann 1992; Erll 2011), which integrates various types of mnemonic theory, and helps demonstrate, in general terms, just how various agents have negotiated memory narratives and systems through time. In the next section, I introduce the model and in subsequent chapters I test it. In so doing, I reveal the roles played by collective memory in the formation of states, beginning in prehistory through present times. Additionally, studying collective memory and counter-memory in multiple contexts exposes the agentive importance of "memory workers" (historians, archaeologists, museum specialists, cultural resource managers, tour guides, etc.) who collect and deliver the material from which national pasts and identities are constructed. Understanding the modern "heritage" industry, its methods, and goals is therefore essential to understanding modern collective memory and counter-memory production, and so current theories of cultural heritage management are addressed in detail in the conclusion to this book (Anheier and Isar 2011; Benton 2010).

AN EXPLANATORY MODEL FOR COLLECTIVE MEMORY PRODUCTION AND STATE FORMATION

The explanatory model I have assembled draws from practice theory and integrates several, key independent variables that must be present for collective remembering (and forgetting) to occur and for (nation-)states to form (see also Galaty 2011). It demonstrates how collective memories are constructed and applied in the state-building process. Though the variables I have included may operate separately, it is when they intersect and merge that hegemonic collective-memory systems, and state systems of governance, appear. The model also reveals the significant roles played by counter-memory and resistance in stimulating sociopolitical change. In subsequent chapters I search the regional (ethno-)archaeological and historical records of Egypt, Greece, and Albania for points of nexus, where the contributing variables met, collective memories materialized, and states formed and, in some cases, were subsequently challenged.

The theoretical underpinnings for my model have been drawn from Bourdieu's (1977) *Outline of a Theory of Practice*. Practice theory helps explain how and why various individuals and groups, from all segments of society, might seek to influence the collective memory-making process. Official collective memory systems are imposed by central governments, in both dictatorships and democracies; they are key components in the nation-building process. But even so, they often stem (or are co-opted) from non-official, traditional sources; they bubble up from below (Misztal 2003: 61). This means that marginalized individuals and groups, even those living at the far edges of the nation-state, may contribute to, and contest, collective memory narratives. Collective memories, like all state ideologies, are the result of dynamic, reciprocal interactions between individuals and groups located at all levels of society (Comaroff and Comaroff 1991: 19–27). To explain collective memory production, and state formation, therefore, it is necessary to understand the agentive construction of cultural knowledge.

Bourdieu (1977: 167–69) makes a distinction between the cultural fields of *doxa* and *opinion* (figure 1.1). The field of doxa encompasses the "universe of the undiscussed," composed of ideas and behaviors that are inviolate and taken for granted. The field of opinion encompasses the "universe of discourse," wherein new and competing ideas and behaviors are subjected to evaluation. In the realm of opinion, most new ideas and behaviors are rejected in favor of established, "orthodox" ways of thinking and doing, whereas other, "heterodox" ideas and behaviors may be accepted, and used to challenge the status quo. It is typically those individuals who are dominated who introduce heterodoxy into the system and those who dominate who resist it in favor of orthodoxy. It is also within the realm of opinion that individuals—the "moral entrepreneurs" (Ben-Yehuda 1995: 23) and "do-it-yourselfers" (Wachtel et al. 1990: 10) mentioned above—may bend or break cultural rules, and "improvise," thereby producing challenging, new riffs on old cultural norms and values. According to Bourdieu (1977), it is this generative process that creates and renews culture, and, I would assert, collective memory. And, as it happens, collective memory lends itself exceedingly well to control and manipulation by authorities and those who would challenge them.

Processes of collective memory production unfold within the field of opinion, with corresponding effects on the *cadre matériel* of memory, and while most collective memories operate within the cultural field of doxa and are not discussed, in particular in simple societies, some, under the right conditions, may slip into the realm of opinion. Because collective memories are constructed, they may remain contested, are thus open to discussion, and may evolve. As described above, memory may be used by those with power to achieve political ends, to create and maintain (nation-)

state systems of governance, for example. Or it may be used by those with little or no power to push or resist various political agendas. Today, in some parts of the world, the process of counter-memory making is working overtime, as individuals, like great jazz musicians, compose through improvisation new forms and interpretations of their national pasts. Most of these compositions lodge in the realm of heterodoxy, but some gain wider appeal, and a select few may be hijacked by the state and granted official, orthodox status. Some may work to help topple governments. It is this movement, this shifting of new cultural knowledge, cultural memories in particular, from heterodoxy to orthodoxy—in Bodnar's words (1992), from the "vernacular" to the "official"—that builds nations, and will be addressed in the rest of this chapter.

My agentive model of collective memory production can be operationalized through the addition of six variables—crisis, nostalgia, imagination, identity, nationalism, and time—that together determine the nature and success of any given memory- and nation-building process. According to Appadurai (1996: 30, following Jameson 1989), all people, modern ones included, feel nostalgia, often for a past they never experienced. This is especially true during or following periods of crisis, which, according

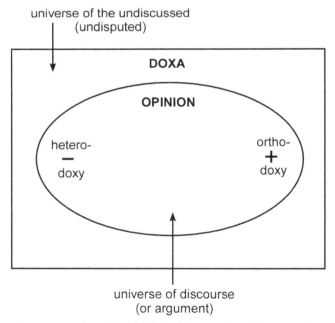

Figure 1.1. The cultural fields of doxa and opinion. Based on Bourdieu 1977: 168. *Source:* M. L. Galaty.

to Bourdieu (1977: 169), are necessary prerequisites for agentive change. For example, throughout history, with almost cyclical regularity, Mediterranean nations, like Egypt, Greece, and Albania, have experienced crisis, often as a result of invasion, but also caused by internal political strife (e.g., the Egyptian "Revolution of January 25," the Greek Civil War, and the collapse of communism in Albania). Crisis prompts nostalgia, and nostalgia encourages intro- and retrospection. It is during such periods of national turmoil that new, heterodox memory tropes are created—or retrofitted for current consumption—and tested by those in power, those without power, and, most importantly, those aspiring to power. New memory tropes are the imaginative products of individual minds, but may take on collective, intra- and inter-structural lives of their own. We may therefore refer to both individual imaginations, as well as, in Appadurai's (1996: 31) terms, a "collective imaginary" or *imaginaire*. A particular landscape may offer the symbolic cues necessary to construct and maintain a collective sense of imagination, or these may be drawn from artistic or historical sources. Once piqued, the collective imagination may function as a potent source of memory material and may help individuals validate or contest orthodox systems of collective memory. Memory thus sits at the source of all imaginative, agentive attempts to reinforce or throw off hegemonic power structures.

According to Anderson (1983: 6), nations are themselves products of nostalgic imagination, and, as imagined communities, are wholly dependent on ideologies that create for citizens a shared national identity. National identity may be constructed by emphasizing a group's shared ethnic origins, supported by linguistic and religious similarities, or by emphasizing its historical claim to a piece of territory. For example, Egyptians, Greeks, and Albanians all stress their autochthonous right to the territories they currently occupy, despite overwhelming historical evidence for the almost continuous movement of different peoples in and out of the lands they now control. Narratives of ethnicity and ethnic belonging thus constitute particularly powerful national ideologies, and are always, to some degree, imagined. Building these ideologies, and therefore building nations, is thus a memory-making endeavor. Consequently, national identity and nationalism depend strongly, if not almost entirely, on constructed versions of the past, versions that have been moved out of the realm of opinion and into the realm of doxa. Shackel (2001) argues that through memory people may create and commemorate three different forms of the past: an exclusionary past; a patriotic or celebrated past; and a past that enables or sanctifies a particular current social or political situation. In all three cases, conflict may ensue, as different memory communities are encouraged, or forced, to subsume traditional forms of identity. This is usually accomplished by the state over time through processes of "leveling, sharpening, and assimilation" (Ben-Yehuda 1995: 24). First, heterodox constructions of the past are leveled; that is, they are simplified and made accessible to the masses. Next, they are sharpened; the message is honed to meet particular nationalistic goals. Finally, they are assimilated into the nation's collective memory, and thus rendered orthodox.

Memory systems are constructed and contested over the course of time (Halbwachs 1980: chapter 3). An *Annales* historical approach works well to structure the human experience of collective memory through time. Braudel (1972) identified three temporal scales at which human history unfolds—the event, conjuncture, and longue durée—or as Fowles (2002) glosses them—intra-generational, multi-generational, and long-term. Intra-generational processes unfold over the course of a single human lifespan. Consequently, individual humans may be aware of and able to influence intra-generational processes (Fowles 2002: 24). At this scale, individual memories may be made, shared, shaped, and tested against existing, orthodox collective-memory narratives, which often span lifetimes and are multi-generational. Multi-generational historical processes, and memories, are "composite" and take on structural meaning (Fowles 2002: 25). Consequently, they cannot be as easily controlled and changed by individuals. Multi-generational memories are supported by various forms of memory regime, depending on context. Traditional societies typically use oral mnemonic systems to preserve memories over multiple generations, whereas complex societies use written ones. Both also employ various types of material and embodied mnemonic cues. Once memory becomes multi-generational it typically becomes fixed in the cultural field of doxa; it can be challenged, but, as described above, this usually requires some kind of crisis. Finally, some historical processes are long-term. They develop over spans of time that are too long to be perceived by individual humans. They are not propelled by human goals and desires, but rather are the consequence of undirected human action (Fowles 2002: 26). Over time, human collective memories may break down and fail, or be transformed into myths, which transcend time. Writing may help support memory over the long term and is therefore essential to state control of collective memory systems. Exactly how collective memories are made and then applied to the nation-building process depends to a large degree on the temporal scale or scales at which they function.

In order to determine the role of memory in the state formation and nation-building process in any given cultural context, it is necessary to estimate the strength with which the six independent, interconnected variables are operating. Doing so serves to delimit the particular form collective memories will take, how they might subsequently evolve, and their effects on systems of governance and resistance. The relationship between the independent variables, the mediating variable of memory, and the dependent variable of state organization is not simply linear, but rather is recursive and multidimensional; change in one variable will precipitate change in all others, in different directions, and with different degrees of intensity. It is thus helpful to picture a causal model that measures change across all six variables at once (figure 1.2).

When the six variables operate narrowly, the state is able to gather and maintain more control over memory systems, thereby encouraging the nation-building process. The cultural field of doxa hardens and that of opinion shrinks, and the possibility for change through resistance is reduced. Centralized, hierarchical memory regimes become common. When the six variables operate widely, the state loses control over memory systems. Orthodox constructions of the past can be questioned and heterodox constructions gain ground. Distributed, parallel-processed, heterarchical memory networks, such as those that existed prior to state formation, flourish when political control wanes.

We can begin with crisis. When crisis is absent and society is stable, state control of memory is enabled. When times are "good," official versions of the past are accepted and not questioned. Memories of a "golden age," when the nation was founded, are constructed, and these are used to legitimate the actions of the state and its leaders in the present. Marginalized groups will have little or no ability to effect ideological change; their protests will bounce back. However, when crises do occur, as a result of war, disease, and famine, for example, state-sponsored memory narratives become more vulnerable to attack, leading to a net loss in ideological control. Marginalized groups may attempt, therefore, to precipitate crisis by destabilizing the state. This is a common strategy on the part of terrorists, who may have as their ultimate goal the displacement of official constructions of the past. In some cases, crisis can galvanize citizens and lead to patriotism, such as when the homeland is attacked. But even when crisis leads to solidarity, gaps will be opened in official memory narratives. Such was the case in the United States after 9-11, for example, when anger and grief gave way to fear and suspicion, and ideologies of invincibility, based on constructed memories, were questioned. It is quite likely that crisis functioned similarly in prehistory, helping chiefs appropriate traditional memory regimes and create systems of social inequality, a precondition for state formation. In times of crisis, cultural behaviors rendered unacceptable, or forbidden, by tradition became acceptable: old gods could be abandoned; rituals embodying memory, suspended; and social systems, reorganized.

When crisis is high, nostalgia may be high as well, but, importantly, people may become nostalgic for a past that is not that of the state. Memories of the nation's "golden age" often ring hollow during times

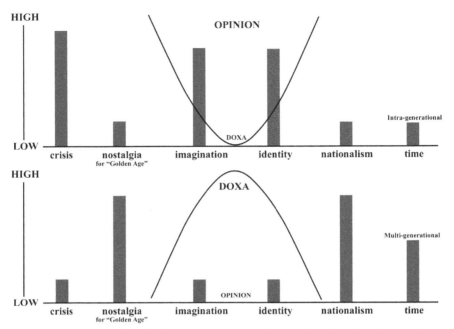

Figure 1.2. Two models of collective memory production based on the changing input of six interacting cultural variables and their effect on the fields of doxa and opinion. In the lower model, collective memory production is limited and can be more easily controlled by the state. In the upper model, collective memory production operates more dynamically and is less easily controlled by the state. *Source:* M. L. Galaty.

of crisis and heterodox memories of other possible pasts may proliferate. That said, nostalgia is necessary to the nation-building process. It helps activate the shared sense of imagination that underpins national identity. As described by Anderson (1983: 6), the "nation," like all human communities, is a construct, a product of collective imagining. What distinguishes nations is not their relative truth or falsity—they are all similarly constructed and thus similarly false—but rather "the style in which they are imagined" (Anderson 1983: 6). Consequently, the models sketched in figure 1.2 will appear different when applied to different nations, and to the same nation at different times in its history. Different nations have different means of imagining, and explaining, their origins and so each will deploy imagination differently. Like nostalgia, states must manage and channel imagination; if it operates too widely, heterodox versions of memory, and community, will be devised. States thus work hard to shape collective imagination. State-owned or monitored media and state-run schools are particularly important in this regard. In prehistory, for states to form, chiefs would likewise have had to channel the collective imagination, away from traditional pasts and toward very different futures. One way to do this was to co-opt those individuals—the artists, storytellers, shamans, and elders—who did most of the imagining and also instructed the young. In this way, the first states were probably much like modern nations. Nostalgic imaginations were used to construct collective memories, which supported new forms of identity, transcending local affiliations and allegiances.

The ultimate goal of a nation's *imaginaire* is to create forms of identity based on homogenized ethnic histories that leave no room for difference and dissent. When states tightly control imagination, ethnic identity remains narrowly defined and collective memory is circumscribed. In extreme cases, ethnic groups that do not belong may be removed; they may be driven out or exterminated. Alternatively, ethnic groups will be assimilated into the dominant national culture. This entails erasing or resetting the heterodox collective memories associated with minority ethnic populations, and this almost always requires coercion. Nations that allow wide systems of collective imagination must accommodate alternative ethnic identities and memories, which may threaten territorial integrity. Early states experienced similar problems integrating diverse ethnic populations, but tended to employ different solutions. Instead of destroying or assimilating ethnic groups, which was costly, early states appropriated ethnic identities, including beliefs and practices. The early Egyptians and Greeks (and in later times, the Albanians) were especially adept at adopting other peoples' gods, rituals, material culture, and memories. This strategy had the similar result of narrowing identity and, simultaneously, centralizing disparate collective memory systems. Narrow systems of imagination and identity in modern nations invariably lead to nationalism: deep-seated, even fanatical, support for a nation and its leaders, policies, and practices. High levels of nationalism bring dogmatic adherence to state-sponsored systems of ideology. Those citizens who are nationalistic often believe strongly in the nation's constructed memory and mythic past. They are typically members of the dominant ethnic group and may seek to enforce, sometimes violently, the nation's perceived ethnic purity. Examples of nationalism in ancient times are rare, but certainly the leaders of early states demanded loyalty from their subjects. This was most often accomplished through forms of ideological control, religious in particular. Citizens of ancient states appear to have obeyed their leaders both because they had no (or little) choice but also because they had some degree of faith in state-sponsored religious systems. In archaeological terms, it is particularly evident and interesting when such religious systems failed and the people rose up against them, defacing religious icons and tearing down temple structures.

Finally, we must add to the model the key component of time. Intra-generational systems of memory lend themselves to manipulation and control. Because they unfold over the short term, they operate actively within the cultural field of opinion. Leaders of states, whether early or modern, try to shrink the pool of intra-generational memory tropes, in ways described above. At the same time, they support certain memories, and histories, in particular those that underwrite their claims to power. Once such memories and histories become "official," that is public and accepted without question, they may become multi-generational, inter-structural, and passed on through time. To advance new, orthodox, multi-generational collective memories, states will often destroy or appropriate mnemonic cues that worked to trigger traditional, non-state memory systems through time. One way to do this is to prohibit traditional peoples from speaking their native languages, so that elders cannot pass on knowledge and memories to the young. Another is to ruin or deny access to sacred places, which are necessary for the conduct of important rituals. The colonial Christian practice of building cathedrals on top of pagan temples or Pueblo kivas is a good example of this. Ethnic minorities will often fight such state-sponsored tactics, since loss of language and access to material mnemonics often signals the death of a culture. Once collective memory is gone, it is almost impossible to reconstruct. All that remain are myths, which may operate over the long-term, but myth without memory is sterile and bereft of meaning.

The variables included in the memory model operate along continua. They typically do not function in simple positive or negative fashion. Depending on the historical context, some variables may settle at the extreme ends of continua, as depicted in figure 1.2, but usually they migrate back and forth between poles, through time. We can best demonstrate the model at work, however, by using it to analyze an example of collective memory production under extreme circumstances: the Bosnian Pyramids.

THE BOSNIAN PYRAMIDS

Bosnia was a member state of the former Yugoslavia, a nation created for the "South Slavs" by the Great Powers following World War I. It turned communist after World War II and was ruled for several decades by Josip Broz Tito, who died in 1980. Tito de-emphasized regional and religious ethnic identity and encouraged all citizens, including non-Slavs, like the Kosovar Albanians, to be good, dedicated Yugoslavs, first and foremost. National historical ideology reinforced pan-Slavism, imagining a medieval "Golden Age," when Slavic peoples dominated the Balkans and were rich and united. Events that reinforced a shared Slavic identity were taught and commemorated, such as the Serb-led, collective defense of the Balkans against Ottoman conquest, which failed at the Battle of Kosovo in 1389. Yugoslavia was stable and prospered under Tito, especially compared to other Eastern European states, like Albania. Communities throughout the nation were largely integrated across ethnic lines and ethnic and religious intermarriage was common. A seemingly modern, tolerant Yugoslavia was put on display for all the world to see during the 1984 winter Olympic Games, held in Sarajevo.

Yugoslavia fits very well the closed model of collective memory production presented in figure 1.2. Following World War II and through the 1980s, the country was stable and levels of crisis were low, particularly relative to the period of the first and second Balkan Wars, which preceded World War I, when ethnic strife was extremely high. The communist state was a totalitarian one and exercised direct control over the national imagination. Ethnic, religious, and linguistic differences were de-emphasized and a Yugoslav identity was invented. Yugoslav nationalism was celebrated through various pan-Slavic folklore festivals, in museums, and in art, songs, and poetry. Village-based loyalties (and loyalty to the traditional Slavic extended household or *zadruga*) were undermined as the nation urbanized and industrialized. Local, intra-generational memory systems were gutted and replaced by state-sponsored, collective systems of memory. Under Tito, there was very little room for counter-memory production. Those ethnic groups that were non-Slav, such as the Albanian minority, were forced to learn Serbo-Croatian, and could not show non-Yugoslav ethnic pride (by flying the Albanian flag, for instance). At the same time, minority groups were granted special political status and rights. Vernacular counter-memories that did appear were confined to the realm of opinion and official, state-sponsored memory systems hardened into orthodoxy, or so it seemed.

Beginning in 1989, Bosnia and several other Yugoslav states declared independence. The so-called modern Balkan Wars, which cost thousands of lives, culminated in the Kosovo War of 1999, which pitted Serbs against Kosovar Albanians. In Bosnia, Orthodox Serbs fought Muslim Bosniacs (and, to a lesser extent, Catholic Croats). Sarajevo was besieged by Serbian heavy artillery and snipers. What Tito had built over a period of decades collapsed in a matter of years. The collective memory of an integrated, prosperous nation of South Slavs, which had seemed solid and incontrovertible, crumbled rapidly as localized ethnic memories proliferated. Ethnic hatreds that had seemingly disappeared generations ago reappeared, as villages burned, internment camps were built, and the world community watched. The war in Bosnia (and Croatia) ended with the Dayton Accords, which were signed in 1995. Bosnia and Herzegovina, now an independent nation, has yet to recover and reintegrate.

The Bosnian Pyramids were first "discovered" in Visoko, Bosnia's medieval royal capital, in 2004, in the aftermath of the Bosnian War. They are supposed to have been built 10,000 years ago, but outside geologists and archaeologists have demonstrated that they are in fact natural hills. Despite expert testimony to the contrary, however, the idea of the Bosnian Pyramids has spread (helped along by a savvy media campaign and website), and they are now visited by thousands of international tourists annually. Much of the national budget for archaeology, and heritage management in general, was shifted to the "Pyramid of the Sun Foundation," to support excavations in Visoko and development of the site for tourism. State-funded archaeological research projects ceased and in 2012 the National Museum of Bosnia and Herzegovina, which had been open in Sarajevo for 124 years, was closed indefinitely. What had been a homegrown, vernacular construction of the Bosnian past—built around a "memory" of pyramids and a deep, prehistoric, ultimately Illyrian past—has now been co-opted by the national government and rendered official. I contend that the "pyramid" trope constitutes a neutral source of collective imagination and, therefore, identity, which all Bosnians can share regardless of ethnic origin. The pyramids are, of course, a farce and a scam, but also a vibrant source of collective memory cues, written visibly and dramatically into the Bosnian medieval landscape. Groups of men and women gather each summer to dig together in Visoko, destroying real archaeological sites in the process, but simultaneously building pride in a new, special Bosnia.

Modern Bosnia and the Bosnian Pyramids present a good, albeit extreme, example of radical, collective counter-memory making. Modern Bosnia fits well the open model of collective memory presented in figure 1.2. Bosnians emerged from the war traumatized. The nation experienced, and continues to experience, high levels of crisis, both economic and political. Ethnic enclaves have been carved out, separating Orthodox Serbs from Muslim Bosniacs, and they rarely manage any kind of cooperation. The former Yugoslav collective memory is all but dead. In its place, localized, vernacular, ethnic memories have been (re-)constructed, often built around fabricated histories that emphasize regional ethnic purity. These new, old forms of collective memory have been drawn (literally) from medieval songs and maps, and from the landscape itself. Re-traditionalization is common, pushed along by so-called turbo-folk rock music and dance, which appeals to young people and celebrates ethnic identity. In interesting ways, the Bosnian Pyramids represent a counter-counter-memory, aimed at re-establishing a shared Bosnian identity that transcends ethnic identity. Given the current state of political flux, and the inability of the nation to shape public opinion, memory production is working wide open. Bosnian cultural imagination currently allows a large number and variety of heterodox ideas to compete in the field of opinion, including many outlandish, pseudoscientific conspiracy theories, not least the idea that Paleolithic proto-Illyrians built pyramids larger than those at Giza.

The Bosnian example, while extreme, demonstrates well the tight link between state systems of social and political control and collective memory production (figure 1.3). When control is high, memory production slows and narrows. When control is low, memory production accelerates and widens. The same relationship between politics and memory would have held in the first states as well. As archaic states, like those in Mesopotamia, formed, controlling traditional memory systems would have been of paramount concern. State administrators would have found it advantageous to limit cultural imagination, focus nostalgic attention on the state's mythical origins, and create a national identity that transcended traditional, localized, possibly "ethnic" identities and histories. The primary means of meeting these goals would have been to disrupt the heterarchical, parallel-processed, intra-generational memory systems upon which incorporated peoples depended. Killing or co-opting memory workers was one way to do this, as was uprooting material mnemonic cues, those located in the landscape in particular.

In the next three chapters I describe these very processes for early and later states in three regions: Egypt, Greece, and Albania. With reference to figure 1.2, in all three test cases we can apply the memory-production model I have developed and track shifting approaches to collective memory and counter-memory production through time. This effort clearly reveals the important roles played by collective memory in non-state and state-level societies, during state formation and in modern nation building. Ultimately, explaining how collective memory works is critical to understanding the current global situation, one in which nations proliferate and various marginalized peoples seek recognition and power, sometimes violently.

SUMMARY AND CONCLUSION

To summarize, I have argued in this introductory chapter, following Halbwachs (1980, 1992), that collective memory is necessary to the creation of individual human memories, and vice versa. Memory-making is a social process. Moreover, I have insisted that collective memory systems are structured and function in ways very similar to the structure and function of individual memory systems. This is not mere analogy, rather there is an ontogenetic relationship between the two; collective memory develops out of and is dictated by individual human memory and brain organization. As described in some detail above, all memories, whether individual or collective, are constructed. The human brain employs dispersed systems of parallel processing and recall, as do cultural memory systems. Likewise, the human brain requires mnemonic cues to remember, as do cultural memory communities. And in both cases, forgetting is absolutely necessary to proper memory function. For these reasons, collective memories are always politically charged, whether in traditional or more complex societies. Counter-memories can be deployed in traditional societies and states, but both tend to tamp down dissent, though in different ways. Traditional cultures employ extremely effective forms of enculturation, so that subjective identities tend to align with group identities. States employ equally effective forms of enculturation, but they are mandated and operated by the state, reinforcing national identities and fostering nationalism.

Traditional societies deploy various oral memory regimes, which help organize social relations across generations. States employed writing, which gave them a distinct advantage in terms of directing memory production across multiple generations. Both traditional and state societies have employed various inscribed and incorporated (embodied)

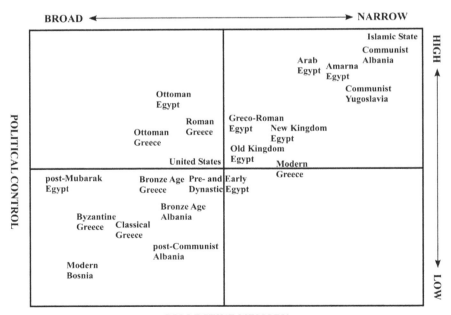

Figure 1.3. Chart demonstrating the positive relationship between political control and collective memory. States that exercise low levels of political control generally allow broad systems of collective memory production. *Source:* M. L. Galaty.

memory systems (Jones 2007), but those of states tend to be hierarchical and centralized, facilitating control. Figure 1.3 charts the positive relationship between higher levels of political control and narrow systems of collective memory production. Contemporary Bosnia falls at one end of the scale; political control is low and collective memory production is broad and highly unorthodox. Communist Albania, which experienced extremely high levels of political control under the Hoxha government, falls at the other end of the scale; political control was high and collective memory production was narrow and highly orthodox. In fact, depending on the offense, contesting state-sponsored collective memories in Hoxha's Albania was punishable by death. Other states on the chart were more or less politically open depending on historical circumstance and trajectory. The United States, for example, currently falls near the center of the chart, since political control is moderate, and changeable, and collective memories are open to some debate. There are limits, though: viz. the vociferous debates about the Vietnam Veterans Memorial (i.e., the Wall) in Washington, D.C. and the Smithsonian's plans to exhibit the *Enola Gay*.

In chapters 2 through 4, I describe the collective memory systems of Egypt, Greece, and Albania at different points in their history and chart the evolving relationship of collective memory to political control. As depicted in figure 1.3, the evolutionary development of states is not governed by a simple linear progression from low to high levels of political control and a narrowing of collective memory; on the contrary, processes of state formation and organizational change are situational, and seemingly stochastic. That said, states, whether ancient or modern, never experienced high levels of political control and broad systems of collective memory production. Nor, conversely, did they experience low levels of political control and narrow systems of collective memory production. These combinations appear to have been (and remain) untenable, not just for states, but for human societies generally. Stable, healthy systems of governance—those that last longer than a few generations—may well require moderation along both political and mnemonic axes (and therefore cluster toward the middle of figure 1.3). Ancient states pulled to either extreme, such as Amarna Egypt or the Classical Greek poleis, have tended to be short-lived and/or characterized by high levels of flux and conflict. Likewise, modern nations characterized by high levels of political control and very narrow collective memory systems, like communist Albania, have tended to fail. It is when modern nations are pulled to either extreme—to the upper right or lower left of figure 1.3—that they experience stasis or chaos, respectively, and, eventually, collapse. Clearly there are lessons to be learned from a careful study of collective memory and nation building through time and across regions.

2

Egypt
Unification

Well, we're nearly there, Hermippos.
Day after tomorrow, it seems—that's what the captain said.
At least we're sailing our seas,
the waters of Cyprus, Syria, and Egypt,
the beloved waters of our home countries.
Why so silent? Ask your heart:
didn't you too feel happier
the farther we got from Greece?
What's the point of fooling ourselves?
That would hardly be properly Greek.

It's time we admitted the truth:
we are Greeks also—what else are we?—
but with Asiatic affections and feelings,
affections and feelings
sometimes alien to Hellenism.

It isn't right, Hermippos, for us philosophers
to be like some of our petty kings
(remember how we laughed at them
when they used to come to our lectures?)
who through their showy Hellenified exteriors,
Macedonian exteriors (naturally),
let a bit of Arabia peep out now and then,
a bit of Media they can't keep back.
And to what laughable lengths the fools went
trying to cover it up!

No, that's not at all right for us.
For Greeks like us that kind of pettiness won't do.
We must not be ashamed
of the Syrian and Egyptian blood in our veins;
we should really honor it, take pride in it.

—Constantine P. Cavafy,
"Coming Back Home from Greece"
(1992 [1914])

Figure 2.1.   Cavafy's bedroom, Alexandria, Egypt. *Source:* M. L. Galaty.

Perhaps no poet captures the depth and complexity of collective memory in modern Egypt better than Constantine Cavafy (1863–1933), a Greek from Alexandria (see map, figure 2.2, page 41). Cavafy repeatedly evokes in his poems a nostalgic longing for days gone by, when Greeks ruled the world, but he was very much an Egyptian. Alexandria, of course, had been founded by Alexander the Great, albeit on indigenous foundations, those of Rhakotis, "that which is built up." From the start, the city was a teeming, multicultural mix—a capital of memory, if ever there was one—as reflected in Cavafy's poetry, which is strewn with historical references. The symbols of old, Ptolemaic Alexandria were the *pharos*, a giant lighthouse, and a library, the greatest in the ancient world. It was burned repeatedly and finally destroyed (perhaps by Caesar, possibly by Arabs), only to be reborn again, like a phoenix, as the Bibliotheca Alexandrina, built in 2002. Words and fire, wind and waves, love and violence, all converging on the far shores of the Mediterranean, that great green "corrupting" sea, the poet savored them all. "Cavafy became his own place, period, paraphernalia, persona, poem simultaneously and his youthful Eros matured into Agape" (O'Grady 1993: 9). He understood memory and "historical imagination," and used them to paint a vivid, diachronic picture of his beloved Alexandria and ever-changing Egypt (O'Grady 1993: 8).

Cavafy's family arrived in Egypt during the reign of the "Albanian" dynasty, founded by Mehmed Ali (1769–1849). His father worked as a merchant, importing and exporting goods, as did many members of the Greek diaspora to the Ottoman Empire. Trade brought wealth, with which the Egyptian Greeks built and embellished churches. Today, throughout Egypt, their numbers are shrinking. Many move back and forth from Alexandria to Athens, a peripatetic existence that Cavafy would appreciate, though he himself spent the last 22 years of his life within the three-block radius of an apartment on the Sharia Sharm el-Sheikh. He worked as a civil servant, and so must have been fluent in Arabic, as are the bilingual Greeks of Egypt today. Their great Orthodox churches, dripping in gold, carry inscriptions and dedications in both languages, Greek and Arabic, as do the tombs of their dead. But priests will no longer come to Alexandria, seat of the African patriarchate, and when they do, they are from south of the Sahara, young, and black. *Kalo padhia*. Good boys, the old Greek-Egyptian women murmur, as they enter the churches to light candles and pray, under the stern gaze of strange desert saints.

The Greek experience of Egypt is nothing compared to that of the Jews, hundreds of thousands of whom once lived in Alexandria and Cairo. They arrived in Egypt following expulsion from Jerusalem and, later, Spain, and in large numbers under Mehmed Ali. Today, there are scarcely a couple hundred left. Their cemeteries are abandoned and their synagogues have been turned into museums, protected by armed guards. Like the Greeks, the Jews have a deeper, pre-modern connection to Egypt and to Egyptian collective memory, as described in the Old Testament, a connection recognized and explored by Freud (1939). For Freud, and, more recently, Assmann (1997), the ancient Egyptian memory of Moses and the Jews was a traumatic one, tied to echoes of the Hyksos domination and Akhenaten's heresy. Indeed, the ancient Egyptians were obsessed with memory, in life and in death, an obsession inherited by their Greek and subsequent Roman conquerors, who rapidly Egyptianized. Later, under the influence of early, "paleo"-Christianity, ancient Egyptian beliefs and practices morphed and were preserved in various syncretic, Coptic traditions, which also emphasize memory and divine intercession. The Coptic worldview can be compared to that of the Arabs, who were Muslim and conquered Egypt in AD 639. According to Connerton (1989: 46–47), Islam is a hyper-historical and thus non-ritualized religious system, one not characterized by "inscribed" and "incorporated" forms of collective memory. Given these contrasts, exactly how multicultural Egypt experienced the Ottoman administration, in particular under the liberalizing government of Mehmed Ali and his descendants, bears on the question of collective memory formation generally and its effects on the modern Middle East.

This chapter traces the role of collective memory in Egypt through time, beginning with the Predynastic period, during which the Egyptian state formed. I focus on the origins and evolution of Egyptian funerary practices as manifestations of distributed memory systems, as described in chapter 1. In prehistoric, trans-egalitarian Egypt, the bodies of ancestors were preserved, at first accidentally and later purposefully, through mummification, functioning as powerful mnemonic cues. In life, Egyptians occupied a spiritually charged world, filled with supernatural energy and beings. Upon death, they entered an afterlife where they might intercede with the gods and spirits on behalf of the living. It was this supernatural world and its coupled interactive afterlife that early priests and pharaohs co-opted and sought to control. Evidence for this process of appropriation exists for the Early Dynastic period, during which Upper and Lower Egypt were unified and integrated. Unification itself left an indelible imprint on Egyptian collective memory. Through the centuries of the Old and New Kingdoms, across dynasties and despite interregnal interruptions, kings worked to channel collective memories, sometimes cooperating with priests, sometimes not. To this end, they distorted earlier histories, literally erasing the names and images of their predecessors. Such was the fate of Hatshepsut, the first and only female pharaoh. Common people responded to the official memory system by making counter-memories, as did some pharaohs. I argue that in founding his new monotheistic religion and moving the Egyptian capital to Amarna, Akhenaten attempted to exercise final, autocratic control over orthodox memory systems, to the expense of all other systems, priestly or otherwise. The ultimate response to Akhenaten and his program was their total eradication from Egyptian collective memory and a new 19th dynasty of powerful, expansionist pharaohs, including Rameses the Great. It was presumably sometime during this period that Moses and the Jews were expelled from Egypt.

The Ptolemaic kings and, later, the Romans adopted Egyptian habits, including their propensity for collective memory making and forgetting.

They created a syncretic culture, one Cavafy recognized and memorialized in his poetry. Gods and goddesses were mixed and matched, tombs and temples used and reused, and Egyptian collective memories accessed, processed, and conflated, by royals and commoners alike (Meskell 2003). But it was through Christianity that Egyptian forms of "embodied" ritual and religious practices were preserved, as heterodox counter-points to Greek and Roman paganism and Byzantine dyophysitism. Building Coptic Christianity did require, however, the repurposing of Egyptian *lieux de mémoire*, which happened across Egypt, at sites like Philae in Aswan. By the time the Arabs arrived, Egypt was a Christian nation, one with deep mystical roots in desert monasteries, where monks mimicked earlier Egyptian ascetic and oracular practices.

Islamic Egypt was, compared to Byzantine Egypt, equally cosmopolitan, drawing immigrants from throughout the empire, reaching a crescendo during the Mamluk period. The Mamluks, who were "Circassians," in seeking to justify their rule, once again turned Egyptian collective memory to their needs, this despite the caliph's near-absolute control of Egypt's memory regimes, through Al-Azhar University, for example, the oldest in the world. Mamluk power was challenged by the Ottomans, who conquered Egypt in 1517, but they were not fully destroyed until March 1, 1811, when Mehmed Ali lured them to the Cairo Citadel and massacred them all. The massacre of the Mamluks has become a touch point in Egyptian history and the Citadel a key *lieux de mémoire*, marking for many Egyptians the foundation of modern Egypt. Throughout the Islamic and into the modern, Republican period, Egyptian national identity was constructed against that of the Bedouin, Nubians, and Sudanese, who constituted significant ethnic minorities, just as ancient Egyptian identity was constructed against that of "Asiatics," Canaanites, and Jews.

In this chapter, I follow the development of Egyptian collective memory and memory making processes through time, paying particular attention to state formation and nation-building efforts. At key points, I run Egyptian memory regimes through the explanatory model constructed in chapter 1, noting the configuration of the six independent variables that compose the model and together determine the structure of collective memories vis-à-vis political control (figures 1.1–1.3). Doing so reveals several important diachronic trends: *coevolution* (i.e., of Egyptian state politics and collective memory, which were tightly linked from the period of state formation through modern times); *stability* (i.e., of orthodox collective memory engrams that formed during Pharaonic times, persisted through periods of foreign rule, and were only rarely challenged); and *friction* (e.g., between memory and history, which came to a head during the period of Arab rule).

MEMORY AND THE ANCIENT EGYPTIAN STATE

Wilkinson (1999: 31) has suggested that the history of hierarchy and state formation in Egypt is one of "growing differentiation and elaboration of mortuary provision." Egypt became Egypt through public practices and celebrations of death and dying, which were used to create and unify an Egyptian state. This process began during the Egyptian Neolithic (the Badarian, 5000–4000 BC) and came to a head during the Predynastic (during the Naqada IIC-D phase, 3650–3300 BC), culminating in the foundation of the Egyptian nation-state and the first dynasty, *circa* 3050 BC (see chronological table 2.1). The kings of ancient Egypt generated the "binding force" that held the state together (Wilkinson 1999: 58–59, 183). They championed unification, symbolized bodily and through public ritual, and protected the nation from chaos, represented in Egyptian iconography by various foreign (i.e., non-"Egyptian") peoples (e.g., Asiatics, Libyans, and Nubians) who threatened to infiltrate Egyptian territory. State-sponsored xenophobia was used to build a national ideology in which the king, represented by Horus, was responsible for interceding with the gods on humanity's behalf. Absent such intercession, the Nile's waters failed, outsiders attacked, and the state collapsed. Memory was the primary tool employed by kings in their efforts to maintain the Egyptian state, and their own power, and it was wielded both in life and, most effectively, in death.

Several scholars have described Egyptian concerns for memory, memory making, and the dissemination and control of memory systems. Meskell (2002, 2003, 2004) has written extensively of memory in later periods of Egyptian history, Roman in particular. Assmann (1997, 2002) has applied the concept of cultural memory to developments in Old and New Kingdom Egypt. And more recently, Wengrow (2006: 83) has reinterpreted early Egyptian history in terms of the "urbanization of the dead," which "may have been more important than the urbanization of the living, the density of social memory more vital than the massing of permanent dwellings." All three are addressed in reverse order below.

Pre- and Early Dynastic Egypt

The unification of Upper and Lower Egypt, of the Nile Valley with the Delta, occurred during the Egyptian Early Bronze Age and involved processes of both cultural and political integration (figure 2.2, table 2.1). In the centuries prior to unification, Upper and Lower Egypt apparently charted very different courses, marked by quite different material-culture assemblages and by very different burial practices. Beginning in Naqada I (*circa* 4000 BC) Upper Egyptian burials became more and more lavish, including many imported prestige goods. By late Naqada II (by *circa* 3300 BC) Lower Egypt had adopted similar mortuary practices, at sites like Minshat Abu Omar in the Delta (Wengrow 2006: 83–84). The traditional interpretation of Egyptian Predynastic history thus assumes that an early "king" operating out of Upper Egypt, probably Narmer, attacked and subdued Lower Egypt, perhaps seeking to gain control of lucrative trade routes that connected Egypt with the Levant, as depicted in the Narmer Palette (e.g., Quibell and Green 1902). This process of military subjugation and social integration is thought to have led to the political unification of Upper and Lower Egypt sometime around 3100 BC.

Political unification may have been encouraged by increased urbanization at Middle Egyptian sites like Hierakonpolis, Naqada, and This during the Naqada period (e.g., Hoffman et al. 1986; Kemp 1989; Wilkinson 1993), accompanied by competition and episodes of "chiefly cycling" (Flannery and Marcus 2013: 402-406), and the eventual founding of a new capital at Memphis, at the boundary between Upper and Lower Egypt. Wilkinson (1993) was the first scholar to chart the Predynastic

Table 2.1. Egyptian Chronology

Period	Date	Dynasty
Neolithic	5200–4000 BC	
Predynastic		
Naqada I	4000–3500 BC	
Naqada II	3500–3200 BC	
Naqada III	3200–3100 BC	
Early Dynastic	3100–2686 BC	0–2
Old Kingdom	2686–2181 BC	3–6
First Intermediate Period	2181–2025 BC	7–11
Middle Kingdom	2025–1700 BC	11–13
Second Intermediate Period	1700–1550 BC	13–17
New Kingdom	1550–1069 BC	18–20
Third Intermediate Period	1069–664 BC	21–25
Late Period	664–525 BC	26
First Persian Period	525–404 BC	27
Late Dynastic Period	404–343 BC	28–30
Second Persian Period	343–332 BC	
Macedonian Period	332–305 BC	
Ptolemaic Period	323–30 BC	
Roman Period	30 BC–AD 640	
Islamic Period	640–1517	
Ottoman Period	1517–1805	
Khedival Period	1805–1919	
Monarchy	1919–1953	
Republic	1953–present	

state-formation process from start to finish, but his evidence is not drawn primarily from settlement excavations; rather it stems from the funerary and later written records, which emphasize the lasting importance and impact of ideologies of unification. The monumentalization of tombs at sites like Abydos (e.g., a shift from mud brick to stone with the addition of stairs) began during the 1st Dynasty reign of Den (2970–2928 BC) (Wilkinson 1993: 75). This was accompanied by the first use of the royal title *nswt-bíty*, "he of the reed and bee," and the first depiction of the double-crown, both of which signified unification (Ibid.). Thus, from the start, the king embodied and reinforced, in death and in life, the historical importance of unification and kept its memory current in various ways. Rituals of kingship, such as the *sed* festival, typically held once during a king's reign, celebrated integration, rejuvenation, and continuity, emphasizing unification through the display of both Upper and Lower Egyptian gods along the edges of the festival grounds (Wilkinson 1993: 213). Heirlooms, such as stone bowls, inscribed and re-inscribed with the names of earlier kings, were carefully curated and buried in royal tombs (Wilkinson 1993: 84), providing a lasting, visceral display of permanence and stability. The standard interpretation is thus one of steady, cultural-evolutionary change, characterized by urbanization and increased social complexity, linked to warfare, and, finally, Early Dynastic incorporation and domination of Lower by Upper Egypt.

Wengrow (2006) has questioned this reading of Pre- and Early Dynastic history, arguing that early Egyptian culture, both Lower and Upper, including portions of Lower Nubia (see also Wilkinson 1993: 175–82), was rooted in Neolithic practices of pastoralism, characterized by high levels of mobility, which mitigated against "rootedness" and therefore urbanization. His review of Predynastic habitation sites, including Hierakonpolis, indicates almost no permanent domestic architecture (Wengrow 2006: 76–82), thus leading him to suggest that it was instead the mortuary landscape that was "urbanized" (Ibid.: 83). It was this practice—monumentalizing burial at the expense of domestic architecture—that moved north from Upper to Lower Egypt at the end of the Naqada phase, along with a prestige-goods mortuary economy that depended on non-Egyptian imports. Thus the foundation of the Egyptian nation-state must be explained through study of shifting beliefs related to how bodies were treated and used both in life and, particularly, in death. According to Wengrow (2006: 121–23), treatment of living and dead bodies, including that of the king, in Pre- and Early Dynastic Egypt, enabled creation and elaboration of new, changing Egyptian identities. This process of identity formation, which depended on the manipulation of collective memory, was later co-opted by the state.

The manipulation of memory and the disruption of traditional distributed memory systems by Upper Egyptian elites began almost immedi-

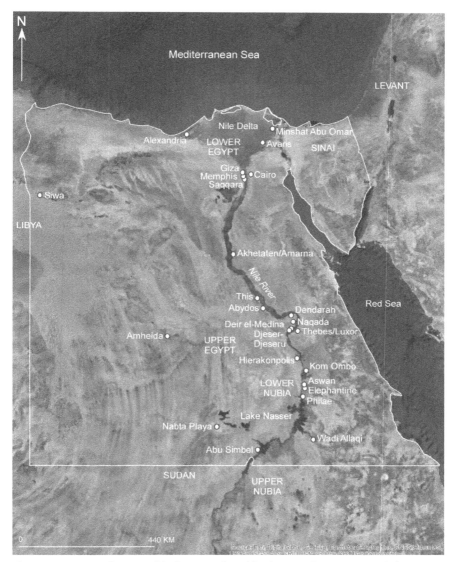

Figure 2.2. Map of Egypt with sites mentioned in the text. *Source:* M. L. Galaty.

ately following unification and were linked to changes in mortuary practice and, more generally, regional economy. During the Naqada period, dead bodies were subjected to exposure, dismemberment, secondary reburial, and significant manipulation (Wengrow 2006: 116–20). Body parts were presumably curated and used by living individuals as mnemonic cues, triggering collective episodic memories, building social solidarity in highly mobile pastoral communities. However, beginning in Naqada II, there was a shift away from pastoralism toward a leavened bread- and beer-based subsistence economy, centrally controlled at sites like Hierakonpolis, signaled by the introduction of new ceramic forms (Wengrow 2006: 92–98). According to Wengrow (2006: 98), "By the end of Naqada II leavened bread and beer had become socially necessary for the proper commemoration of the dead in Egypt" leading to a "significant loss of autonomy" for individuals who did not have easy access to their production. By the end of Naqada II, the practice of dismemberment had waned, to be replaced by mummification and preservation of the deceased. Wengrow (2006: 123) argues that mummification served a purpose similar to that of dismemberment, "by transforming the body into an image" and making possible "its replication and extension into wider chains of signification." Just as the new bread-and-beer, prestige-goods mortuary economy facilitated elite control of burial ritual, mummification enabled state-sponsored disruptions of traditional forms of commemoration and ancestor worship. These disruptions expanded during the Early Dynastic.

Egyptian graves were marked by wood (later stone) stelae that facilitated visitation of the dead by the living, during which offerings would have been made and ancestral lineages recited (Harrington 2013). Simple graves, however, were prone to loss and disturbance, which drove monumentalization. At first, low mounds of sand and rock (perhaps symbolizing the original creation mound) were built over graves and grave groups (e.g., from Neolithic Nabta Playa in the north [Flannery and Marcus 2013: 396; Wengrow 2006: 57] to Lower Nubia in the south [Wengrow 2006: 54]). Later (by Naqada III), subterranean tombs were constructed of mud brick to house the dead, becoming stone built by the reign of Den. During the 1st Dynasty, royal tombs (e.g., of Djet and Semerkhet) attracted hundreds of subsidiary burials that were "poorly finished and crudely inscribed" (Wilkinson 1993: 235, 237; see also Wengrow 2006: 252–55). These graves likely held the bodies of sacrificed retainers, many of them well-to-do members of the king's entourage (Morris 2008). By the end of the 1st Dynasty, the practice of subsidiary burial had died out, and many individuals were left without access to proper disposal and funerary ritual (e.g., mummification, burial in a mud-brick tomb with bread and beer, and deposition of prestige goods). By the 2nd Dynasty (*circa* 2800–2650 BC), tombs were clearly meant to imitate domestic structures, functioning as homes for the souls (*ka*) of the dead (Wilkinson 1993: 241). Originally, these were composed of two separate architectural elements: an enclosure and the tomb itself. Enclosures served as loci for private funeral rituals, including libation, sacrifice, and prayer, celebrated by families. By the 3rd Dynasty (*circa* 2650–2580 BC), enclosure and tomb had been combined and moved below ground (Wilkinson 1993: 231). Large *mastabas* (mud brick monuments) were built over the top of elite graves, eventually developing into stepped pyramids. The stepped pyramid complex at Saqqara, built by Netjerikhet (Djoser), was accompanied by a shrine, where authority passed from the old to the new king in the presence of the assembled ancestors, symbolized by a white baboon, the ḥḏ-wr (Wilkinson 1993: 285). With the development of the royal pyramid complex, the evolution of Egyptian mortuary rites and their linked memory systems away from individuals and families and toward state-sponsored political control was complete. By the end of the 3rd Dynasty, the Egyptian king had been transformed into a deity, supported by complex royal rituals that commemorated orthodox understandings of Egyptian history and disenfranchised traditional memory systems. As such, a key responsibility of the king was to suppress dissent and thereby hold back chaos (Wilkinson 1993: 223). The goddess Mafdet, portrayed as a lioness or large cat, served as protector and avenger of the king, her primary task to punish rebels (Wilkinson 1993: 290), who were portrayed as enemies of unity and, thus, memory.

Key allies of the king in these efforts were the priests who operated out of shrines and temples. Throughout the Early Dynastic, state-sponsored and local shrines were maintained separately and served different deities (Wilkinson 1993: 272). Priests were part-time specialists, descendants of shamans, who, like later *s(t)m*-priests, wore leopard skin robes (Wilkinson 1993: 273). Unlike state-sponsored temples, though, local shrines were open to the public and thus supported local, distributed memory systems, as did traditional funerary practices. By the 5th Dynasty (beginning 2465 BC), however, even local priests had become full-time specialists, and by the end of the Old Kingdom, the state actively sought to appropriate local shrines (Wilkinson 1993: 172). The appropriation of local shrines, particularly those of Lower Egypt, was accompanied by the incorporation of local Lower Egyptian deities into royal titles (Wilkinson 1993: 292), and the creation of estates on Delta lands (Ibid.: 117). Many of these royal estates supported the new mortuary cults of deceased kings, and consequently the professional priesthood. The founding of estates began in the late 3rd Dynasty and was immediately preceded by the construction of small step pyramids throughout Egypt, by the pharaoh Huni, symbolizing unification of the country and centralization of its economy (Wilkinson 1993: 277).

> An estate of Huni is listed on the Palermo Stone in the reign of the Fifth Dynasty King Neferirkara; this indicates that the memory of Huni was still revered. And at least one of his foundations still in existence, a century-and-a-half after his death. (Wilkinson 1993: 104)

By the Old Kingdom, then, autocratic control had been extended by kings and associated elite over the whole of the Two Lands. Control was effected through manipulation of ideologies related to death and dying, tied to religion and economy, embodied by the king both in life and in death. Central to the proper functioning of this system was the substitution of ethnic borders with national ones based on territorial control (Wilkinson 1993: 180). At the beginning of the 1st Dynasty a fortress was built on the island of Elephantine, signaling a new, aggressive policy toward Nubia, a key component of the developing ideological program of national unity (Wilkinson 1993: 180). At the same time, portions of the southern Levant were colonized, and the pack-mule trains through the Sinai were seized and marine routes expanded (Wengrow 2006: 138). Wadi trails from the Nile Valley to the Red Sea were embellished and an "administrator of the desert," *'d-mr zmit*, was named (during the reign of Qaa, 2916–2890 BC), charged with maintaining the buffer zone between Egypt and Libya (Wilkinson 1993: 143). By the Old Kingdom, Egypt had become a nation-state defined in contra-distinction to non-Egyptian territories and peoples, potent sources of memory and counter-memory production.

The above (pre-)historical outline can be run though chapter 1's memory model with interesting results. With reference to figure 1.1, state formation in Egypt involved shifting memory systems out of the realm of opinion and discourse to that of doxa. Heterodox memory systems that originated in early Neolithic pastoral communities and were rooted in the curation and transformation of human remains, thereby supporting open-ended ideologies of identity and belonging, were captured and altered by early state authorities (beginning in Naqada II). Priests, acting as agents of the state, formalized death rituals and linked them to new, orthodox conceptions of nationhood, which revolved around unification. The unity of the body and its preservation through mummification, that of the king in particular, came to symbolize the unity of the state and its defense. The new ideologies of death and political unity, which came at the expense of Lower Egypt, were enshrined (during the Old Kingdom) in novel myth systems, such as that of Osiris, who was murdered and dismembered by his brother Seth (a Lower Egyptian god), an enemy of unity, memory, and, therefore, the state. Osiris was resurrected by his wife, Isis, who gave birth to Horus, the falcon-headed god who personified and symbolized royal divinity. Ideologies of death and unity operated recursively and were reinforced over time through various memory practices (such as lamentation; Wickett 2010), limiting counter-memory production. By the Early Dynastic, proper burial required beer, bread, and prestige goods, obtainable only from the state. Tombs were monumentalized, further reinforcing the permanence—the immovability—of the new memory systems. The net effect was the inversion of cultural variables linked to once-open memory systems (i.e., Neolithic death as a vehicle for identity exploration versus Early Dynastic death as a source of organic solidarity).

Turning to figure 1.2, early Egyptian memory systems generally moved from open to closed through time as they were co-opted by the state and the social spaces available for imagination and identity formation were truncated. The closure of distributed memory systems can be identified archaeologically in the shift from impermanent communal tombs that facilitated ancestor worship (early Naqada) to individualized forms of burial that encouraged private ceremony (by Naqada III), and in the shift from domestic cults to regional shrines and, eventually, temples (see figure 2.3, adapted from Harrington 2013: 102). Family tombs and shrines acted as "distributed memory stores," staffed at first by shamans and then by part-time priests; public access was high. Later, tombs and temples became important *lieux de mémoire*, sacred sites that broadcast the new Egyptian state's constructed past; public access was limited. Cultural memories were triggered during elaborate rituals, encouraging forms of both "inscribed" and "incorporated" cultural memory creation (Connerton 1989: 72–79). Temples were covered with carvings and paintings, commemorating past events. Tombs, and the mummies in them, served as retrieval cues, triggering cultural memory engrams. As the Egyptian state formed, different regions were incorporated into the *nome* system of administration, national borders were reinforced, internal and external sources of conflict were reduced, and alternative sources of imagination and identity formation were curtailed. At the same time,

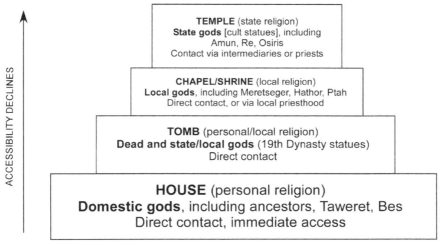

Figure 2.3. Chart depicting Egyptian religious structures and the decline in accessibility across space and through time. Adapted from Harrington 2013: 102. *Source:* M. L. Galaty.

nationalism and nostalgia swelled. To love the nation of Egypt was to love its post-unification past and the royal personages who underpinned that past. State-sanctioned histories were transmitted more and more often using hieroglyphic writing, such as in the form of "year-names" written on "year-labels," which were attached to royal tomb offerings, creating a form of "monarchic memory" (Wengrow 2006: 134). Monarchic memory was linked to social memory through royal death cults that served to reproduce publicly the nation, in perpetuity, through reference to the exploits of past pharaohs. Their death estates were established at sites throughout Lower Egypt, employing citizens directly in the state's memory-making industry.

Old (and Middle) Kingdom Egypt thus lands directly in the center of figure 1.3: political control was moderate, yet autocratic, and so memory systems were narrow, without being completely closed. The history of the Old Kingdom is one of stability and growth, interrupted by the First Intermediate Period, but carrying into the Middle Kingdom. This stability was shattered by the Hyksos invasion, ushering in the Second Intermediate Period, during which Egyptian unity was torn asunder. The New Kingdom pharaohs doubled down on ideologies of unity, further encouraging xenophobia and creating an expansive empire, thereby inching Egypt's memory systems towards closure.

From Old to New Kingdom Egypt

The primary cultural memory engram of Old (and Middle) Kingdom Egypt was that of unification (and therefore stability and harmony), recalling the powerful, mythic pharaohs of the Pre- and Early Dynastic periods who—militarily or otherwise—integrated Upper and Lower Egypt. Unification was supported through the creation of a network of regional estates that produced and consumed manufactured goods, linking the state's ideology to political-economy (Wengrow 2006: 145–146). Shrines and temples served as nodes in a decentralized system of administration that spanned the nation and interconnected far-flung nomes, building and supporting unification. Individuals were employed in this system, helping to construct and maintain shrines and temples, working on royal estates, funneling wealth into royal tombs while their own became more and more impoverished (Wengrow 2006: 152–53). Bodies—mummies—themselves symbolized unification, its tangible, lasting permanence, and sacred stability. Threats to that stability, whether human or supernatural, were dealt with directly, by deploying force or by appealing to gods and ancestors. An ancestor who was properly buried and propitiated lived on in the afterlife and could be expected to render help to the living. Thus, the average Egyptian household remained whole and healthy by regulating its members and remembering forebears. The royal household did likewise, reciting—and, eventually, recording—a list of kings going back to the divine, primal ancestor (Wengrow 2006: 130). The kings of the past, who had successfully defended unity, could be visited at their impressive pyramid-tomb complexes, which functioned as massive *lieux de mémoire*, projecting potent messages of order over chaos, life conquering death, and continuity.

This nested, state-sponsored memory system left little room for counter-memory production. Once, between the Old and Middle Kingdoms, during the First Intermediate Period (2181–2050 BC), unification faltered, primarily as a result of succession disputes. Lower Egypt overthrew Upper Egypt, nome fought nome, but the memory system held. It is perhaps no accident that when centralized control was finally re-established, Osiris became the most popular deity (Assmann 2002: 157–59). It was during the Second Intermediate Period (*circa* 1650–1550 BC), however, that true damage was done to the Egyptian state memory system.

The Second Intermediate Period began when Semitic peoples called the Hyksos (a Greek transliteration of *heqa khaseshet*, "ruler[s] of the foreign countries") took political control of Egypt, ruling from the northern city of Avaris (Knapp 1988: 168–71). Foreign rule undercut the traditional Old Kingdom narrative of unity, and the defeat of the Hyksos (in 1540 BC) set the stage for transformations in New Kingdom ideology. Whereas the Middle Kingdom pharaohs saw the First Intermediate Period as an internal failure (caused by a shortage of *ma'at*, i.e., "solidarity"), the New Kingdom pharaohs emphasized the danger of external forces and focused on foreign policy (Assmann 2002: 198–99). Hyksos domination was fixed in the Egyptian memory system alongside unification, and Seth was retooled as an Asiatic god, symbolic of "otherness" and instability (Assmann 2002: 199–200). Thus, to have and maintain unity, foreign powers and their gods should be conquered and assimilated. Unlike the Old and Middle Kingdom, during which the focus was systematization of politicized memory regimes, emphasizing traditional "social virtues" (and judgment—i.e., of the dead by Osiris) (Assmann 2002: 156), the New Kingdom was a period of imperial expansion, during which external peoples—not only Semites, but also Hittites, Libyans, Nubians, and others—were framed as the primary threats to the state and the state's memory. The historical reality of foreign domination (e.g., that of the Hyksos) had, therefore, to be committed to cultural memory orthodoxy. This was done in a variety of ways, but primarily through the deification and presentation of Ahmose, the great "warrior king" who defeated the Hyksos, as the savior of Egypt.

The first New Kingdom pharaohs (those of the 18th Dynasty), who followed in Ahmose's footsteps, undertook military campaigns that created a wide buffer zone between Egypt and its Asiatic neighbors. Tuthmosis I pushed north and east as far as the Euphrates River. Kings were depicted as victorious generals in New Kingdom public art, smiting their enemies and conquering cities in Syria, and beyond (Assmann 2002: 201). Some pharaohs, however, retreated from the new expansionist ideology, emphasizing dialogue and trade. One of these was Hatshepsut, a female pharaoh who reigned from 1508–1458 BC. Hatshepsut sought to rule as both Horus and Seth, reconciling the civilized world of Egypt and the barbaric worlds beyond (Assmann 2002: 43):

> I united the two lords, that is, their parts,
> by ruling like the son of Isis [Horus]
> and being strong like the son of Nut [Seth].

After her death, the cartouche and images of Hatshepsut were chiseled away, including from her funerary monument at Djeser-Djeseru, a form of Egyptian *damnatio memoriae*. It had long been argued that this was done by her stepson and successor, Tuthmosis III, because Hatshepsut was a woman, but recently Tyldesley (1996: 225) has argued that her unconventional reign was an "offense against *maat*" (i.e., solidarity, stability) and therefore had to be erased from history if the political ideology of the New Kingdom was to hold. Hatshepsut had, in a sense, challenged Egypt's orthodox memory systems, both unification and foreign domination, systems in which many priests and politicians, including Tuthmosis III, had a vested interest. Tyldesley (1996: 223) also notes that the eradication of Hatshepsut from the material record was very poorly executed, such that in some cases, although her body was chiseled away, an associated inscription bearing her name was still readable. This seemingly inconsistent behavior makes sense, though, if Hatshepsut's crime was perpetrated against memory; as noted in chapter 1, the absence of a once-present image may act as a powerful memory cue. The missing Hatshepsut would have elicited a cultural-memory engram related to Egyptian unity in the face of Hyksos rule, which had ended a mere century earlier.

In New Kingdom Egypt, space for counter-memory production was limited. The traumatic cultural memories linked to the Second Intermediate Period were still fresh, and official memory systems and workers, such as priests, could not be easily challenged. Hatshepsut's treatment indicates as much, but also that different factions must have interpreted Egyptian collective memories differently and used them to their advantage. Assmann (2002: 250) describes war and peace parties, hawks and doves, which vied for control of the New Kingdom political machine. One of these parties eventually managed to place a man on the throne who, unlike Hatshepsut (or even the Hyksos kings), was willing to abandon completely the Egyptian collective memory system: Akhenaten.

Pharaoh Amenhotep IV ruled for 17 years (*circa* 1351–1334 BC). By the start of the sixth year of his reign he had taken the name Akhenaten, meaning "Beneficent-one-of (*or* for)-the-Aten" (Montserrat 2000: 21). The new name highlights the pharaoh's role as primary intermediary between humanity and the gods, and further emphasizes his own divinity vis-à-vis the Aten, the sun disc, source of all life (Ibid.). Shortly thereafter, words and images evoking Amun, patron god of Thebes and the royal family, were mutilated throughout Egypt and a new city was constructed in the Middle Egyptian desert, Akhetaten, "Horizon of the Aten," called Amarna today (Ibid.). Worship of all gods other than the Aten was outlawed (Hornung 1999: 48–49).

Akhenaten likely had many reasons for developing a new, monotheistic religious doctrine. Some scholars have suggested that a simple, economic rivalry between Akhenaten and the priests of Thebes pushed him to establish a new state religion and move the capital to Amarna (e.g., Redford 1984: 158–64). Assmann (2002: 214), however, doubts this explanation, since there is no documentary evidence for a conflict leading up to the founding of Akhetaten; rather, something more profound may have been at work. Following Breasted (1906), Assmann (2002: 15) describes a shift in worldview prompted by the imperialist policies of the Tuthmosids and the need for a more "ecumenical" Egyptian divinity, who could rule over all the peoples of the earth, making Egypt the cosmological center of the universe. Indeed, for Hornung (1999: 125, italics in the original) the Amarna religion was nothing short of revolutionary:

> For the first time in history, an attempt was made to explain the entire natural and human world on the basis of a *single* principle. Like Einstein, Akhenaten made light the absolute reference point, and it is astonishing how clearly and consistently he pursued this concept in the fourteenth century B.C.E., making him the first *modern* human being.

I would argue, though, that economy and ideology, alone and in combination, do not explain fully Akhenaten's actions, if we understand his primary motivations to be political, not strictly religious, aimed at strengthening regional control. In fact, the Amarna state represents the logical outcome of memory trends and systems that had moved steadily toward closure, beginning in the Early Dynastic (see, again, figure 1.3). Akhenaten sought to bring under his purview all forms of Egyptian collective memory production and all memory workers, both physically, at Akhetaten, and philosophically, by proposing a single, all-powerful divine force, the Aten, from which all things stemmed, including thought and, thus, memory. The pantheon of gods, including Osiris and Horus, that underpinned ideologies of unification was banned. Prior history (e.g., of the Hyksos) was irrelevant; a new historical cycle began with Akhenaten's ascension.

Akhenaten's iconoclastic counter-memory revolution was short-lived. When he died, evidence of his reign was absolutely erased. Amarna was largely abandoned, temples to the Aten were torn down, and names and images of Amun and the other gods were restored. As Assmann (1997: 4, 25) describes, Akhenaten's revolution was ultimately traumatic (a trauma compounded by a deadly plague that swept the land, subsequently referred to as "the Asiatic illness" because it supposedly began in Syria) and consequently was fully expunged from Egypt's collective memory. So complete was this cultural amnesia that the history of Amarna was not recovered until the late 19th century, when it captured the Western world's popular imagination (Montserrat 2000), prompting Sigmund Freud (1939) to write his last book on Akhenaten, titled *Moses and Monotheism*. In it, he used the new archaeological evidence from Amarna to reconstruct the long-suppressed memory of Akhenaten, and to argue that Moses was an Egyptian and worshiper of the Aten who brought monotheism to Israel. The associated Hebrew sojourn in Egypt and the Exodus were Jewish cultural memories of the Hyksos occupation and expulsion (see also Maeir 2015). Thus, a mnemo-historical arc stretching from Egyptian unification to imperialism to monotheism connects Egypt to Israel and from there to Christianity, Islam, and the modern world (Assmann 1997).

In the aftermath of the Armana era, a line of powerful kings, the Ramessids, took the throne and war became the primary means of forestalling *isfet* (chaos). The start of this period was dominated by geopolitical struggles with the Hittites, which ended with the Battle of Qadesh, fought and won by Rameses II in 1274 BC. The Hittite defeat ushered in sixty years of relative peace and an Egyptian renaissance of sorts (Assmann 2002: 279), characterized by intense inter-regional interaction, trade, and migration. This cosmopolitan era brought Egypt into contact with a host of different Mediterranean ethnic groups, including the Mycenaean Greeks, and ended in conflict with the so-called Sea Peoples, who were defeated by Rameses III in 1175 BC. The New Kingdom closed with the end of the 20th Dynasty *circa* 1100 BC, followed by the Third Intermediate Period and an Eastern Mediterranean Dark Age.

As was done for Pre- and Early Dynastic Egypt, the above outline of Old and New Kingdom history can be run through chapter 1's memory model. During the Amarna Age, Egypt's orthodox memory systems were seriously challenged. A heterodox counter-memory system built around monotheistic worship of the Aten was forcibly transferred into the doxic realm by Akhenaten. Interestingly, it was not crisis that precipitated this shift, which may be why it failed: when crisis is low, memory systems tend toward stability (see figure 1.2). Rather, Akhenaten sought to move Egyptian memory systems hard to the right, while at the same time greatly narrowing opportunities for political discourse (see figure 1.3). In the aftermath of the Hyksos invasion and its existential threat to Egyptian unity, Akhenaten's heresy caused serious damage to the national psyche, so much so that, unlike Hatshepsut, who had only lightly challenged the state's ideology, Akhenaten was fully erased from Egyptian collective memory. So complete was Egypt's cultural amnesia that Freud (1939) used Amarna as the primordial example of repressed traumatic memory.

Despite the military character of New Kingdom Egypt, there is some evidence for counter-memory production, even during the repressive rule of Akhenaten (e.g., images of domestic gods have been recovered from excavations of non-elite houses at Amarna itself) (Montserrat 2000: 23). During the New Kingdom, the basis for Egyptian collective memory systems was still religious in nature, linked to ideas of life and death. Mummified royals and their retainers were buried in the Valley of the Kings in massive underground tombs. These tombs, their contents, and the paintings covering their walls served as raw material for the construction and promulgation of new memory engrams. Some tombs were robbed, presumably by common people, who did not care that robbing tombs disrupted memory systems (Meskell 2004: 45). Other tombs and tomb contents were appropriated by new occupants when memories of the original inhabitants faded (Cooney 2012). That tombs could be visited is made evident by the large amounts of later graffiti cut into tomb paintings, a kind of running collective-memory commentary (Navrátilová 2011).

Shifting ideas about death can be further traced in the lamentations sung at Egyptian funerals. Images of female mourners, who unplait and tear out their hair, wail, weep, scratch their faces, rip open their clothes, dance, and throw their arms in the air, can be traced to the Naqada II (Wickett 2010: 157). Unlike other Neolithic death rituals that were strongly linked to collective-memory production (see above), which disappeared (or were transformed) in the aftermath of unification and state formation, lamentation continued and was particularly popular among non-elites. Wailing women helped the dead cross the boundary between life and death, filling a liminal, intermediary position akin to that of priests and the king himself. In New Kingdom lamentation texts, wailing women are clearly distressed by and pessimistic about death (Wickett 2010: 165):

> You that are beloved (who would) talk to me
> You are silent
> You reply not

For the common people, the afterlife was a barren, unhappy place, and thus lamentations constituted a potent source of improvised counter-memories that called into question official ideologies (cf. Harrington 2013: 112, who refers to laments as "heretical"). This can be contrasted to the state-sponsored, orthodox conception of death, expressed in religious documents and presented in tomb iconography: a smooth transition to the afterlife reinforced social stability (*ma'at*). Interestingly, lamentation and other forms of heterodox mortuary behaviors carried through the periods of Assyrian, Persian, Greek, and Roman occupation and into both Coptic and Muslim practice. In fact, the Greek and Roman periods in particular did not cause mnemo-historic ruptures in Egyptian ideologies of unification and xenophobia, as had the Hyksos domination and Akhenaten's heresy. Rather there was continuity in terms of beliefs and practice. Assmann (2002: 282) attributes this continuity to the power of the Egyptian idea of statehood, which foreign conquerors, such as the Greeks, adopted. In so doing, they also adopted Egypt's collective memory systems.

Ptolemaic and Roman Egypt

The Third Intermediate Period (1080–664 BC), during which political power was divided between Upper and Lower Egypt, was characterized by a decisive break with the past (Assmann 2002: 289). Prompted by internal crises, the expansionist military ideologies of the Ramessids were fully abandoned; memories of unity and empire remained while the state itself de-centralized. Domestic, personal piety and divine intercession through the practice of magic became the primary means of ensuring safety in an unsafe world (Assmann 2002: 309). The Third Intermediate Period (which ended under Nubian control) was followed by the so-called Late Period (664–333 BC). It was marked by foreign invasion and a return to unified rule, that of the Assyrians, and, subsequently, Persian domination (525–333 BC). The "Saite Period" (664–525 BC), corresponding to the 25th and 26th Dynasties, is characterized by remarkable nostalgia for Egypt's distant past, which encouraged the study and curation of papyri and the "excavation" of ancient buildings, at Memphis in particular. During this time, Osiris was reaffirmed as the most important Egyptian god, signaling a return to the memory of "unification," as celebrated in local and national festivals of renewal (Assmann 2002: 349). Such "memory work" laid the foundations for the Persian and Macedonian conquests of Egypt and the beginnings of the Alexandrian Age.

The Persians consciously chose to link their administration to the Egyptian priestly class and thus the Pharaonic past, thereby attempting to legitimize (ultimately unsuccessfully) their occupation. Oracles were consulted, temples (*lieux de mémoire*) rebuilt, festivals held, and rituals observed (Assmann 2002: 367). Alexander the Great, who conquered Egypt in 333 BC, did no less. Having been crowned pharaoh in Memphis, he rebuilt temples at Karnak and Luxor, consulted the oracle at the Siwa Oasis in the western desert, which named him the "Son of Ammon" and therefore fit to rule, and established the city of Alexandria (Green 1991: 272–75). By portraying himself as a "savior king" and liberator, Alexander linked his rule to traditional Egyptian collective memory and dispelled that of the Persian occupation (Assmann 2002: 372–73). Likewise, his successors, the kings of the Ptolemaic dynasty, did all they could to assimilate and rule as proper pharaohs (Hölbl 2001). For instance, Egyptian art was not Hellenized and Egyptian gods were blended with, not replaced by, Greek gods (Assmann 2002: 374–75). Furthermore, in support of Egyptian memory work, they established the famous Library of Alexandria, which functioned as a teaching academy, educating elite youth in Egyptian and, more generally, "world" history. In this ecumenical context, the cults of Serapis and Isis were spread across the Mediterranean basin. In the end, though, Egypt was for the Greeks—and the Romans to follow—primarily a bread basket: taxes were kept high and the end of the Ptolemaic period was marked by repeated rebellions (Lewis 1986). Yet, despite the turmoil of the Late and Ptolemaic periods (which was eventually attributed to the god Seth), Egyptian collective memory and memory practices morphed and survived, both in official, orthodox forms (e.g., through the proliferation of Greco-Roman Osiris rites) and, in particular, among the common people.

Changing Egyptian memory regimes, from the New Kingdom to Roman conquest, have been closely studied by Meskell (e.g., 2002, 2003, 2004), with a focus on the workers' village at Deir el Medina. Despite repeated "disjunctures," during which various memory traditions were conflated, in all periods villagers retained key, domestic commemorative practices (Meskell 2003). These practices revolved around images, such as statues, which resided in households and served as living referents to the deceased (Meskell 2004: 7). Egyptians placed "enormous emphasis" on such images, appeals to which could effect change and ward off evil, and so their iconoclastic destruction was a powerful, negative act (as in the obliteration of all images of Akhenaten) (Meskell 2004: 8). According to Meskell (2004: 60–61):

> In New Kingdom Egypt ancestral images were prefigured as congealed memory and also operated as contextual technology, a pre-science, or technics, of communication and effective change.

Beliefs in the magical power of mnemonic images dominated Egyptian memory and counter-memory practices through the Roman period. And yet, evidence from Deir el Medina also indicates that at least as early as the New Kingdom and continuing into the Roman period, family memory rarely stretched more than two generations into the past (Meskell 2002: 203). As described above, distributed memory practices linked to the state's orthodox, collective-memory regimes had been gradually displaced from homes and family tombs as early as the Predynastic period and relocated to temples and shrines. Generalized commemoration of the dead, such as the setting of ancestral stelae, helped to reinforce Egyptian orthodoxies writ large, attached to idealized notions of a dutiful life and beautiful death, and *ma'at* (Meskell 2002: 205), but did not contribute to the collective-memory engrams of the social organism per se (Meskell 2003: 34). Despite the participation of large numbers of people in funerary rituals, there were precious few opportunities for counter-memory production in the New Kingdom and later Egypt, one notable exception being lamentation (see above), a behavior that lay squarely within the female domain (Meskell 2002: 189–93).

With the end of the Pharaonic age, the state's memory systems, fully under foreign control for the first time in Egyptian history, were finally completely divorced from traditional, domestic memory work, the outcome of a process that had unfolded over the course of three millennia. Most Greeks and Romans living in Egypt experienced Egyptian mnemo-history as tourists. They roamed ruins like Deir el Medina, marveled at its remains, and left *proskynemata* (written expressions of awe), thereby creating "new, hybrid forms of commemorative practice" (Meskell 2003: 50). At the same time, the Greek and Roman kings of Egypt performed Pharaonic rites in rebuilt temples and sponsored religious festivals that had been reinvented for a new, cosmopolitan age; native Egyptian elites, who were largely kept out of the Greco-Roman ruling class (Lewis 1986), could only watch and feel nostalgia for a glorious past they no longer controlled (Assmann 2002: 386). In this context, knowledge of Egyptian orthodox memory systems were preserved and accessed only because they were recorded in various visual media, such as in temple and tomb paintings. Egyptian heterodox counter-memorial beliefs and practices should have faded away, or been completely reconfigured vis-à-vis the new Hellenistic worldview, and to some degree they were. That they survived at all is surprising, and, ironically, it was Christianity that saved them.

MEMORY AND THE MAKING OF THE MODERN EGYPTIAN STATE

Egypt entered the Common Era possessed of an orthodox memory regime that had been transformed but was still similar in structure and function to that of the Old and New Kingdoms: political control was moderate, but now tied to foreign occupation, and memory systems were narrow, though not completely closed (figure 1.3). If anything, the introduction of Roman culture to Egypt encouraged more religious experimentation, opening the door to enhanced counter-memory production. Roman tolerance for other religions did not, however, extend to Christianity, which was viewed as a political movement and, given its appeal to the poor and disenfranchised, a threat. Indeed, Christianity became such a fertile source of heterodox counter-memories that the Romans eventually had no choice but to appropriate it and raise it to the level of state-sanctioned doxa, which happened during the reign of Constantine (AD 306–337). Nonetheless, it was Coptic Christianity that through a process of religious syncretism preserved something of ancient Egypt's collective memory system and practices. This system was not seriously disrupted and changed until the Arab conquest of Egypt in AD 639 and the spread of Islam.

Coptic Christianity

Christianity gained an early toehold in Egypt. According to Coptic tradition, the Gospel was first preached in Egypt by the Apostle Mark, who was martyred in Alexandria in AD 68 (Meinardus 1999: 28). And Jesus, Mary, and Joseph had, of course, sojourned in Egypt to escape Herod's "Massacre of the Innocents" (Meinardus 1999: 13–28). Their travels in Egypt are recorded in a mnemo-topographic network of Coptic churches dedicated at those locations where the Holy Family had stayed or where Jesus had performed miracles (Ibid.). Given Egypt's early adoption of Christianity, it is perhaps no accident that many of the Church's foundational traditions developed there. In fact, many Coptic Christian beliefs and practices stem from earlier, pharaonic beliefs and practices that had been preserved in counter-memory communities opposed to Greco-Roman domination.

For example, Alexandrian theologians eventually determined that Christ was possessed of a single, divine nature, the so-called mono- or mia-physitic position (Meinardus 1999: 39–40). However, following the Council of Chalcedon in AD 451, the Western and Eastern Orthodox churches officially adopted the dyophysitic position, that Christ was both human and divine, leading to a lasting schism with the Oriental church, including the Copts (Ibid.). Importantly, these religious controversies were not mere academic disputes, but rather affected Byzantine geopolitics and caused riots in Constantinople (Norwich 1997: 58–59). To this day, two different popes reign in Alexandria: the Coptic (non-Chalcedonian) and the Melkite/Greek Orthodox (Chalcedonian) (Meinardus 1999: 53–54).

Such paleo-Christian theological controversies were rooted in much earlier debates among Egyptian, Jewish, and, later, Greek philosophers about the relationship of God/gods to humans generally. For Egyptians, these discussions had revolved around the divine nature of the pharaoh—god or son of god?—and the disposition of one's soul (*ba*) in the afterlife. The divinity of the pharaoh was typically framed within the context of the Osirid myth cycle. Osiris represented the divine principle and as judge of the dead, helped enforce *ma'at*. As discussed above, he also embodied unification, having been dismembered by Seth (an Asiatic god) and then resurrected by his wife, Isis. His son, Horus, symbolized the pharaoh, who became like Osiris in death. Thus, the Osirid myth system takes a largely monophysitic position, not unlike that of early Egyptian Christians regarding Jesus. Essentially, the dyophysitic position of the non-Oriental churches, adopted by the Roman Empire as dogma, was that of Akhenaten, who presented himself as the one true god's chief representative on Earth (i.e., his son, possessed of both human and divine characteristics). Eighteen hundred years later, the Egyptian church fathers still could not bring themselves to support the Amarna heresy. Christianity, which had formed as a heterodox response to Roman rule, was thus co-opted by the West, and the pope in Rome named God's infallible interlocutor. In response, Egypt's Copts employed pagan Egyptian orthodoxies, knowledge of which persisted, as counter-memorial responses to Roman colonization and Egyptian ethnocide. If not for the Copts, ancient Egyptian culture, including the Egyptian language, would have completely disappeared. It is no accident, then, that, just like Osiris and his pharaohs, the Coptic pope carried a crook as a symbol of his rule (Wilkinson 1999: 160), as do many other Christian bishops today, with the telling exception of the pope in Rome.

Many other early Christian practices have their origins in Coptic Christianity, and therefore in ancient Egypt. For Coptic priests, knowledge of these practices lent them "traditional" authority, alongside conventional Biblical authority (Meinardus 1999: 40); but they also rooted Coptic Christianity in vernacular memory communities, tied to distributed memory stores and specialists. For example, ancient Egyptian mortuary rites were potent sources of Coptic Christian counter-memorial (i.e., counter-colonial) activities. Ancient Egyptians believed that the dead lived on after death and could be influenced by their descendants (Harrington 2013: 28–33). As described above, images of the dead were kept in homes and used to facilitate communication between individuals and their ancestors (Meskell 2004: 7). Various ritual activities eased the deceased's passage into the afterlife, including proper burial with certain provisions, such as food and drink (Harrington 2013: 113). As also described above, lamentations were sung at the time of death by women, who also wept, tore their hair, and rent their clothing (Harrington 2013: 109–112; Wickett 2010: 146–59). In ancient Egypt, the primary locus for funerary activities was the outdoor courtyard in front of underground tombs, which were sometimes accompanied by a chapel (Harrington 2013: 86–99). Each of these ancient Egyptian practices is mirrored in Coptic Christian practice.

Coptic Christians, like many Christians generally, continued to believe that the dead—saints in particular—might intercede with God on their behalf, to heal illnesses, for example (Meinardus 1999: 119–22). Images of saints—icons—were painted, hung in churches and homes, and venerated, mirroring the ancient Egyptian practice of ancestor worship. The practice of lamentation continued into the Christian and Muslim eras and functioned as a domestic female counterpoint to male-dominated funeral activities (Wickett 2010: 107). Lamentations were composed by female specialists and sung at various times to aid recollection of the deceased. Mortuary complexes used by Christians (and Muslims) mimicked those of ancient Egypt, with the exception that the tomb was moved above ground and combined with the chapel. Like the idea of a monophysitic Christ, many of these practices were anathema to the Roman church. Icons caused major strife between those who supported their use and those who did not, so-called iconoclasts ("the smashers of icons"), who believed that their adoration amounted to the worship of false gods (Norwich 1999: 111–12). Lamentation, along with other female-controlled religious rituals, was curtailed (Geary 1994: 52–59). And pagan burial rites were stricken from the church liturgy. These actions on the part of the Occidental church were not simply attacks on the schismatic Oriental church, but rather amounted to attacks on heterodox memory systems generally, which aided the medieval state-building process. In Egypt, they were construed as colonial attacks on Egyptian culture, and rejected.

Perhaps the most important and lasting gift given by Egypt to Christianity was the tradition of monastic life. Egyptian mystics had always lived in the desert, as had communities of priests who maintained oracles, such as at Siwa (see above). Additionally, in the Late Period groups of priests moved into temples (Assmann 2002: 411–14), forming "textual communities" (Stock 1987). These temple-dwelling priests were dedicated to the study and preservation of esoteric knowledge related to Egyptian religious traditions. They were not dissidents; rather they were official representatives of the priestly class, charged with developing a corpus of orthodox religious records. As such, they were forerunners of the Coptic "schools" founded in Alexandria (alongside the great library), and of the great Coptic monasteries built both in Alexandria and throughout the country, beginning in the fourth century AD (Meinardus 1999: 143).

The early Christian schools and monasteries, along with churches, formed the backbone of a Coptic community that by the sixth century AD had syncretized with traditional Egyptian religious practices and preserved the Egyptian language, serving as the primary locus for Egyptian nationalist sentiment through the modern age (Meinardus 1999: 81). That is not to say that the Coptic Church retained Egyptian collective memory fully or always correctly, or that there was not a certain degree of animosity held toward "pagan" religious practices and places. The memory engrams of "unification" faded, but the antagonistic relationship between Upper and Lower Egypt remained. The Hyksos domination was forgotten, but foreign conquest continued to stimulate Egyptian xenophobia, especially toward desert peoples, like the Bedouin, and Egypt's traditional nemesis, Nubia. Many of the Egyptian temples were re-purposed as Christian churches, an excellent example being Philae, now located on an island in Lake Nasser. Temple paintings and carvings were often mutilated by Christian priests, as at Dendarah (Crawford 2007: 29–31). Nevertheless, while ancient Egypt's orthodox memory system slowly disappeared, along with its *lieux de mémoire*, to be partially preserved only in tomb paintings and old papyri, the distributed memory stores that had survived Egyptian state formation were grafted onto Coptic culture, and persisted. Thus, with the exception of the Amarna Age, we can chart a remarkable stability in official Egyptian collective memory systems, from the period of state formation, through the Persian and Greco-Roman occupations, and into the Byzantine era, during which ancient Egyptian beliefs and practices became sources of heterodox counter-memory production directed at foreign occupiers, who threatened to erase any evidence for a once-independent Egyptian nation. This process of erasure was accelerated following the Arab conquest and the introduction of Islam, which was, unlike Christianity, largely intolerant of traditional Egyptian memory practices. In short, the Muslim theocratic state managed to do what Akhenaten and a string of foreign powers had not: narrow Egypt's political system to the point of complete collective-memory closure (see figure 1.3). As such, the Egyptian memory system remained sealed, with little or no possibility for counter-memory production, through the late Ottoman period, when Mehmed Ali, the "Father of Modern Egypt," took power.

Arab and Mamluk Egypt

In AD 639, when an Arab army under the command of Amr ibn al-As conquered Egypt, it was a Christian nation, ruled by a Byzantine governor who resided in Alexandria (Marsot 2007: 1). By that point, Egyptians had lived under foreign rule for over 1,000 years, and while a distinct Egyptian identity had somehow survived, the vast majority of Egyptians were completely alienated from their country's government (Ibid.). The Persians had transformed the *nomes* of Egypt into satraps, building a decentralized administrative network staffed by non-Egyptians. This network was expanded by the Byzantines, who instituted a harsh system of taxation that the Arabs then appropriated (Marsot 2007: 4). The Arab system taxed Jews and Christians at a higher rate than Muslims, which encouraged conversion to Islam, and was particularly unfair to Delta farmers, who paid additional land taxes (Ibid.). Inexorably, native Egyptians lost their property, becoming *fellahin* (i.e., peasant sharecroppers), and what had been a Christian populace became majority Muslim. Consequently, what remained of Egyptian collective memory systems were dealt nearly fatal ideological blows.

By the advent of the eighth century AD, under the Umayya dynasty, Arabic had displaced Coptic as the official language of Egypt. Copts were forced to learn Arabic if they hoped to have any access to new economic and political systems. All tax registers were recorded in Arabic, new Arabic-style coins were struck in Damascus and shipped to Egypt, and an Arabic postal service was created (Marsot 2007: 6). The loss of the Coptic language and script, which henceforth was used in the Coptic Church only, marked a serious setback for Egyptian memory specialists, who had always employed Egyptian language and writing in rituals of commemoration. Even more damaging to Egyptian collective memory systems were the tenets of Islam itself. Converts to Islam became citizens of a global Muslim community (the Ummah) that transcended national borders. For Egyptians, this ran counter to their primary means of ethnic identification, which was strongly tied to place—the Nile Valley—and led to an us/them mentality. Moreover, many traditional Egyptian memory practices, which had merged with Coptic Christian practices, were especially offensive to Islam. For example, the esoteric, flamboyant activities of ancient Egyptian temples, which lived on in Coptic churches, were diminished under Islam. Festivals and processions, during which images of gods and (later) saints were carried through the streets, often ending at the family tombs of ancestors, ceased or were co-opted by Muslims. Indeed, the mere idea that God could be somehow depicted in images ran completely counter to Islamic dogma, stoking iconoclastic activities in both Egypt and Byzantium. In fact, according to Connerton (1989: 46–47), early Islam, unlike Christianity and Judaism, was "hyper-historical" and non-commemorative, and thus non-ritualized. Whereas Christians and Jews grounded their practice of religion in perpetual memory work, making it relatively open to interpretation, Islamic practices (and beliefs) stemmed from a single text, the Koran. Islamic orthodoxies could not be questioned, except by a small number of religious specialists, such as, for example, those at Cairo's Al-Azhar University, founded in AD 970. Thus, Islam became the perfect vehicle for colonial state building, since it afforded strict political control and did not depend on collective memory making (figure 1.3). Under these circumstances, traditional Egyptian memory systems withered and almost died, a process greatly hastened by the Mamluks, who took power in AD 1250.

The Mamluks were Turkic-speaking mercenary-slaves—first brought to Egypt by the Ayyubis (the heirs of Saladin)—who, rather quickly, wrested control of the country from the Arabs (Marsot 2007: 28). Whereas Egyptians had gradually adjusted to life under Arabic rule, the Mamluks brought with them a new, alien language and culture. More than ever, native Egyptians were excluded from government posts, which were reserved for Turkish speakers. Given their "tribal" origins, the Mamluk administration quickly factionalized based on systems of patronage. Wealthy houses acquired huge tracts of land, worked by poor *fellahin*. The property of Copts and of the Coptic Church, including monasteries, was confiscated. Consequently, the Coptic community suffered, and only much later, in the nineteenth century, did it begin to recover (Meinardus 1999: 65–66). The Mamluks also convinced members of various non-Egyptian ethnic groups to relocate to Egypt in large numbers, including (even more) Greeks, Jews, and Armenians, who filled specialist roles in the Mamluk administration. As a result, native Egyptians were fully disenfranchised in the years leading up to Ottoman rule, which began in AD 1516. Egyptian language and culture were further eroded, to the extent that collective memory engrams of Egyptian "identity" and "unity," once promulgated by the Coptic Church, were completely contradicted by events on the ground. Egypt—now known by its medieval name, Misr—thus entered the Ottoman period a nation in name only. And for that nation to rise again, Egyptian collective memory systems would need to be reconstructed and/or refashioned, a process that began in earnest in the late Ottoman period, under the unlikely guidance of an Albanian *pasha* named Mehmed Ali.

Ottoman Egypt

> Can anyone mention Cairo without the phantom of Mehmed Ali leaping to his mind? Doesn't he, till this day, hover high above you from his citadel, defending and protecting you?

This quote, from a novel called *The Sphinx Confides in Cairo*, published in August 1949 by Egyptian nationalist writer Mahmūd Taymūr (quoted in Fahmy 1997: 15), captures the attitude of most Egyptians on the 100th anniversary of Mehmed Ali's death. Taymūr's book describes his discovery and translation of a love letter from the Sphinx to the city of Cairo, written in hieroglyphics. The Sphinx, an ancient Egyptian *lieux de mémoire* if ever there was one, praises the city for surviving years of foreign rule, only to be rescued from the Mamluk "tyrant" by the Albanian "genius." Indeed, Mehmed Ali's massacre of the Mamluks at the Citadel in Cairo on March 1, 1811, stands as *the* defining collective memory of the modern Egyptian nation, capping centuries of Ottoman struggles with the Mamluk great houses, clearing the way for the rebirth of an Egyptian nation.

Whereas the Arab rulers of Egypt, under the influence of Islam, had almost fully closed Egyptian memory systems, the Ottomans slowly reopened them, a process that gained momentum under Mehmed Ali in the liberalizing context of the Early Modern period. Mehmed Ali was born in 1769 in Kavala, now in northern Greece, to Albanian parents (Fahmy 1997: 14–15). He worked his way up the ranks of the Ottoman army and, in the wake of the short-lived French occupation under Napoleon (see Dykstra 1998), was sent to Egypt. Supported by Albanian troops, he eventually took power and in 1805 was named *walī* (governor) of Egypt. Over the next several decades, he increasingly distanced himself from the Ottoman Sultan, running Egypt like an independent state, one he was determined to "modernize" (Mitchell 1988). Modernization entailed nation-building, a process already well under way in most 19th-century European states. To build a modern Egyptian nation, Mehmed Ali first sought to erase ethnic divisions, which had built up over centuries of foreign rule, and construct a new, inclusive "Egyptian" identity. To do so, he promoted individuals in his administration, including native Egyptians, based on merit rather than ethnic origin or family connections. He also built a large conscript army, one in which native Egyptians served, ending the Egyptian government's dependence on mercenary and slave soldiers (Fahmy 1997). He restructured the Egyptian economy by redistributing land from private to government ownership, building factories, and monopolizing trade (e.g., of spices being moved through the Red Sea), and he built schools (Fahmy 1998). Finally, like most Ottomans, Mehmed Ali practiced a mystical form of Islam, called Sufism, which was much more tolerant of other religious traditions (Winter 1998: 25–27). This allowed for the beginnings of a Coptic fluorescence, which tapped traditional memory stores in the Coptic Church. The net effect of these many changes was a secularized, neo-Egyptian (re)unification, built along Pharaonic lines, which transcended cultural, religious, and geographic differences. Once again, unity and social stability were defined in opposition to those on the outside, and so Mehmed Ali's expansionist foreign policy is key to understanding the formation of the modern Egyptian nation.

Having built a modern military, Mehmed Ali became both an asset and a threat to the Ottoman sultan in Istanbul. Repeatedly, he marched his army into the Near East, putting down revolts, occupying territory in Syria-Palestine, as had pharaohs of old, thereby kindling nostalgic recollections of past Egyptian empires (see, again, figure 1.2). Egyptian nationalism soared, rooted in collective memories of a glorious Golden Age, evidence for which had been uncovered by Napoleon's archaeologists. However, given that Egypt was still a province of the Ottoman Empire, such reconstructed memories were deemed heterodox and ran counter to the imperial ideology of absolute submission to the Sublime Porte on the part of provinces and provincial officials, who could be recalled to Istanbul at any time.

In 1821, the Greeks rose in revolt and declared independence from the Ottomans. In response, the Sultan commanded Mehmed Ali to move his military assets, including his brand new navy, to Greece to put down the revolt, which he did, reluctantly, in 1825 (Fahmy 1998: 157). The Egyptians met fierce resistance from the Greeks and in 1827 the Ottoman fleet, including Mehmed Ali's navy, was destroyed by an allied force of British, French, and Russian vessels in the Battle of Navarino. The Ottomans lost Greece, but did manage to curtail Mehmed Ali's growing power. In response, Egypt once again turned inward, as it had during the Old Kingdom; having formed a unified, nominally independent state and having secured its borders, Mehmed Ali and his heirs worked to create durable governmental systems. As it turns out, one of the main challenges to these systems came from Islamic fundamentalists, the Wahhabis, based on the Arabian Peninsula, who practiced an overly historicized, "obsolete" form of Islam and therefore objected to Egypt's secular turn (Ibrahim 1998: 198–99). Consequently, Egypt's Arab Spring pit Mehmed Ali's secularized Egyptian nation, which spawned the military dictatorships of the twentieth century, against the Arab fundamentalists of its recent past. That struggle, which is often characterized as a clash between modern and medieval worldviews, is in reality a struggle over collective memory and its control.

Using chapter 1's memory model, we are now in a position to compare the modern Egyptian state's various phases of development in terms of collective memory production. The Greco-Roman rulers of Egypt maintained orthodox memory systems that had developed in the Nile Valley over the course of several millennia. These systems and the collective memory engrams they supported formed along with the Egyptian territorial state. They worked to enforce regional unification and enabled social solidarity. It is no surprise, then, that foreign administrators readily adopted them. At the same time, traditional memory regimes, with roots in Predynastic times, persisted and continued to generate counter-memorial activity aimed at preserving native Egyptian identity. Boozer's (2010) comparison of Roman to native (or "hybrid") Egyptian houses at Amheida illustrates this point well; the latter produced a different, "traditional" material culture, including amulets of Bes, and evidence for consumption of native, non-Roman foods. Generally speaking, then, during the Greco-Roman period, Egypt experienced low levels of crisis and considerable nostalgia for the Pharaonic past (figure 1.2). Under these circumstances, memory systems remained relatively closed (figure 1.3), except among Egyptian "nationalists," who strove to save something of their Egyptian identity in the face of non-Egyptian appropriation. Eventually, Christianity emerged as the primary source of Egyptian counter-memorial activities. Through a remarkable process of syncretism, the Coptic Church managed to protect some orthodox and many heterodox (i.e., non-official, vernacular) Egyptian memory practices. Priests and monks acted as memory specialists and Egyptian memory cues were embedded in Coptic churches. These cues prompted collective memories of Egyptian religious primacy. For example, the "memory" of the Holy Family's sojourn in Egypt, marked in the Nile landscape by Coptic churches, was draped over earlier, Pharaonic myth cycles, of the Egyptian pantheon and its origins (Meinardus 1999: 13–28).

Egyptian collective memory systems thus remained intact through the Byzantine period, across generations. The Arab conquest, however, marked a sea change. The Arabs and Islam completely overwhelmed the Coptic Church and destroyed what remained of Egyptian memory systems, orthodox and otherwise. This final memory crisis was not resolved in the realm of opinion, leading to a new Egyptian *imaginaire*; rather a novel Arab-Egyptian identity was forged, as *fellahin* converted to Islam and the Egyptian language was lost. Islam encouraged a transnational worldview and its historicized theology obviated the state's need to mold collective memory. In effect, under Arab control, Egyptian collective memory ceased to exist as an orthodox ideological concern. What little counter-memory activity remained in Egypt during the Arab period was confined to the much-diminished Coptic community. And any counter-memory activity among Muslim Egyptians was swiftly and easily staunched by government agents, who were largely non-Egyptian. Anti-Egyptian sentiment reached a crescendo under the Mamluks and Ottomans, when all government workers, including soldiers, were required to be Turkic-speaking or of Turkish descent. In this context, any sense of Egyptian identity, and a non-Muslim Egyptian past worth memorializing, might have disappeared once and for all, if not for Mehmed Ali's efforts to detach Egypt from the Ottoman Empire, which required a process of modern nation building. To build a modern Egyptian nation, Mehmed Ali and his immediate successors encouraged political discourse, stoked nostalgic memories of Egypt's Pharaonic Golden Age (a strategy greatly aided by the advent of modern archaeology), and fanned nationalist flames. Schools and museums were built, Egyptian arts were encouraged, and the Coptic language was resuscitated (albeit ultimately unsuccessfully). Within the space of a century and a half (*circa* 1805–1952), Egyptian identity was entirely reimagined and reconstituted, at which point the political system was closed. These new, modern memory systems then became the primary ideological tools of the Egyptian Republic, led by generals Naguib, Nasser, Sadat, Mubarak, and, now, el-Sisi.

CONCLUSION

The role of memory and archaeology in the formation of the Egyptian Republic and in the short-lived Egyptian Revolution of 2011–2014 will be discussed in chapter 5. Here it is enough to say that collective memory has always played a dominant role in the functioning of the Egyptian state, beginning in Early Dynastic times. Looking at Egyptian history in full, we can identify several key trends with regard to collective memory formation. First of all, through time, local distributed collective memory systems, with Neolithic roots, were undermined and increasingly tethered to the Egyptian state. State officials took control of regional political systems while, at the same time, institutionalizing orthodox memory regimes. Second of all, once in place, these regimes—which stimulated memory engrams of "unification" and "solidarity" in the face of foreign threats—were not easily dislodged. The most significant challenge to Egyptian memory regimes and specialists came during the Amarna Age, under Akhenaten. I contend that the Amarna heresy was indeed an affront to memory, but also amounted to a failed political gambit. Thus, in the Egyptian state, and perhaps all ancient states, collective memory and politics coevolved and were codependent. Changing one changed the other, and vice versa. Finally, in Egypt, the Arabs succeeded where Akhenaten had failed. They did so not by challenging the collective memory system per se, but by rendering it unnecessary. The Arab-Islamic state was grounded in a politics of history not memory, and as such, state-level memory work became irrelevant. The politics of history carried through the Mamluk and Ottoman periods and was only displaced when Mehmed Ali came to power and set about building an Egyptian nation, based on European models.

Egypt thus teaches us that nations and national identity form when history is transcended and collective memories are (literally) made. This process is similar to the process whereby a human being constructs a sense of self. It remains to be seen, however, if the trends identified for Egypt hold in other places, like Greece, where states also formed. Clearly, Greece and Egypt were linked during some periods (e.g., during the Hellenistic Age), and again when both countries were incorporated into the Roman and Ottoman empires. But (*contra* Bernal 1987, 1991, 2006) during the key periods of state formation, the Neolithic through Bronze Age, when collective memory systems would have been actively appropriated and shaped by state authorities, Greece was relatively disconnected from Egypt. As we will see, compared to Egypt, Greece forged a different path to state formation and, ultimately, experienced Ottoman rule very differently, without the overt memory break caused by mass conversion to Islam. As a result, the Greek nation was built on collective memories of Byzantine glory, amplified by echoes of the Classical age, sustained through the period of Ottoman rule, forming the foundations for Greek independence.

3

Greece
Diversification

Give me your hands, give me your hands, give me your hands.

I have seen in the night
the sharp peak of the mountain,
seen the plain beyond flooded
with the light of an invisible moon,
seen, turning my head,
black stones huddled
and my life taut as a chord
beginning and end
the final moment:
my hands.

Sinks whoever raises the great stones;
I've raised these stones as long as I was able
I've loved these stones as long as I was able
these stones, my fate.
Wounded by my own soil
tortured by my own shirt
condemned by my own gods,
these stones.

I know that they don't know, but I
Who've followed so many times
the path from killer to victim
from victim to punishment
from punishment to the next murder,
groping

the inexhaustible purple
that night of the return
when the Furies began whistling
in the meager grass
I've seen snakes crossed with vipers
knotted over the evil generation
our fate.

Voices out of the stone out of sleep
deeper here where the world darkens,
memory of toil rooted in the rhythm
beaten upon the earth by feet
forgotten.
Bodies sunk into the foundations
of the other time, naked. Eyes
fixed, fixed on a point
that you can't make out, much as you want to:
the soul
struggling to become your own soul.

Not even the silence is now yours
here where the mill stones have stopped turning.

—George Seferis, "Mycenae" (1967 [1935])

Figure 3.1. The Treasury of Atreus, Mycenae, Greece. *Source:* M. L. Galaty.

Like Egypt, Greece is a land where the past is always present and memory casts long shadows. George Seferis (1900–1971) knew this to be true. He had been displaced from his ancestral home of Smyrna (Izmir) in 1922 after Greece's failed invasion of Turkey under Venizelos (see map, figure 3.2, page 74). Memory—and a sense of loss—thus informs many of Seferis's poems, as it does the Greek consciousness. The Venizelist agenda itself was memory work on a grand scale: the Megali Idea, to reclaim Constantinople and re-establish the Byzantine Empire.

The subjugation and occupation of Constantinople by the Ottomans in 1453 was just the latest in a string of Greek defeats—the end of the Bronze Age, the collapse of the Athenian Empire, the death of Alexander, the Roman conquest—each of which was committed to collective memory, each of which added to the Greek sense of loss and longing, or, as Cherry (2001: 253) describes it, "belatedness": in a place like Greece, it "proves almost impossible to avoid dreaming of a past that has already passed into myth." This mythic Greek past did not generate centripetal memory engrams of "unification" and "solidarity" as was the case in Egypt; rather, Greek mnemo-history is one of centrifugal "unfolding," a constant "becoming" that never quite arrives. Whereas Egyptian identity and language suffered under foreign rule, Greeks held fast to Greek identity and language. As Seferis put it in his acceptance speech, upon winning the Nobel Prize in Literature in 1963:

> I belong to a small country. A rocky promontory in the Mediterranean, it has nothing to distinguish it but the efforts of its people, the sea, and the light of the sun. It is a small country, but its tradition is immense and has been handed down through the centuries without interruption. The Greek language has never ceased to be spoken. It has undergone the changes that all living things experience, but there has never been a gap.

Continuity in memory purpose, despite a lack of political unity, characterizes Greek memory work, from earliest times to the present. When examined alongside Egyptian collective memory systems, those of Greece can be seen to be distinctly different, leading to very different outcomes in modern times, despite a shared Mediterranean ancestry.

Like Egypt, analysis of Greek collective memory systems can begin with the Neolithic Age (*circa* 6000–3100 BC), when agriculture was imported to Greece from the Near East and villages formed (table 3.1, page 72). As a general rule, during this period deceased individuals were interred in intramural fashion: that is, within villages and often under house floors. Burials were sometimes primary, but more often than not, skeletons were subjected to various forms of secondary treatment, including exposure, collection, curation, and reburial, deposition in ossuaries, and scattering. These secondary treatments of the dead likely informed collective memory production in societies that were largely egalitarian and dominated by broadly distributed, non-formalized memory systems, similar to those that operated in the Neolithic Near East and Egypt. In Egypt, these systems were undercut and appropriated during state formation, in service to processes of territorial unification, but they never completely disappeared. Likewise, in Greece, distributed memory systems were captured by early states (both Minoan and Mycenaean) and applied to state-building efforts. However, Greek Neolithic memory practices and specialists appear to have fared rather better than their Egyptian counterparts and, over time, traditional collective memory behaviors became synonymous with Greek identity, helping to preserve Greek culture through centuries of foreign domination.

The state formation process began in Greece at the start of the Bronze Age (3100 BC). By about 1900 BC, "palace"-centered states had coalesced on Crete, associated with the so-called Minoan civilization. Similar societies formed on the mainland beginning about 1650 BC, the so-called Mycenaean civilization. The Minoan and Mycenaean states were certainly in contact with one another, and Egypt, and yet were organized very differently. The Minoan states were corporate polities, whereas the Mycenaeans were networked (Parkinson and Galaty 2007). Corporate polities depend on a "cognitive code that emphasizes a corporate solidarity of society as an integrated whole, based on natural, fixed, and immutable interdependence between subgroups and, in more complex societies, between rulers and subjects" (Blanton et al. 1996: 6). In contrast, networked polities encourage "ancestral ritual that legitimates the control of society by a limited number of high-ranking individuals and households" (Ibid.). The Minoan and Mycenaean states thus required and deployed very different collective memory strategies, and drew differentially from the available Neolithic and Early Bronze Age memory substrate. Minoan collective memory systems bear some similarity to those of the Egyptians, but this is a result of parallel evolution, not colonization of Crete by Egyptians.

The Minoans were conquered sometime around 1400 BC by Mycenaeans, who occupied the Palace of Minos at Knossos. Beginning about 1200 BC—shortly before Rameses III defeated the Sea Peoples—the Mycenaean palaces themselves were destroyed, one after another. Greece and the Eastern Mediterranean were plunged into a Dark Age, roughly coinciding with the Egyptian Third Intermediate Period (1080–664 BC). The Linear B writing system was abandoned, and yet Greek collective memories of their Mycenaean past were somehow preserved through the Dark Age, to be recorded in the works of Homer. That being the case, we can assume that Bronze Age distributed memory systems, which functioned outside Mycenaean state control, survived the collapse and helped bridge the Iron

Age literacy gap, laying the ideological foundations for the formation of the Greek city-states (*poleis*).

The development of Classical Greek memory systems and their elaboration under Roman imperial rule have been described in detail by Alcock (e.g., 2002), a pioneer in the archaeological study of memory generally. Having survived the Dark Age, Greek memory systems evolved in numerous, heterodox directions. Each city-state boasted its own mythic history, supported by highly visible *lieux de mémoire*. Prominent temples and burial monuments—such as the Parthenon in Athens and the tumulus at Marathon—cued collective memory engrams that were particular to each city-state and yet understood by all. As such, collective memory making in Classical Greece was a competitive process and disputes over memory could launch wars, as described in detail by Herodotus. The decentralized nature of Greek political systems thus caused, or allowed for, very broad memory systems and opened various social spaces for counter-memory production. As Alcock (2002: 137) describes, even the Messenian helots, having been freed from generations of Spartan domination, "were well able to enumerate and praise their ancestry, their heroes, their mythic history."

For the Greeks, then, remembering was an active, open process and attempts to curtail that process were typically met with resistance. Consequently, the open nature of Greek memory systems was maintained as the Greeks converted to Christianity. As was also the case in Coptic Egypt, during the Byzantine period Greek traditional memory behaviors, some with prehistoric roots, and specialists were gradually assimilated by the Greek Orthodox Church, and preserved. The church consequently acted as the primary defender of Greek culture and identity during the long centuries of Turkish domination. During the Tourkokratia (i.e., the roughly four centuries of Ottoman rule that began in Greece in 1453) the Greeks rebelled repeatedly, always unsuccessfully, until 1821, when they finally, effectively declared independence. The Greek War of Rebellion lasted for eight years, during which Mehmed Ali's navy was sunk at the Battle of Navarino. The First Hellenic Republic was finally recognized by the European powers as an independent state in 1832. In the aftermath of the war, Greek collective memory systems shifted into overdrive, creating a unified nation where there was none (Herzfeld 1986). This process of nation building continued unabated through World War II and involved countless acts of commemoration, and forgetting. Numerous stories of defiant Greeks (often women), who fought all comers, were enshrined in Greek collective memory and recorded in the new nation's landscape. There were, for example, the Souliote women, who in 1803 (literally) danced off the cliffs of Zalongo, Epirus, rather than surrender to the besieging Turks. Or, the women of Diros, Mani, who in 1826 repulsed Ibrahim Pasha and his marauding Egyptians, armed only with scythes. Or, the women of the Aegean island of Kalymnos, who in 1935 fought Italian occupiers, with nothing more than rocks (see Sutton 1998). At the same time, the decisive part played by Albanians in the Greek War of Independence was conspicuously struck from Greek collective memory.

Rocks and stones often play prominent roles in Greek myths and memories. For Seferis, the stones of Mycenae elicited Greek cultural memories of toil, tyranny, and murder, and a "cyclical pattern of violence" from which Greece could not escape (Beaton 2003: 137). A mnemonics of violence is particularly evident in the Mani region of Greece. There, in one of Greece's poorest, most remote *nomoi*, the Maniates preserved traditional memory practices linked to blood feud and death, the most prominent of which was the singing of *mirologia*, lamentations.

> Eh, Lazaros and Panayis,
> And you, Fokas and Theodoris,
> What are you waiting for?
> The killer of Panagos
> Is staying in Yerakia.
> Tie up your belts,
> Pick up your guns,
> And hunt the killer,
> Sunwards, in Yerakia.
>
> —(recorded in Seremetakis 1991: 129)

Mirologia are sung by women at domestic mourning ceremonies (*kláma*) held in advance of a funeral (*kidhía*). Once composed, these "stories of vengeance" are preserved and "handed down from generation to generation as a cherished instalment in the family's poetic memory" (Greenhalgh and Eliopoulos 1985: 41). Interestingly, Egyptian and Greek lamentations could not be more different, reflecting very different underlying memory systems. Egyptian lamentations are meant to ease the dearly departed into the afterlife, from which they might act as advocates for the living. Greek lamentations celebrate the life of the dead individual and promise revenge. Egyptian lamentations help reconstruct social solidarity in the aftermath of death, whereas Greek lamentations reinforce social divisions, often in the face of violence.

As was done for Egypt in chapter 2, in this chapter I chart the development of Greek collective memory and memory-making processes through time, with a focus on the Mani region, which represents Greek memory systems in microcosm. At intervals, I run Greek memory regimes through the explanatory model constructed in chapter 1. Greek collective memory and political systems, like those of Egypt, also *coevolved*, but the relationship was continuously renegotiated and thus marked by considerable ins*tability*. Greek memory systems prompted social segmentation, factionalism, and *friction*, not between memory and history, as was the case in Arab Egypt, but rather between competitive memory communities. The decomposable nature of Greek collective memory systems rendered them both powerfully creative and difficult to manage. As a recent *New York Times* article put it, with reference to the Greek rejection of a European Union bailout plan:

> Whether Greeks' overwhelming rejection on Sunday of the latest European loan deal proves to be a master stroke or a monumental blunder remains to be seen. What is clear, experts and analysts say, is that it sprang from a deep cultural and historical strain of defiance in apparently hopeless situations, honed over centuries under Ottoman rule and nurtured by the telling of heroic tales from one generation to another.
> —"Greek 'No' . . . , July 6, 2015)

The consequences for the Modern Greek nation of Greek "defiance" are further addressed in chapter 5.

MEMORY AND THE ANCIENT GREEK STATE

As was the case in Egypt, Greek memory systems and practices stretch back into the deep past, to the Neolithic Age, having formed prior to the first states (figure 3.2; table 3.1). Evidence for their origin and development can be found in Greek Neolithic mortuary practices, which were complex, symbolically charged, and varied across space and time (Souvatzi 2008: 186–93; Stratouli et al. 2010; though see Perlès 2001: 281 for a different interpretation). Formal cemeteries dating to the Neolithic are rare; only a handful exist. Rather, the deceased were usually buried inside or near houses, within the bounds of the village, occasionally cremated. Grave goods are generally absent. Children were typically buried inside pots, whereas adults were inhumed in rough graves and their remains subjected to various kinds of secondary treatment. Skulls and long bones of multiple individuals were collected and redeposited in pits or, more rarely, built ossuaries. Secondary treatment may have occurred in the course of normal village activities (e.g., when digging turned up human remains), but ritual exhumation and reburial of body parts seems more likely. Either way, during the Greek Neolithic the dead were very present in the lives of the living. Triantaphyllou (1999: 131) suggests, based on evidence from Neolithic Makriyalos, located in north Greece, that communal, secondary burial installations likely reinforced the importance of groups, versus individuals, to mechanical, egalitarian social systems.

Table 3.1. Greek Chronology

Period	Date
Neolithic	7000–3100 BC
Early Bronze Age	3100–2000 BC
Middle Bronze Age	2000–1600 BC
Late Bronze I–II	1600–1390 BC
Late Bronze III	1390–1070 BC
Iron Age	1070–800 BC
Archaic	800–480 BC
Classical	480–323 BC
Hellenistic	323–146 BC
Roman	146 BC–AD 330
Byzantine	330–1453
Ottoman	1453–1821
War of Independence	1821–1832
Monarchy	1832–1924
Republic	1924–present

Greek Neolithic mortuary practices can be usefully compared to those of the Near East and Egypt, described in chapters 1 and 2. Like plastered skulls in the Near East, human remains in the Greek Neolithic also served as memory cues. Their curation and ritual reinternment validated beliefs about the age and continuity of the social organism as a whole, signaling shared title to land and property. Conversely, Near Eastern plastered skulls likely represented known individuals (at least in the short-term, i.e., one to two generations) (Kuijt 2008), the ancestral leaders of competitive social segments in trans-egalitarian societies. A shift to similar individualizing mortuary behaviors occurred in Greece in the subsequent Early Bronze Age, when burial in extramural cemeteries was introduced. Graves would have been marked on the landscape and visited by family members of the deceased, highlighting social differences. Egyptian Neolithic mortuary practices were initially similar to Near Eastern and Greek practices, but were quickly co-opted by early state officials, during the Naqada II, to be replaced by mummification and burial of powerful individuals in large built tombs (Wengrow 2006: 123). State-level appropriation of Greek memory systems happened first on Crete, in the Middle Bronze Age, where Minoan state authorities amplified rather than replaced Neolithic "corporate" ideologies. By contrast, the Mycenaean appropriation of memory systems was rife with conflicts. Unlike Egypt and Minoan Crete, Mycenaean state collective memory systems were not used to build solidarity; rather they underpinned "networked" individualizing modes of political rule, similar to those promoted (unsuccessfully) by Akhenaten. This process—the shifting of Mycenaean memory systems from corporate to networked orthodoxies, with reference to their Neolithic origins—can be profitably traced in the Mani region of Greece, and can be juxtaposed to the quite different, Minoan experience.

From Neolithic to Bronze Age

Three peninsulas extend south from the Peloponnesus: Messenia to the west, Lakonia to the east, and between them the Mani. The Mani terminates at Cape Tanairon, the southernmost point in continental Europe. The Mani is rocky and dry: "a dead, planetary place, a haunt for dragons" (Fermor 1958: 23). The peninsula is split by the forbidding Taygetos Mountains. To the west of the mountains and south of the town of Areopolis is the so-called Inner or "Deep" Mani. To the east is the Lower Mani. To the northwest, north of Areopolis, is the Outer or "Messenian" Mani. Historically, the Mani was the poorest, most remote province in Greece, only recently made accessible by motor vehicle, occupied by the Maniates, who proudly boast of having never been conquered by the Ottomans. Generally speaking, the Mani has received little attention from archaeologists and so its prehistory is poorly known, with the exception of Alepotrypa (Fox Hole) Cave, located close to the shores of Diros Bay in the Inner Mani.

Alepotrypa Cave was discovered in 1958 and opened to tourists in 1961, at which point evidence for early human habitation was recognized. This prompted excavations that began in 1970 under the direction of Dr. George Papathanassopoulos, now in his 90s, and have continued through the present day (e.g., Papathanassopoulos 1996; see also Papathansiou et al. n.d.). The cave system is gigantic, over 300 meters long and composed of several chambers, the deepest and largest of which includes a lake. In nearly five decades of work at the cave, Papathanassopoulos and his team have determined that it was settled throughout the course of the Neolithic, having collapsed, become sealed, and been abandoned about 3000 BC, just after the start of the Bronze Age. From the beginning, it was clear that people both lived and worked in the cave and were buried there, accompanied by various mortuary rites. In this sense, Alepotrypa is superficially similar to most Greek Neolithic settlements generally, composed of living quarters with graves interspersed. But the size and length of the occupation, the large number of burials, and the scale of the mortuary rituals performed there make Alepotrypa altogether different from anything attested anywhere else in Neolithic Greece. Not only did numerous people live in the cave, primarily in the first chamber, but a large number of deceased individuals was buried there: 161 at minimum, the largest number from any Neolithic site in Greece (Papathanasiou 2001). The majority of skeletal elements were recovered from two ossuaries (labeled I and II), three primary

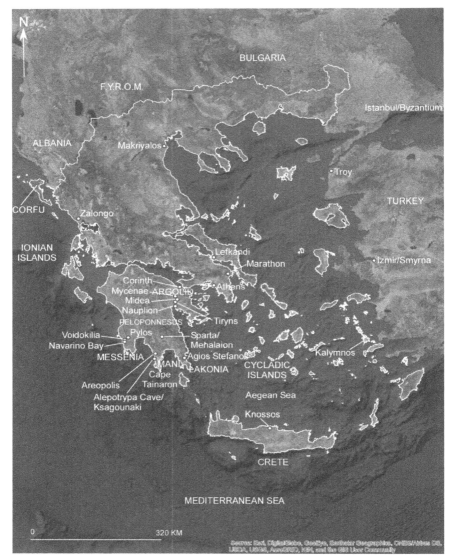

Figure 3.2. Map of Greece with sites mentioned in the text. *Source:* M. L. Galaty.

graves (one with multiple bodies), and one cremation (of two children). Grave offerings are rare, but limited excavation of the cave's settlement contexts (e.g., trench Beta 1) produced a wide range of artifacts, including trade goods from elsewhere in Greece, the Mediterranean, and the Balkans, such as obsidian tools, marble figurines, Spondylus shell bracelets, copper axes, and a silver pendant. Other parts of the cave generated a discontinuous surface backscatter of human bones and dramatic evidence for chthonic ritual practices. In a smaller, deeper chamber (labeled area Zeta), which overlooks the cave's largest room and lake, Papathanassopoulos excavated a deep deposit of black, ashy soil. Recent analyses indicate that it was produced by the burning of dung in very large quantities over the course of hundreds of years (Karkanas 2018; Tsartsidou 2018). In one section of the chamber, the ashy soil was mixed with nearly 100 polychromatic pots that had been deliberately smashed. We can therefore imagine a large cavern, occupied for thousands of years, by hundreds if not thousands of people, both living and dead, attracting exotic trade goods, and prompting a raft of ritual activities, which involved fire, smoke, and the manipulation of human skeletal remains.

We now also know that Neolithic occupation extended outside the cave proper, at least in some periods. Recently, members of the Diros Project, designed to survey the landscape of Diros Bay, have documented an equally large, similarly impressive settlement, called Ksagounaki, located to the north of and above the cave entrance, on a promontory, which likewise produced living quarters and a number of intramural burials, including burials of a child and infant in Final Neolithic pots and the grave of a spooning male and female couple (Parkinson et al. 2017; Pullen et al. 2018). Settlement remains cover several hectares and are bisected by later terraces that follow the contours of a gentle slope. However, running across these terraces are large, "megalithic" stone walls, which abut and support Final Neolithic structures, presumably houses. These walls are unique for the entire Greek Neolithic and, together with the cave, signal the special character of the site. Survey data indicate that during the Neolithic, Alepotrypa and Ksagounaki constituted the only settlement in the Diros Bay catchment and that after the cave's collapse, no new settlement occurred there prior to the Classical Age.

Altogether then, Alepotrypa Cave anchored a Neolithic landscape of memory in the western Mani, one that attracted and integrated people from throughout the wider region. Chemical data gathered from bones deposited in the cave indicate that at least some of the inhabitants of Alepotrypa were not local (Giblin 2018). Rather, they had traveled (or been brought) to Diros from afar. It may be that following death and primary exposure elsewhere, their skulls and long bones were gathered up and transported to the cave for secondary internment. As suggested by Papathanassopoulos, it is possible that Alepotrypa was a Neolithic pilgrimage site, attracting visitors from throughout southern Greece and abroad, who brought and deposited offerings, including the bones of revered ancestors. Alepotrypa might mark, therefore, the original source of Greek myths of the underworld. However, once the cave collapsed there was no reason to visit Diros and no reason to live there: Ksagounaki was abandoned. But the idea of the underworld and the memory of Alepotrypa Cave lived on in the minds of visitors and Ksagounaki's former occupants, who, presumably, moved away and joined other communities elsewhere. With Aleoptrypa's closure, the main entrance to Hades shifted south to Tanairon, where it was located in Classical times.

That Alepotrypa Cave was an important place and lingered in Greek Bronze Age cultural memory is indicated by evidence for surprising, unexpected Mycenaean activity at the site of Ksagounaki (Parkinson et al. 2017). Surface collections at the settlement prior to excavation produced a single Mycenaean obsidian arrowhead and no Mycenaean pottery at all. And yet, about a meter below the surface the Diros Project identified an unusual Mycenaean burial feature that had been cut into Neolithic levels. Most Mycenaeans were buried in cist graves or, if wealthy, in chamber or tholos tombs. At Ksagounaki, though, a large number of bones, representing many individuals, were deposited in a large circular ossuary. The bones, including those of men, women, and children, were found in very bad condition, having been collected elsewhere and reinterred. Two episodes of reburial were evident, separated by layers of small beach stones. Several whole Mycenaean pots—bowls, jars, and cups—were also found, mixed in among the bones, as were various prestige goods—a large ivory hair pin, several exotic stone beads, and a bronze dagger. The tomb's wealth alone makes the Ksagounaki ossuary unusual, but the mortuary context is completely unprecedented, unlike that of any other Mycenaean tomb known. It cannot be a coincidence that a unique Mycenaean ossuary was inserted into a much earlier, Final Neolithic village, one associated with a sacred cave, at which secondary burial in ossuaries had once, long ago, been practiced. As such, Ksagounaki presents the distinct possibility that Mycenaean people, who lived during the palatial period (i.e., Late Helladic IIIB, 1300–1200 BC), preserved collective memories of Final Neolithic burial practices over the course of nearly two millennia, and mimicked them, a truly remarkable example of collective memory creation and retention.

It may well be that Bronze Age mortuary behavior in Mani is exceptional, compared to the rest of the Mycenaean world. At the moment, we do not have enough archaeological data to know. But there is, in fact, some amount of meaningful variation in Mycenaean burial practices, generally, related to differences in sociopolitical organization, and indicative of the early formation of very different regional memory communities. During the Greek Bronze Age, we can chart increasing social complexity and inequality through time, beginning in the Early Bronze Age, when the first formalized cemeteries appeared. In the Middle Bronze Age (2000–1650 BC), some proto-Mycenaeans were buried in tumuli (mounds), a practice that likely spread south from the western Balkans—from Albania, for example—where tumulus burial was common. Greek tumuli contain the graves of important individuals, probably the leaders of ranked lineages. They are most common in Messenia, in western Greece, and are rather rare elsewhere, where cist graves were preferred. Sometime in the Late Bronze Age (Late Helladic IIA, *circa* 1500 BC), the tholos ("beehive") tomb was adopted in Messenia, having been introduced from Crete, signaling Messenia's early, intimate relationship with the Minoans (Korres 1984). Small tholos tombs were built throughout the region, sometimes replacing mounds as the preferred venue for competitive corporate burial. This process of mortuary change is well represented at the Messenian site of Voidokilia, where a Middle Bronze Age tumulus was built over the top of a small Early Bronze Age village only to be replaced in the early Late Bronze Age by a tholos tomb (Korres 1990), indicating some form of regional, long-term collective memory, manifested in the landscape, in ways at least fleetingly similar to Ksagounaki. During the course of the Mycenaean period, Messenia's tholos tombs gradually went out of use or were destroyed, until they were employed only at the Palace of Nestor or at secondary sites, like Nichoria, that were strongly affiliated with the palace (Bennet 1995). Thus, sociopolitical change in Messenia, related to state formation and consolidation, drove changes in mortuary practice. Changes in collective memory systems and memory making can also be strongly implicated in this process.

Messenia can be compared to the Argolid, where at least three different Mycenaean states formed, centered on the palatial sites of Mycenae, Tiryns, and Midea. Tumulus burial never caught on in the Argolid; rather most elite individuals were buried in cist graves. At the very end of the Middle Bronze Age/beginning of the Late Bronze Age, cist graves were enlarged into shaft graves at several pre-Mycenaean sites, the most important of which was Mycenae, where shaft graves associated with two grave circles, A and B, contained exceptional wealth, including large amounts of gold. Tholos tombs were introduced to the Argolid, but there were far fewer as compared to Messenia, and those built were much larger and were concentrated at the primary centers (e.g., nine at Mycenae). Most wealthy individuals were buried in chamber tombs.

Messenia and the Argolid thus practiced very different mortuary customs, beginning as early as the Middle Helladic (beginning *circa* 2000 BC). Messenia was strongly influenced first by the north, through the introduction of tumuli, and later by the Minoans, leading to a more "corporate" system of political organization, and burial. Power was shared horizontally between various competing families or factions, each operating out of a different settlement, each, eventually, with its own tholos tomb or tombs. When Pylos took over, late in the Mycenaean period (*circa* 1300 BC), and extended regional political control to the whole of Messenia, strongly "networked" political-economic systems were instituted and tholos tombs at once-independent settlements throughout the region were forced out of use. This radical restructuring of elite mortuary systems represents a reconfiguration of regional memory systems in service to the new state. A similar reconfiguration did not happen in the Argolid, since the Argolid states were strongly compartmentalized, and networked, from the start, each boasting its own built memory landscape. Mycenaean Greece—a relatively small place, much smaller than Egypt—thereby boasted remarkable variety in terms of collective memory systems (and mortuary practices), all of which were relatively unstable, especially those at Pylos, where orthodox regional memory systems had been jettisoned.

Mycenaean political, mortuary, and memory systems thus can be fixed along continua running from strongly networked to strongly corporate, individualizing to collective, and closed to open, with large amounts of variation from region to region, and marked change through time. As early as the early Late Bronze Age, the Argolid states had become compartmentalized, networked, and competitive, an outcome most visibly demonstrated by the Shaft Graves at Mycenae. By the palatial period, Argolid burial practices were individualizing, emphasizing "royal" personages, families, and their ancestors. Collective memory systems were harnessed by the state and used to support and legitimize social and political inequalities. They therefore remained relatively closed; opportunities for counter-memory production were limited. Messenia charted a different course. Early, sustained interaction with Adriatic peoples (e.g., during the Cetina period, 2200–2000 BC) and later close contacts with the Minoans encouraged the formation of corporate identities and regional interdependence, marked by the construction of many small tholos tombs. Collective memory systems were open and shared across many interacting social and political units; opportunities for counter-memory production existed, to be discussed in more detail below. If Ksagounaki is any indication, the Mani fell somewhere beyond Messenia along each of these continua. Traditional (i.e., "Neolithic") sociopolitical, mortuary, and memory systems persisted. Anonymous, collective burial was emphasized, powerfully symbolizing corporate, trans-egalitarian political systems. A palace has not been identified in the Mani, so it may well be that it operated outside state-level systems of administration and economy. Memory in the Mani ran deep and had not yet been subjected to elite control, as had happened early (perhaps as early as the late Middle Bronze Age) in the Argolid, and by 1300 BC in Messenia, under the direction of Pylos.

As described briefly above, the Minoan states were quite different from the Mycenaean states in terms of political organization, emphasizing corporate versus network ideologies. For example, whereas Mycenaean palaces were (in all cases) centered on throne rooms, Minoan palaces were (in all cases) centered on large courtyards, leading some archaeologists to suggest that they were not, in fact, palaces. Whereas there exist many images of Mycenaean kings and the Mycenaean king is identified in Linear B—the so-called *wanax*—there are no images of Minoan kings. Moreover, there are arguably "royal" Mycenaean burials, but no "royal" Minoan burials. And finally, the Minoan states were interacting, relatively non-confrontational peer polities. When they were destroyed at the end of the Neopalatial period (1390 BC) only one was reoccupied, that of Knossos, and it appears to have been under Mycenaean control. Tellingly, a throne room was added to the complex.

The process whereby Mycenaean memory systems formed and were appropriated by states can be pieced together through careful study of changing mortuary behaviors, with reference to Linear B records. Because Mycenaean states were "networked" (see above), leaders would have worked to construct personal pedigrees, linked to ancestors, which legitimized their attempts to control once-independent sociopolitical systems. One way they did this was through the display of "inalienable" objects, with known biographies, linked to important personages. As discussed by Schon (2010: 220–21), these objects were typically exotic, often of foreign origin, and appear to have circulated in and out of communal tombs, as they were opened and closed during burial rites. Necklaces of glass and amber beads, for example, could be removed from tombs and fragmented, allowing numerous members of ruling families or lineages to possess and exhibit ancestral heirlooms (Ibid.; see also Hamilakis 1998: 117). One result of this behavior is that many Mycenaean tombs are found to be empty upon excavation, bones pushed aside, grave goods missing (Cavanagh 2008: 339). Such tombs were not looted; empty tombs are the products of properly functioning memory systems. A full tomb represents collective memory's failure, the tomb or ancestor having been forgotten.

Memory behaviors like these, which appear during the period of state formation (i.e., during the Early Mycenaean [Middle Helladic IIIB-LH II]), are inherently diacritical, meant to differentiate individuals and families in increasingly hierarchical social systems. They are unlike the "corporate" memory behaviors practiced in Minoan Crete (e.g., before LM II Knossos, when wealthy individualizing burials become common) and those represented for the Mani by the Ksagounaki ossuary. That bones were gathered up elsewhere and reinterred at Ksagounaki along with wealth goods indicates that in the Mani, collective memory systems were still distributed in ways that worked against the creation of "networked," individualizing political systems.

Hamilakis (1998) has argued that Aegean Bronze Age funerals were venues for ritualized collective memory making. More specifically, mortuary feasts that occurred at the time of death fueled a distinctive "political economy" of "memory and forgetting" (Hamilakis 1998: 118). Feasts in general served as powerful loci for performative memory behaviors, at death but also for the living, throughout the course of a calendar year. Mycenaean feasts involved eating and drinking, but probably also the distribution of gifts, and certainly the telling of tales, perhaps by professional bards (Wright 2004). Moreover, there are strong indications that Mycenaean feasts were diacritical in nature, meant to reinforce the hierarchical social structures of Mycenaean states (Bendall 2004). In fact, a reconstruction of Mycenaean feasting at Pylos, based on analysis of Linear B records, reveals the social tensions (and opportunities) inherent in Mycenaean society, at all levels (Nakassis 2012). Tensions likely developed between different, competitive social factions (Wright 2001), but, generally speaking, by the palatial period they appear to have been most common between ordinary people, represented by the *damos* (probably a village council of sorts), and palatial authorities, represented by the *wanax*. Recently, Lupack (2014) has characterized disputes between damos and wanax, and between various factions, as contests over ancestry and, therefore, memory. As the wanax sought to separate himself from other regional chiefs, the so-called *basilees* (sing. *basileus*), he would have legitimized his right to rule by emphasizing his connections to the semi-divine "ancestral wanax," the first to sit the throne (Lupack 2014: 170–71). The need to support collective memory of an ancestral *wanax* can be used to explain Mycenaean mortuary behaviors in general, but also explains why Grave Circle A at Mycenae was preserved in LH IIIB when the city walls were expanded. Mycenae's leaders refurbished the grave circle, which predated the LH IIIB by several centuries, re-erecting grave stelae, and employed it as a highly visible *lieux de mémoire* (Lupack 2014: 171; see also Cavanagh 2008: 340). We can thus implicate several mnemonic behaviors in Mycenaean state formation: ancestor worship (which probably included the creation of fictive kinship relationships) leading to and/or in the face of factionalism; feasting (both mortuary and otherwise), at which social positions related to ancestry were both asserted and challenged; and the manipulation of mortuary monuments and rituals, creating what Cavanagh (2008: 331) has called a Mycenaean "war of the tombs," whereby "rival families competed to express variously their status, leadership, traditional authority, or links to the powerful elsewhere."

The Mycenaean "palace" period, during which palatial officials administered territorial states—and memory systems—lasted only a few centuries, at most, and only one century in Messenia (1300–1200 BC). Beginning about 1200 BC, the Mycenaean states collapsed, one after the other, until by 1050 BC they were no more. Greece was plunged into a Dark Age. The Mycenaean collapse was part of a much larger, regional collapse of cities and states that engulfed the entire Eastern Mediterranean at the end of the Late Bronze Age. Some, like Egypt, were spared, but suffered considerable instability. Others, like Troy and Hattusa, were destroyed. Possible causes for the collapse include mass migrations and warfare (Drews 1993), earthquake storms (Nur 2008; Nur and Cline 2000), and drought (Langgut et al. 2013), but, ultimately, a combination of factors, including social instability and shifting international trade patterns, likely contributed to widespread "systems failures" (Galaty et al. 2009: 49–51).

Whether or not a particular state ultimately survived the end of the Bronze Age may be linked to the strength and resilience of its collective memory systems. Egypt, for example, experienced a Third Intermediate Period following the collapse, marked by political decentralization, but the collective memory engram of "unification" was retained, encouraging continuity. Conversely, the Mycenaean states were independent and competitive, and thus did not possess a shared collective memory engram equivalent to Egyptian unification. The absence of integrated Mycenaean memory systems amplified the effects of collapse, encouraged regionalization, and laid the groundwork for the formation of the compartmentalized city-states of Archaic and Classical Greece. Coherent collective memories of the Mycenaean period were scarcely retained by the Classical Greeks, though they did share a sense of nostalgia, best represented in literature. The epic poems of Homer, for example, record certain kinds of very specific information about the Greek Bronze Age (e.g., regarding the geography of Mycenaean states) but largely misrepresent Mycenaean society. Descriptions of Mycenaean palatial administration and economy are completely missing, as is any record of Linear B writing. Interestingly, use of the term *wanax* was retained in Homeric Greek only, whereas *basileus* became the standard Greek word for "king" (Palaima 1995). Collective memories of the Mycenaean wanax did not survive the Dark Age. Those collective memories that did survive from the Mycenaean period did so primarily because localized distributed memory behaviors and systems were retained into and through the Iron Age, within very different, non-state systems that had more in common with Greek Neolithic societies, and, perhaps, with the Bronze Age societies of the Mani, than they did with Mycenaean states. Thus, whereas for Egyptians the Hyksos domination remained a traumatic memory, a cultural-historical touchstone, through the course of the New Kingdom, the Mycenaean collapse was recast by later Greeks as an important, transformative first step towards ideal, democratic societies. Tyranny was jettisoned, while the moral-ethical character of the Homeric heroes was retained.

We can now apply chapter 1's memory model to prehistoric Greece. Neolithic communities in Greece depended on widely distributed collective memory systems and employed human remains as memory cues. In this, they were not unlike Egyptian Neolithic communities. However, whereas during Naqada III (sometime after 3300 BC) Egyptian individuals managed to co-opt collective memory systems and specialists, in part by changing the practice and ideology of burial, thereby leading to state formation, a similar process did not unfold in Greece until much later and when it did, it generated regional variability, not unification. Some regions, like the Mani, appear to have maintained Bronze Age memory systems that were open and Neolithic in character, perhaps because they were not incorporated into early Mycenaean state systems (i.e., they were geographically remote and/or able to resist incorporation). Other regions, like Crete, produced states—beginning *circa* 1900 BC, at the start of Middle Minoan IB—that were independent "peer polities" (Cherry 1986), but shared intersecting state-level memory systems. Widespread memory cues, embedded in Minoan architecture and material culture and found at all Minoan sites, including palaces, likely triggered collective memory engrams, which underpinned corporate political ideologies. With reference to figure 1.2, the Minoan states deployed orthodox systems of memory that were stable over long periods of time, leading to a shared "Minoan" identity, and low levels of crisis. By contrast, Mycenaean states, which formed much later (i.e., as late as 1300 BC in Messenia) and were networked, deployed numerous heterodox memory systems linked to the ancestral histories of individual *wanaktes*. Mycenaean collective memory systems allowed, even encouraged, factionalism and counter-memory production and, as a result, were inherently unstable. Conflict between different memory communities would have led to high levels of crisis. Consequently, no single memory engram tied Mycenaean states together across time and space.

The diversity in Mycenaean memory systems is reflected in Mycenaean burial practices, which were also diverse, varying across regions (i.e., the Argolid versus Messenia). Generally speaking, Mycenaean mortuary rituals appear to have included *prosthesis* (mourning of the deceased on a bier) followed by *ekphora* (carrying of the bier to the grave site), as depicted on pictorial vases (Cavanagh 2008: 338–39, plate 13.2). Mourning women are portrayed with shorn hair and scarred or tear-stained faces. They dance and, we can assume, sing lamentations. The practice of singing lamentations together with public procession provided numerous opportunities, for women in particular, to fashion and present counter-memorial narratives. If Modern Greek lamentations are any indication (see above), Mycenaean Greek lamentations likely praised the deceased while at the same time encouraging social segmentation and factional confrontation (Seremetakis 1991). In this way, they were unlike classical Egyptian lamentations, which might question official religious ideologies (i.e., regarding the nature of the afterlife), but were not typically used to contest the social order. Importantly, unlike many aspects of Mycenaean culture, Bronze Age mortuary practices appear to have survived through the Dark Age and bear some similarity to Classical practices, indicating continuity in distributed memory systems.

The Mycenaean (and Minoan) states can be situated close to the center of figure 1.3: political control was moderate and memory systems were relatively broadly construed. They were more similar to Pre- and Early Dynastic Egypt than they were to Old and New Kingdom Egypt. They certainly never experienced political unification, as did the Egyptian state, and were never pulled toward memory-system closure, as was Egypt under Akhenaten. The decentralized nature of Mycenaean memory systems carried through the Dark Age, and laid the foundations for the heterogeneous states and memory systems of the Classical period. As was also the case in Egypt, the Romans assimilated Greek memory systems. Unlike Egypt, however, this process did not threaten Greek identity and language; rather, the Greeks eventually appropriated the Eastern Roman Empire, including Egypt, and forged a new, "Byzantine" identity and empire. And yet, even under imperial rule, Greece itself maintained wildly diverse memory communities. This diversity, with origins in prehistory, was encouraged and maintained by Christianity. Whereas Christianity helped preserve Egyptian collective memory and memory practices, if only in part, in Greece it amplified regional memory systems that were alive and well and promoted memory communities that, more often than not, competed with one another. This was particularly true of memory communities in the Mani.

Classical and Roman Greece

The precise nature of Greek Dark Age (1100–750 BC) communities is difficult to determine. Some parts of Greece, like Messenia, were completely depopulated. Others, like the Argolid, supported Dark Age settlements that were much smaller and seemingly less sophisticated than their Bronze Age predecessors. Some regions, though, such as central Greece and the Ionian islands, experienced growth. Dark Age communities may have been semi-sedentary and pastoral, having largely abandoned the settled ways associated with the Mycenaean states. This did not prevent them from amassing considerable wealth, as demonstrated at sites such as Lefkandi, where a Dark Age "chieftain" was buried at the center of a large tumulus (Popham et al. 1982). Nevertheless, for the Greek Iron Age we can draw a distinction between those who lived in proto-*polis* (i.e., walled cities) and those who lived in *komai* (i.e., small, un-walled villages), recapitulating the differences between those Mycenaeans who lived at palaces and those who did not (Papadopoulos 2014). It is therefore likely that the memory conflicts that characterized the Mycenaean period, between wanax and damos, continued to plague Iron Age societies, exacerbating processes of regional fragmentation. Collective memories of the Mycenaean palaces largely evaporated, along with the wanax ideology, while regional memory systems, built around enduring mortuary practices (e.g., prosthesis and ekphora), persisted. The formation of true poleis at the start of the Archaic (750–500 BC) depended on processes of collective memory making that built solidarity and new systems of identity, often operating against those distributed memory systems associated with komai and ethnic (i.e., "tribal," from the Greek *ethnos*) political organization. Greek city-states concocted elaborate origin stories, tapping ancient myth systems. They then expanded their purview by conquering other poleis and through colonization of tribal zones, both outside of (e.g., in Illyria) and within Greece. Conquered and colonized peoples were folded into the collective memories of their Greek mother cities.

Sparta provides a good example of collective memory making and polis formation. The province of Lakonia supported one or two Mycenaean palaces, definitely at Agios Stephanos and possibly at the Menelaion in Sparta. Following the collapse, Lakonia was largely depopulated and settlement did not rebound until the early Archaic, *circa* 750 BC (Cavanagh et al. 2002: chapter 5). Spartan origin myths linked their arrival to the Doric invasions of the Early Iron Age, making them newcomers. Seeking legitimacy, the leaders of Sparta later recast their arrival in Lakonia as a return, that of the Herakleidai in the aftermath of the Trojan War (Malkin 1994: 15). This same tactic was used by the leaders of all Classical poleis, each of which was joined to a returning Homeric hero: an imaginative, generative form of collective memory work. At the same time, like many Archaic-period city-states, Sparta founded colonies (*apoikia*) throughout the Mediterranean, but also sought to expand its control of Greek territories. Sparta, for example, conquered adjacent Messenia sometime in the late eighth or early seventh century BC. The Messenians became helots, Spartan slaves.

Spartan social organization distinguished between Spartan citizens, helots, and the perioichoi, the "dwellers around," who may have performed skilled labor. The Messenian helots appear to have lived difficult lives: they were disenfranchised and, if later histories are to be believed, tortured and humiliated by their Spartan masters (Alcock 2002: 134–36). Whereas we know where the Messenian helots lived (in Messenia) and what they did (farm work, presumably), we do not know exactly where the perioichoi lived and what they did. Some perioichoi appear to have occupied dependent poleis and developed patron-client relationships with Spartans. Of an estimated 17 definite perioikic poleis in Messenia and Lakonia combined, as many as six may have been located in the Mani (Shipley 1997). Doubtless, poleis that were dependent on the

Spartans would have had a difficult time developing meaningful heroic genealogies of their own. Perioikic identity—and therefore Maniate identity—would have been subordinated to Sparta. And yet, as Alcock (2002: 138) argues based on an analysis of landscape and monuments, the Messenian helots managed to produce "some form of collective identity" despite their subjugation, which served them well just prior to and following liberation in 370/369 BC. The Maniate perioichoi likely did so as well. However, whereas the freed Messenians documented their newly constructed—or finally recovered—identity and collective memory in numerous monuments and inscriptions, and by founding a capital city at Messene (as described in detail by Alcock 2002), there is no record of similar activities on the part of the Maniate perioichoi: no existing monuments, no inscriptions, no new cities, nothing. I submit that this is because the Messenian helots, while slaves, had lived within and around state-level systems for generations, prior to their liberation. Their manipulation of Messenian landscapes and construction of various *lieux de mémoire* betrays a deep, meaningful understanding of and appreciation for the importance of collective memory to the nation-building process. In contrast, the Maniate perioichoi operated outside the bounds of the Spartan, or any, state. When the helots gained their freedom, Messenian perioichoi joined them in creating a new, Messenian identity. Little changed for the Maniate perioichoi and no equivalent Maniate identity appeared, that is, until much later.

Alcock has further argued that helots—and Messenian perioichoi—prior to and following liberation, participated in tomb cults and worshiped at small, possibly open-air shrines, unlike their Spartan overlords, who favored temples. An example of post-liberation Messenian tomb cult is that of Thrasymedes, located at Voidokilia (Alcock 2002: 150). This is the same Voidokilia, described above, where a Middle Bronze Age tumulus had been built over the top of an Early Bronze Age village to be replaced by a Late Bronze Age tholos tomb. Thrasymedes was the son of old king Nestor, ruler of Pylos, a Messenian ancestor *par excellence*. That the Messenians placed his tomb cult at Voidokilia represents an incredible example of memory work, drawing a direct, albeit imaginary, line between freed helots and the original Homeric heroes of the region. Given these practices in Messenia, we might expect and reconstruct similar kinds of activities in Mani—tomb cults and worship at open-air shrines—thus explaining the general lack of monuments and temples, compared to elsewhere in Lakonia, and in Messenia itself. Indeed, if Diros is any indication, the Maniate perioichoi may have sought, like the Messenians, to connect themselves to the earlier, Mycenaean inhabitants of the region. No one seems to have lived at Diros, in proximity to Ksagounaki and Alepotrypa Cave, following their abandonment at the start of the Bronze

Age, until the Classical period, when a substantial settlement, discovered by the Diros Project, appeared at the head of the bay, possibly serving as a port for the inland, "perioikic" polis of Pyrrichos (Shipley 2006: 63). Substantial amounts of Classical pottery were also found by the Diros Project at Ksagounaki, mixed in with the excavated terrace fill, overlying the Final Neolithic settlement and Mycenaean ossuary. It is perhaps no accident that Classical settlers, possibly perioikoi, were drawn to Diros, both because of the protected bay and access to the sea—perioikic poleis favored the coast (Shipley 2006)—but also because of the area's prehistoric pedigree, which would have encouraged tomb cult. Maniate perioikic activity at prehistoric *lieux de mémoire*, like Ksagounaki and Alepotrypa, may have laid the groundwork for the later construction there, and throughout the Mani, of small Byzantine churches. By some estimates, there are more small Byzantine churches in Mani than any other region of Greece and many of them stand in proximity to or incorporate Classical spolia, much of it from tombs.

The atomization of memory, landscape, and identity that characterized Classical Greece and continued into the Byzantine period was not forestalled by Hellenism and the efforts of Alexander the Great, nor was it ended by Roman conquest. Alexander himself was a master of memory. Like many Greeks, he used collective memory to his advantage, to legitimize his conquest of the Greek city-states by constructing for himself a heroic ancestry: descended from Achilles on his mother's side, and Heracles on his father's (Green 1991: 40). For their part, the Greeks considered him to be a barbarian, a non-Greek whose right to rule could be questioned:

> The story goes that Alexander, upon his succession to the throne, went into the Peloponnese, where he assembled all the Greeks in that part of the country and asked them for the command of the campaign against Persia, which they had previously granted to Philip [Alexander's father]. The only people to refuse his request were the Lacedaemonians, who declared that the tradition of their country forbade them to serve under a foreign commander; it was their prerogative to lead others. (Arrian, Book One; de Sélincourt 1971: 42)

The Greek reaction to Alexander can be contrasted to that of the Egyptians, described in chapter 2, who declared him the son of Ammon and welcomed him as a liberator and unifier. He adopted Egyptian customs and restored a sense of Egyptian identity that had been threatened under the Persians. The Greeks did not need liberating and, as I have argued above, were never unified under singular rule; Alexander's pan-Hellenism was a threat to democratic principles and collective memories of hard-fought, regional independence, like that of the Lacedaemonians.

Throughout the Hellenistic period, which began with the death of Alexander in 323 BC and ended with the Roman incorporation of Achaia, Mani largely flew under the historical radar. Philip V penetrated deep into its territory in 218 BC and the Temple of Poseidon at Tanairon continued to attract visitors (Greenhalgh and Eliopoulos 1985: 20), but Mani was perhaps best known during this time as a pirate haunt and ready source of mercenaries, a reputation it shed only after the final Roman conquest of Greece in 146 BC. It was during this period, around 195 BC, that a union of 18 "perioikic" cities, mostly in the Mani, including Pyrrichos, was formed and separated from Sparta with the help of the Romans (Ibid.), eventually to become, in 21 BC under Augustus, the Eleutherolakones, the League of the Free Lakonians. Even though many traditional poleis and some leagues, such as the Eleutherolakones, were nominally independent and some were immune from taxation, following the Battle of Actium in 31 BC and the creation of the province of Achaia, "for the first time, all of the autonomous, or largely autonomous, Greek political units were formally and forcibly brought together under an external power" (Alcock 1993: 16). And yet, Greek identity was not subsumed by Roman identity, despite Italian immigration to Achaia, and the mnemonic shatter zone that was Mycenaean and Classical Greece survived into and through the Roman conquest, to emerge again under Byzantium. The first hint of ongoing regionalization, despite the *Pax Romana*, and the continued existence of competitive memory communities is the necessity for "free" cities and leagues at all. The Romans could have forced all Greek poleis to pay tribute equally, but they did not; a divide and conquer strategy was more effective (Alcock 1993: 21–24). Another hint concerns the structure of the "Greek" provinces and the borders between Achaia, Macedonia, and Epirus, demarcated by the Romans sometime in the first century AD. It is no accident that the boundary separating Achaia from Epirus roughly marks the northern extent of true Greek poleis, the Greek character of the frontier city-states having always been questioned. The northwestern border separating Epirus from Macedonia, which ran along the Shkumbin River, marks the divide between Albanian speakers of the Tosk and Gheg dialects. The former was and always had been more closely aligned with the southern, Hellenized world of Epirus. I will return to these distinctions in much more detail in chapter 4, but safe to say that these borderlines did not simply distinguish Greeks from others; rather, they split landscapes of memory that were differently inhabited and variously experienced. Again, tellingly, the island of Crete, which, as argued above, supported Minoan memory systems that were very different from Mycenaean memory systems, was allotted by the Romans in 63 BC not to Achaia, but rather to Cyrenaica, with a capital at Gortyn, not Knossos.

When Akhenaten became pharaoh, he attempted to dislodge millennia's worth of Egyptian collective memory. He failed. When Alexander the Great and, later, the Romans, conquered Greece, they likewise recognized the power of memory to shape empires, but they took a very different approach. Instead of restricting and homogenizing the diverse, heterodox memory systems of Greece, they co-opted them, deeply tapping the Greek penchant for nostalgia (see discussion in Alcock 2002: e.g., 39–41). Both promised to restore a glorious Greek past: Alexander, by defeating Persia and avenging wrongs, and the Romans, by reinvigorating the Greek people, who had become (according to the Romans) weak and mendacious. In both periods, the effects on Greek collective memories were limited. Consequently, Classical and Roman Greece look much like Mycenaean Greece when it comes to their memory systems. With reference to figure 1.2, conflicts between Classical poleis were common and provoked crises. These were often framed in mnemonic terms and normalized through various political and religious practices, such as consulting oracles. Under the Romans, crises were reduced and nostalgia rose. Whereas the Classical Greeks had employed collective memories imaginatively to build individualized urban identities, city by city, such behaviors were curtailed under the Romans, who demanded fealty to Rome. Nevertheless, the Greeks nurtured their language and culture under Roman rule, which lasted several centuries, and eventually turned the tables, appropriating the Eastern Roman Empire and ruling from Byzantium. Christianity had a key role to play in this process. With reference to figure 1.3, Classical Greece's memory systems were relatively more open than those of the Mycenaeans, and political control somewhat less pronounced. Under the Romans, Greek memory systems were constricted some, but not to the point that Greek collective memories, and therefore identities, were seriously threatened. With roots in prehistory, Greek memory systems were too highly distributed to allow direct political control, and overt political control ran counter to Roman imperial strategies anyway, which tended to be relatively decentralized. By the time Theodosius I finally made Christianity the official state religion in AD 380, the Greeks had already transformed the Church into a memory machine, tuned to their needs, but highly flexible and able to accommodate the regionalized structure of Greek memory systems. Once again, a close look at Mani helps make these points.

Byzantine Greece

In AD 324, Constantine the Great moved the capital from Rome to Byzantium, which in 330 was renamed Constantinople. In 325, he inaugurated the First Council of Nicaea, at which Christian bishops and theologians debated the true nature of Christ. As described in chapter 2, it was not until the Council of Chalcedon in AD 451 that this debate was finally settled, in favor of the dyophysitic position: Christ was both human and divine. The Coptic, mono- or mia-physitic position, associated at Nicaea with Arius—that God and Christ were possessed of a single divine nature—was prohibited. As further described in chapter 2, the dyophysitic position was rejected by the Copts because it ran counter to traditional, Egyptian forms of theology and collective-memory making, which supported unification: just as God and Jesus were one, so should be Egypt. It is perhaps no surprise that Constantine and the Great Church (i.e., the Western and Eastern churches together) supported the dyophysitic position, which was preferred in both Rome and Constantinople. Arius himself was banished to Illyria. Thus, the so-called Byzantine period of Greek history began by shifting a theological and political problem from Egypt to Albania. Instability and conflict persisted, however, in part because the Eastern Church continued to be influenced by both the Oriental Church and, later, by Islam. New theological fault lines opened, for instance, around icons. Catholic and Orthodox Christians both used icons, but employed them differently, and any such images were forbidden by Islam. The controversy over icons erupted in AD 726, when Emperor Leo III destroyed the giant icon of Jesus over St. Sophia's Chalke gate, ushering in the practice of "iconoclasm," the smashing of icons (Norwich 1997: 111). I will argue below that iconoclasm represents a larger struggle over collective memory, its place in the Byzantine Empire, and the suitability of Greek memory systems for nation building.

Under the Byzantines, the landscapes of memory that had characterized Classical and Roman Greece, composed of temples and monuments, were slowly replaced by an ecclesiastical landscape of churches and monasteries. In many cases, these were built over the top of, and using stones from, pagan *temenoi*. This new, ecclesiastical landscape did not, however, unite Greece around a singular collective memory system; rather, churches, which operated relatively independently, reinforced the distributed, open memory systems that had characterized Greek culture at least as early as the Bronze Age, with origins in the Neolithic. As described above, a whole suite of memory behaviors evolved in Greece during prehistory, survived into the Classical period, and flourished. They were not dislodged under Roman occupation, because they meshed well with Roman strategies of imperial occupation. Greek memory practices mitigated against nation building through unification, encouraging regionalization and competition between memory communities instead. These practices, which were further elaborated during the Byzantine period, included various mortuary rites, such as lamentations, procession, and commemoration, including libation (Poulou-Papadimitriou et al.

2012). Interestingly, the range of Greek (Orthodox) and Egyptian (Coptic) collective-memory practices employed under Christianity were similar but functioned very differently, despite similar prehistoric origins, having experienced very different developmental histories. For Egypt, the key historical rupture was, of course, the Arab conquest of AD 639. However, the spread of Islam to Egypt, a historical process, and not to Greece is not sufficient to explain the vast differences in memory and nation building that distinguish Egypt from Greece (and both from Albania). Other, sociopolitical processes were at work.

To some degree, the Byzantine struggle over memory was couched within a larger struggle over how the empire should be structured and function, and between "Roman" and "Byzantine" ways of doing things. Whereas the Romans had ruled lightly, the Byzantine impulse was to dominate the provinces, Greece included. Generally speaking, it was the Church, led by the patriarch, and his representatives, the bishops (*episkopoi*), that defended the common people from the worst excesses of the state, led by the emperor (*basileus*) (von Falkenhausen 1997). In theory, patriarch and emperor were independent, cooperating entities. In reality, they were often at odds, to the extent that numerous patriarchs were deposed (or killed) by kings. Eventually, church and state merged, as members of the royal family took elevated positions in the church hierarchy, allowing a more direct assault on traditional memory systems. This long process, which played out over the course of 150 years, began with Justinian (527–565), the "last true Roman Emperor" (Norwich 1997: 97), and ended during the reigns of Basil the Macedonian (867–886) and his son, Leo the Wise (886–912). The Arabs were repulsed, the Balkans subdued, Italy (partially) reconquered, and Greek became the official language of the land. Most importantly, the lingering theological debates that had plagued the early Byzantines were finally laid to rest. For example, during her reign, Empress Theodora (d. 867) made it her personal mission to eradicate iconoclasm once and for all (Norwich 1997: 139). To that end, she sought to centralize ecclesiastical power and harness it by actively promoting a like-minded patriarch, Methodius. But she is perhaps best known for actively persecuting the Paulicians, a monophysitic Christian sect that rejected icons and the Church hierarchy (Norwich 1997: 140). The Paulicians and those like them, such as the Bogomils (who were active in Albania), were religious radicals, but also represent heterodox memory communities, ones that actively resisted Byzantine efforts to assert political, and therefore mnemonic, control. Similar conflicts played out in less extreme form throughout the empire, in places like Mani.

Throughout Greece, during the Late Roman period, churches replaced tomb cults and sanctuaries as loci for commemoration. Despite Byzantine attempts to regulate clergy by controlling the patriarchate, priests continued to act as memory-workers. Typically, they were members of their communities, trusted with curating village memory stores. For example, priests kept a list in the church building of all births, deaths, and baptisms, acting as village genealogists. It was not until the founding of the Modern Greek state that these records were moved to government archives. Priests married and buried people, heard confessions, and mediated disputes. As such, churches reinforced local systems of kinship and provincial ways of life. They gathered centripetal force, turning societies inward, as had the Mycenaean damos and Classical poleis. Whereas the Romans allowed, even encouraged, such forces, the Byzantines sought to stop or, at least, redirect them. If the Byzantine state was to survive, as a Greek nation, it had to overcome millennia of inertia, and the best way to do so was to appropriate and reconstruct Greek collective memories. This strategy failed, which is a good thing, since it was the resilient memory systems of wider Greece that repulsed Ottoman systems of imperial coercion and incorporation, systems that had nearly destroyed Egyptian culture.

Greek Orthodox churches are, by and large, small, dark, smoky affairs. They are chthonic, otherworldly, and cave-like. These very characteristics must have marked Alepotrypa Cave during the Neolithic. Like Alepotrypa, Greek churches are designed to evoke mystery. They are the abode of saints, personified by icons. As described above, many Byzantine churches, including those in Mani, were built in proximity to ruins and incorporate spolia, architectural and sculptural fragments reused from earlier buildings. For example, the Classical site at Diros, which I have associated with ancient Pyrrichos, was superseded by a possible monastery and two churches, dedicated to Ag. Paraskevi and Ag. Theodoroi, indicating long-term interest in the locale. Both churches include spolia, as do most Maniate churches. Papalexandrou (2003) refers to spolia as memory cues, which reference the Classical past, used for nostalgic or apotropaic purposes. Classical Greek inscriptions held particular interest, acting to reinforce Greek autochthony. In later periods, these were sometimes juxtaposed with so-called pseudo-Kufic decorations designed to evoke Arabic script, including in Mani (Mexia 2016). Overall, then, Byzantine churches, including the churches of the Mani—of which there may have been as many as 1200 (Saitas 2009: 392)—functioned as distributed memory stores, cueing local memory engrams linked to patron saints and prominent citizens, reinforced through church liturgy.

Referring again to figure 1.2, Byzantine Greece was much like Classical Greece: crisis was high, as Constantinople lurched from one theological controversy to another. Whereas under the Romans, certain orthodoxies were inescapable (e.g., that the Emperor was divine), with the adoption of Christianity, fertile grounds for heterodox memory production appeared.

Imagination and identity formation ran high, producing numerous heterodox memory communities, like the aforementioned Paulicians. This inhibited Byzantine nationalism and nation building, even in regions, like Greece, that should have supported synergasia. Byzantine Greece thus falls close to Classical Greece on figure 1.3: collective memory systems were relatively open and political control was low (though not for a lack of trying on the part of Byzantine authorities). As I will argue below, it was not until the founding of the modern Greek state, in 1829, with a capital in Nauplion, of all places, that some semblance of Greek national unity was finally manufactured. For places like Mani, though, unity came grudgingly, and with memory strings attached.

MEMORY AND THE MAKING OF THE MODERN GREEK STATE

Modern Greek mortuary practices evolved during the Late Medieval period, but their origins can be traced to Classical, even prehistoric, times. As discussed above, in Greece the Neolithic dead were typically buried within villages and, sometimes, within houses. Bodies appear to have undergone various kinds of manipulation, including exposure and secondary reburial, sometimes focused on particular body parts, such as long bones and skulls, as was apparently practiced at Alepotrypa Cave. Body parts likely served as memory cues, triggering collective-memory engrams related to village ancestry, as was also the case in Neolithic Egypt and the Near East. However, whereas these types of distributed memory systems were co-opted by early state officials in Egypt, supporting new memory tropes of "unification," a similar process did not occur in Greece, where regionalized mortuary systems developed during the Bronze Age, in support of localized, competitive memory systems. These memory systems, later captured by Homer, however fleetingly, in writing, survived the Late Bronze Age collapse, *circa* 1200 BC, and propped up the various, heterodox memory communities of the Classical poleis. Importantly, as the polis "ideal" evolved, so too did burial practices. Morris (1987: 216–17) correlates changes in grave form to changes in the nature of the Greek political system, from autocratic to egalitarian, and back again, a process finally disrupted by the Romans, who dropped all pretenses of equality. Classical mortuary practices, such as public mourning of the dead (*prosthesis*) and procession to the tomb (*ekphora*), continued into and through Byzantine times, and became hallmarks of modern Greek mortuary practices (as described by Danforth 1982). In fact, the tomb cults of the Classical period, as practiced in places like Messenia and Mani, bear a striking resemblance to rituals of adoration and commemoration of the dead in Byzantine and modern Greek cemeteries. It was exactly these kinds of localized, distributed memory behaviors that sustained Greek language and identity during the years of Turkish occupation.

Ottoman and Early Modern Greece

In 1453, Constantinople fell to Mehmed II, the Ottoman Turkish sultan. By 1460, all of Greece was under Turkish control, with the exception of the Ionian Islands and various, other small Venetian holdings. The Mani remained under Turkish suzerainty but was not subject to Turkish administration. To this day, the Maniates proudly claim that unlike the rest of Greece, they were never conquered by the Turks.

Under the Ottomans, Greek Christians, members of the so-called *rayah*, the taxable "flock" or underclass, suffered. They often retained ownership of their land, but were taxed at higher rates than Muslim rayah, and their male children were subject to the *devshirme*, military conscription and permanent separation from the family. One way to avoid these inequities was to convert to Islam, and yet only a very small percentage of Greeks did so (Bialor 2008). This is quite unlike Egypt and Albania, where the majority of Christians eventually converted. Differential conversion rates in all three regions is one result of very different underlying memory systems and, consequently, experiences of Arab and Ottoman conquest. In Egypt, Christian peasants were dispossessed of their land by the Arabs and Arabic became the official language. Egyptians became Muslim out of necessity, but also because by the time of the Arab conquest, they had already suffered over 1,000 years of foreign domination. Egyptian collective memory, which was largely a product of the Egyptian state, was long gone and what memories remained were supported, in large part, by the Coptic Church, which was itself under attack. As will be described in chapter 4, Albanians converted from Christianity to Islam, and back again, with apparent ease. Cryptochristianity—the practice of Christianity in secret—and various forms of religious syncretism were normal. This also happened in Greece, no doubt, but much less commonly. As of the 2011 census, an estimated 60 percent of Albanians were Muslim (Census-AL 2011). As of 2006, the estimated number of Muslim Greeks was only 1 percent, in part due to population exchanges with Turkey in the early 20th century, but largely because very few Greeks converted (United States Department of State 2006). As of 2012, an estimated 90 percent of Egyptians were Muslim (CIA World Factbook 2016).

Interestingly, contemporary Greeks preserve few collective memories of Muslim Greeks, despite their continued presence in the country in small numbers, especially in Thrace. More generally, the Tourkokratia itself is variously remembered, with most Greeks preferring to think of the fall of Constantinople and Ottoman occupation as being the darkest period in Greek history. One thing all Greeks seem to agree upon is that it was the Greek Orthodox Church that "saved" Greek language and culture during the period of Turkish rule, so that today, Orthodox Christianity is recognized in the Greek constitution as the "prevailing" (i.e., official, state) religion of Greece. For many Greeks, churches continue to be primary centers of village life and activity, and collective-memory production, as they must have been under the Ottomans, who generally allowed religious diversity. Ethnohistoric data support this conclusion. In traditional Greek culture, most major rites of passage—baptism, marriage, death—occurred in, or near, churches, reinforcing bonds of kin- and friendship that stretched back generations, counteracting social forces, like migration, that pulled families apart. For example, the institution of *koumbaroi*, whereby men and women sponsored children and friends in baptism and marriage, generated local networks of reciprocity and encouraged insularity, such that one's *patridha* (home village) could be contrasted to all other villages, which were filled with *kseni* (strangers) (Friedl 1962: 72–74, 104). The socio-historical webs that characterized individual Greek villages were materialized in landscapes of memory composed of houses, shrines, paths between them, haunted areas (to be avoided), and cemeteries. On the island of Lipsi, Papachristophorou (2013) documented in detail just such a landscape of memory, which was accessed daily by villagers, who told and retold stories about important people and events in the life of the community, formulating identifiable, shared memory engrams. Sutton (1998) describes similar behaviors on the island of Kalymnos, where residents reinforced collective memories (e.g., of resistance to Italian occupation) by lighting and throwing sticks of dynamite at times and in places of significance. It was these kinds of regionalized, "centrifugal" commemorative practices that, generally speaking, prevented Greek political unity, but helped preserve Greek identity during the Tourkokratia.

Such public memory spectacles reached their height during funerals. As described by Danforth (1982), after death the body of the deceased was displayed in the front hall of the family home. For the next 12–24 hours, relatives and friends gathered to mourn and women sang laments. Just as in Classical times, the deceased's status, and that of the family, was signaled by the number of visiting mourners (Morris 1987: 48). When the priest finally arrived, the body was moved into a coffin and carried in procession to the church, where the funeral was held. Following the funeral, the coffin was taken to the cemetery and lowered into the ground, prompting a final round of mourning. A liminal period then ensued, lasting about five years, during which various memorial services (*mnimo-*

sina) were held, ending with exhumation of the body (Danforth 1982: 43). When the body was exhumed, the expectation was that the bones would be clean, white, and free from flesh, hair, and clothing, which indicated that the individual's sins had been completely absolved. Women undertook the exhumation, sifting the earth and then placing the bones in the village ossuary, "a powerful symbol of the ultimate unity of the village dead" (Danforth 1982: 56).

As was the case in Egypt, laments provided an excellent opportunity for Greek counter-memorial activity, especially on the part of women. As described by Seremetakis (1991: 1), the women of Inner Mani used lamentation as a form of *poesis*, of "making and imagining," an ongoing social process that emerged "from the relation of women to death" and reinterpreted the Mani as a peripheral, fragmented place. Maniate laments were biographical and, as discussed above, could encourage revenge, if, for example, the deceased had been murdered. Female mourning ceremonies (*kláma*), which were held in public, can be juxtaposed to male council meetings (*yerondikí*), which were held in secret, and at which men made political and legal decisions for the clan (Seremetakis 1991: 126). It was through the improvised singing of laments that women actively engaged and challenged male authority and encouraged certain juridical outcomes. They did this by recollecting and describing pertinent people and events, and reminding men of their obligation to pursue feuds. In this way, women acted as primary memory workers—which often put them at odds with priests (Seremetakis 1991: 161)—but also as moral-ethical voices for their communities, keeping men honest. A famous lament, recorded by Seremetakis (1991: 237), goes:

> I am the Verga of Almyros
> I hold and withstand all
>   ill-fated attacks
> For I have the rounded belly of
>   a storage vase,
> I can open the earth and bring all
>   that is up down
> I can throw it in the deep ocean
>   as well.

Verga near Almyros is the location of the 1826 battle that pitted the Maniates against Mehmed Ali's Egyptians, and launched the Greek War of Independence. As noted by Seremetakis (1991: 237), "In Maniat memory, this battle is an event of cosmic proportions." Indeed, the battle is memorialized each year in June by Maniates, many of them expatriates, who gather near Alepotrypa Cave and throw mannequins dressed as Turks off the cliffs. According to historians, Verga was a male victory, but the lament tells a different tale. In reality, the Egyptians were repulsed at Diros—near Alepotrypa Cave—by women armed with sickles. It is women who bring life, but they can also bring death: what is up becomes down, and is thrown into the ocean. Memory devours history, in the rounded belly of a storage vase.

The War of Independence

The Greek War of Independence began on March 17, 1821, when the Maniates raised their flag over Areopolis, capital of the Inner Mani, and declared war on the Ottoman Empire. Soon, the whole of Greece was in revolt, led by bands of warrior *klephts*, armed brigands who operated out of the mountains under the command of *kapetanaioi* (captains). After the war, some of these *kapetanaioi* became leaders of the Greek state: Kolokotronis, Makriyannis, and, perhaps most famous of all, Mavromichalis.

Petros "Petrobey" Mavromichalis (1765–1848) was a Maniate clan leader, well known for his skills both as a warrior and a politician. It was he who brokered peace among the various Greek factions, leading up to the declaration of war. After the war, he was elected to the first Greek senate. An important man, and yet, the first head of state of independent Greece was not Mavromichalis, but rather Ioannis Kapodistrias (1776–1831), an expatriate Greek from Corfu, who did not fight in the war. In fact, the Greek nation needed a non-native leader if it was to survive. Kapodistrias was succeeded by King Otto I of Bavaria (reigned 1832–1862), not by a Greek, and, ironically, Greece, the cradle of democracy, became a kingdom.

As I have argued above, the collective-memory systems of Greece encouraged regionalization and loyalty to one's family, clan, and village before nation. Nowhere was this more true than the Mani. The Maniates, for their part, never supported national unity and rule from Athens—this is one reason why the first capital was established at Nauplion in the Peloponnese, as a concession to the Maniates—and, consequently, Mavromichalis and Kapodistrias did not agree on just how the new government should be structured. Not surprisingly, the former preferred a decentralized federal republic, whereas the latter opted for centralization, arguing that the young nation required "enlightened autocracy" first, and representative democracy later (Brewer 2011: 338). Like Alexander and the Romans before him—and Mehmed Ali in Egypt—Kapodistrias sought to dismantle the traditional, distributed collective-memory systems of Greece—by, for example, establishing a national school system, disbanding local militias, and introducing a national currency—which constituted a direct threat to people like the Maniates, and leaders like Mavromichalis, who valued freedom above all else. Unlike the official Greek motto, which reads

"Freedom or death," the Maniate battle flag reads "Victory or death," because the Mani had always been free.

In 1831, Kapodistrias had Mavromichalis imprisoned, a dire offense to his family and all Maniates. On October 9, 1831, Kostantis and Georgios Mavromichalis, Petrobey's sons, assassinated Kapodistrias on the steps of the Church of Saint Spyridon in Nauplion. The first bullet, which missed, lodged in the church wall and is still visible today, making Saint Spyridon a powerful *lieux de mémoire*. Whereas today there are statues of Kapodistrias all over Greece, including in Athens, Corfu, and Nauplion, and in several countries, there is only one statue of Mavromichalis, in Areopolis. To this day, the Mani remains one of the poorest provinces in Greece.

This very brief, overly broad description of the Greek War of Independence, which does not deviate much from official accounts, masks much complexity. Greek collective memories of the Tourkokratia and War of Independence omit any facts that do not fit the modern, nationalist tropes of Greek unity, territorial integrity, and ethnic purity. For example, most Greeks believe that all *kapetanaioi* were Greek. In reality, many were Albanian—including the only female captain, Laskarina Bouboulina—such that most war councils were conducted bilingually, in Greek and Albanian (see various documents in Clogg 1976). That there were Albanian *kapetanaioi* is not surprising; large numbers of Albanians had migrated into Greece during the Late Medieval period, the so-called Arvanites (Bintliff 2003; Gogonas 2010), most of whom fought in the war on the side of the Greeks. In fact, at the dawn of the modern age, Greece was a very diverse place, as diverse as Egypt, at least, if not more so. In addition to the Arvanites and Greek Muslims, described above, Greece was home to various other ethnic groups, many of whom still remain, including Turks, Vlachs, Roma, Armenians, Jews, and various Slavs. In an attempt to erase evidence for the minority presence in Greece, beginning as early as the 1830s non-Greek (i.e., Albanian, Slavic, even Celtic) place names were converted to Greek (Mackridge 2009). For example, Areopolis, the "city of Ares," where the Maniates declared war against the Ottomans, was once called Tsimova, a Slavic toponym. The name was officially changed to Areopolis in 1912.

Turning once again to figures 1.2 and 1.3, Ottoman Greece appears much like Ottoman Egypt. Political control was high, but not very, and memory systems remained relatively open. The Ottomans allowed local autonomy when it suited them and tolerated religious diversity. By comparison, modern Greece, like many modern nations, is characterized by moderate forms of political control coupled with relatively closed memory systems, which work to reinforce orthodox histories constructed and promulgated after the War of Independence. National unity was not sculpted, block by block, memory by memory, by Greek politicians;

rather, Greek landscapes were emptied, as Greek people moved overseas or to Athens. Separated from their churches, shorn from their *patridhes* (homelands), Greeks finally abandoned their distributed collective-memory communities. The population of the Mani now stands at 13,000. Every year, the Battle of Diros is remembered by fewer and fewer people, who gather there and toss effigies of Turks from the cliffs.

4

Albania
Adaptation

§238. The boundary is constructed with large, towering rocks thrust into the earth and exposed above it. An aged tree may serve as a boundary.

"The boundary stone has witnesses behind it."

§239. The boundary stone has witnesses around it. These are six or twelve small rocks which are buried in the earth around the boundary stone.

§240. When boundaries are fixed, aside from the households concerned, there must also be present Elders of the village, Elders of the Banner, and as many young people and children as possible from the villages of the district, so that the boundary will be retained in memory.

§241. Every tract of land, whether field or meadow, garden or vineyard, small forest or copse, woodland or pasture or house grounds, village, Banner, or house—all are divided by boundaries.

§242. "Once boundaries are fixed, they are never moved again."

§243. In the view of the Kanun, the bones of the dead and the boundary stone are equal. To move a boundary is like moving the bones of the dead.

—*Kanuni i Lekë Dukagjinit*, Book Four: House, Livestock, and Property, chapter 13: Boundaries, LVII "Land Boundaries are not Movable," Gjeçov 1989: 74 [italics in original]

Figure 4.1.   Boundary Stone, Theth, Shala. *Source:* M. L. Galaty.

The *Kanuni i Lekë Dukagjinit* is a body of oral customary law that, according to tradition, was codified, and enforced, by a northern Albanian chieftain, Lekë Dukagjini (1410–1481). Lekë Dukagjini was a contemporary of Albania's greatest culture hero, Gjergj Kastrioti Skanderbeg (1405–1468), who united the Albanian tribes in 1444 at the Council of Lezhë and led a war of resistance against the occupying Ottomans. The *Kanun* was one of many such law codes in operation throughout Late Medieval Albania, and certainly the most famous. The word *kanun* comes from the Greek κανών (canon), "to measure," and was adopted into Albanian from Arabic via Turkish (Hasluck 1954: 14–15). The colloquial Albanian term *doke*, derived from *dukem*, "to behave," was also employed to refer to customary law (Camaj 1989: xiii). Thus, the *doket* were rules meant to determine (or regulate) individual relationships and measure behavior. In the *Kanun*, the primary basis for right behavior is *nder*, honor. Honor itself could be measured, like water in a glass. Men, and therefore families, might have more or less of it depending on their conduct and family history, such as whether they owed blood (*gjak*) in a feud (*gjakmarrje*). According to the *Kanun*, behavior, like a landscape, is bounded and fixed. To transgress a known boundary, or worse yet, to remove a boundary stone, was a particularly egregious sin, comparable to removing the bones of the dead (i.e., rejecting one's ancestry). Boundary stones and human bones can thereby be equated. Boundaries, like graves, must be marked and their locations and meanings carefully committed to memory "by as many young people and children as possible." Likewise, when boundary stones were erected, six or twelve smaller rocks were buried around them, to serve as silent, sacrificial "witnesses" (Tafilica 2013: 155). As such, given their power to inform cultural memory, both stones and bones were considered sacred, and both feature in Albanian folklore and epic songs. According to Albanian custom (and the *Kanun*), the most solemn and terrible oath a man can swear is that sworn on a rock, *beja mbë gur* (Elsie 2001: 242), which following his death then became the marker for his grave (Lambertz 1973: 475). Moreover, as dictated in the *Kanun*, a man who died on another's property as a result of a boundary dispute would be covered with a mound of stones, a *muranë* (cairn), and "no man would dare move the cairn that remains as a boundary, since it is won with blood and a broken skull" (Book Four: House, Livestock, and Property, chapter 13: Boundaries, LIX "The Boundary Won with Blood," Gjeçov 1989: 78). The traditional Albanian epic, the *Songs of the Frontier Warriors*, begins with the hero, Mujo, proving his strength to the *zanas*, the mountain faeries, by lifting heavy rocks (Elsie and Mathie-Heck 2004: 3–9). And Lekë Dukagjini himself, in his final days, having fought the Ottomans for 25 years, retreated to the mountains, to the tribal strongholds of Shala and Shosh, where he ruled from the Castle of Dakaj and defended the Guri i Leks, the Rock of Lek (Lee et al. 2013: 47).

Stones and bones, honor and blood, powered the landscapes and memory systems of Albania. They served as potent memory cues in a nation that did not adopt an official writing system until the Conference of Monastir, held in 1908 in Bitola, Macedonia. A written version of the *Kanun* (comprising 12 chapters) was published posthumously in 1933 by Father Shtjefën Gjeçov, a Franciscan priest and Albanian nationalist, murdered by Yugoslav agents in Kosovo in 1929 (Fox 1989: xviii). Gjeçov realized the deep importance of the *Kanun* to the Albanian people. Adherence to its precepts had helped the *malësorë* (the mountaineers) preserve their unique social system and identity through the long centuries of Turkish rule, which began in 1385 and did not end until 1912. In transcribing and publishing the *Kanun*, Gjeçov hoped to ensure its continued existence. But transforming an oral code into written form proved challenging, for various reasons. The *doket* functioned as living, breathing memory instruments, and the elders (the *pleqni*), who memorized and interpreted them, were memory workers. By enforcing the rules (i.e., of right behavior) and by measuring honor they reproduced the ideological, and therefore the social, system. These same elders also memorized tribal genealogies and kept the tribal history, which stretched back into the mythic past.

That the tribal elders of northern Albanian kept the *Kanun* alive, employing oral systems only, over at least five centuries and down to the present day is a remarkable feat, in and of itself. Their success points to the general resilience of such systems and raises the distinct possibility that the *doket* have ancient roots. Gjeçov clearly thought so. His *Kanun* includes footnoted references to Roman law, and the case can be made for an earlier, indigenous legal system that survived Roman conquest and is reflected in the *doket* (Fox 1989: xvi). Indeed, Papadopoulos (2014) sees evidence for a prehistoric origin of Albanian customary law in excavation results from the Late Bronze–Early Iron Age (*circa* 1300–800 BC) Lofkënd *tumulus* (burial mound), located in south-central Albania. At Lofkënd, more males than females were entombed late in the life of the mound, some of whom were buried together and appear to have died violently, perhaps as a result of a feud. Papadopoulos (2006) further argues that modern *muranë* are distant descendants of Albania's prehistoric tumuli, both of which functioned as "mounds of memory," marking the landscape, signaling ownership by monumentalizing death.

While there is not an easily identified, direct-historical connection linking tumuli to *muranë*, we might well ask why certain kinds of behavior, like burial in mounds of rock and dirt, which died out in Egypt and Greece, continued in Albania. I contend that traditional memory systems survived intact into modern times in Albania precisely because the Albanians, and their ancestors, the Illyrians, did not experience processes of state formation. Whereas the Egyptians underwent state formation, based, in part, on the disruption of traditional memory systems, as early as 3000 BC, and the Minoans and Mycenaeans a millennium later, the Illyrians never formed states. They remained "tribally" organized. Those Illyrians living in southern Albania had contact with the Greeks, who colonized the Adriatic coast at Epidamnus (modern Durrës) and Apollonia, in the seventh century BC, and built polis-like urban centers, but that did not lead to state formation. The Illyrians were eventually conquered by the Romans (between 229 and 167 BC, over the course of three Illyrian wars), and incorporated into the Roman and Byzantine empires, but even then, traditional memory practices survived. Albania later suffered a series of invasions, by Slavs (AD 600), Bulgarians (AD 800), and Serbs (AD 1300). It was during this time that a recognizable "Albanian" ethnic identity emerged. The first references to Albanians (Greek *Albanoi*), who today refer to themselves as Shqiptarë (Sons of the Eagle), are found in the *History* of Michael Attaliates, written in AD 1080.

Christianity arrived in Albania very early. Saint Paul asserted that he had preached the gospel from "Jerusalem all the way around to Illyricum" (Romans 15:19). Nevertheless, few Illyrians appear to have adopted the faith. For example, according to Elsie (2000: 36), there are no ethnic Albanian (i.e., Illyrian) martyrs or saints, though he declines to address why. This is the opposite, of course, of Egypt and Greece, where there are numerous indigenous Egyptian and Greek saints, many of whom were later "imported" to Albania. As discussed above, Christianity played vital, though very different, roles in preserving Egyptian (Coptic) and Greek identities, in particular in response to Islam. I would argue that Illyrians did not adopt Christianity in large numbers because they had little or no experience with state-level systems of cultural memory, including religion, prior to the introduction of Christianity. When Albanians finally did adopt the faith in large numbers, it was because they found themselves wedged between the Eastern (Byzantine) and Western (Italian) churches, both of which actively proselytized in Albania. Even so, they clearly retained many pagan beliefs and traditions, and their practice of religion was instrumental and syncretic. For instance, Bogomilism, a heretical Christian sect with origins in Macedonia, was popular in Albania during the Middle Ages, betraying ambivalence when it came to church authorities and doctrine. Similarly, most Albanians readily converted to Islam under the Ottomans, and back again to Christianity, when it suited them. Skanderbeg himself converted from Roman Catholicism to Islam and back to Roman Catholicism. Religious flexibility under the Ottomans appears to have been a coping mechanism (conversion, for example, lowered one's tax rate). But it may well also be the case that Albanians did not need Christianity in order to protect their language and identity from the Ottomans, as had the Egyptians and Greeks. Rather, they had preserved vibrant memory systems that were deeply inscribed in the landscape and cared for by a legion of memory workers, the elders of the Albanian tribes. Ironically, it was not the Ottomans who ultimately destroyed Albanian memory systems, though they certainly tried. It was the leaders of the first independent Albanian state, formed in 1912, who dismantled them, by, for example, murdering tribal elders. As a result, Albanian traditional memory systems entered the post–World War II period destabilized and weakened. The resulting collective memory vacuum was filled by a repressive totalitarian dictator, Enver Hoxha, who maintained power by exercising complete control over Albanian memory practices. In Hoxha's Albania, to reference the *Kanun*, let alone live it, was punishable by death.

As was done for Egypt and Greece in chapters 2 and 3, in this chapter I chart the development of Albanian collective memory systems through time. At intervals, I run them through the explanatory model constructed in chapter 1, with interesting results. Unlike Egypt and Greece, Albanian collective memory systems and state-level political institutions *did not* coevolve. Even under foreign rule, they remained disconnected. Consequently, traditional Albanian memory systems, with prehistoric origins, survived, even thrived, right down to the present. The key question is, why? Why did states not form in Albania, as they had in Egypt and Greece? Might this be because traditional Albanian memory systems were somehow different, more malleable, and, therefore, resistant to elite control and manipulation? In chapter 2, I argued that Egyptians experienced friction between memory and history, beginning with the Arab conquest (in AD 639), and that this was particularly detrimental to traditional Egyptian memory systems. A monolithic, non-ritualized Egyptian history, viewed through the lens of Islam, facilitated nation building and intensified processes of subjugation, under the Ottomans in particular. This was most certainly *not* the case in Albania, a non-literate society, even under Ottoman rule and with the introduction of Islam. Likewise, in chapter 3, I argued that the Greeks also experienced friction, but not between memory and history, and not as a result of Ottoman occupation; rather there was friction between different, competitive memory communities, going back to Classical, if not earlier, times. This did *not* occur in Albania, precisely because Albanian collective memory practices were specifically designed to deter such competition: "The Kanun of the Albanian mountains does not make a distinction between man and man" (Book Eight: Honor, chapter 17: Personal Honor, Gjeçov 1989: 130). A careful analysis of Albanian memory systems and their development through time throws considerable light on the nature of collective memory in general, and, by contrast, state-level memory systems specifically.

MEMORY IN ANCIENT ALBANIA

As was the case for Egypt and Greece, the origins of Albanian collective memory systems can be found in prehistory (figure 4.2; table 4.1). However, unlike Egypt and Greece, we know very little about the Albanian Neolithic, mortuary practices in particular. There are only six human burials known from the entire Albanian Neolithic (*circa* 6500–3100 BC): three from Early Neolithic Podgorie, in Korçë (Korkuti 2010: 51–53), two from Middle Neolithic Cakran, in south-central Albania (Korkuti 2010: 152–53), and one (poorly dated) example from Late Neolithic Maliq, also in Korçë (Prendi and Bunguri 2008: 26). All six bodies were interred intramurally in rough pits and were not accompanied by grave goods. They thus fit the Greek pattern, though there is no evidence for secondary treatment: no ossuaries, and no removal and curation of skulls or long bones.

Why are there so few Neolithic burials known from Albania, as compared to Greece, for example? Twenty Neolithic sites, both open-air and

Table 4.1. Albanian Chronology

Period	Date
Neolithic	7000–3100 BC
Early Bronze Age	3100–2000 BC
Middle Bronze Age	2000–1600 BC
Late Bronze Age	1600–1000 BC
Iron Age	1000–167 BC
Roman	167 BC–AD 330
Byzantine	330–1385
Ottoman	1385–1912
Independent Albania	1912–1914
Principality	1914–1925
Republic	1925–1928
Kingdom (Zog I)	1928–1939
Italian Occupation	1939–1943
German Occupation	1943–1944
Communist	1944–1992
Republic	1992–present

caves, have been excavated in Albania over the course of several decades, many almost completely, so the dearth of burials cannot be a result of sampling bias or poor excavation techniques only; rather, the Neolithic occupants of Albania appear to have treated their dead quite differently. Neolithic Albanians did not curate human remains in ways that generally concentrated and preserved them, rendering them accessible, as was the case, for example, at Alepotrypa Cave (see chapter 3), which may indicate that body parts, like skulls, were not employed as mnemonic devices. This may mean that Albanian Neolithic systems of land tenure differed from those of Neolithic Greece, and that land use did not require proof of land ownership through periodic display of human remains, but it may also be the case that different kinds of material culture were preferred as memory cues.

For example, whereas clay figurines were popular in Neolithic communities throughout the Balkans (Bailey 2005), including Greece (Marangou 1996), they have been disproportionately recovered from Neolithic sites in Albania (Ruka 2006), especially as compared to Neolithic sites in south Greece. While no fewer than 161 dead individuals were recovered from Alepotrypa Cave, only a very small number of figurines were found—Papathanassopoulos illustrates only seven in his 2011 catalog—and many of them are Cycladic marble imports. By contrast, most Albanian Neolithic sites produced at least ten figurines, many of them anthropomorphic (versus animal), and no human skeletal remains (Korkuti 2010). Those dating to the Middle Neolithic (e.g., from Dunaveç in Korçë) are particularly

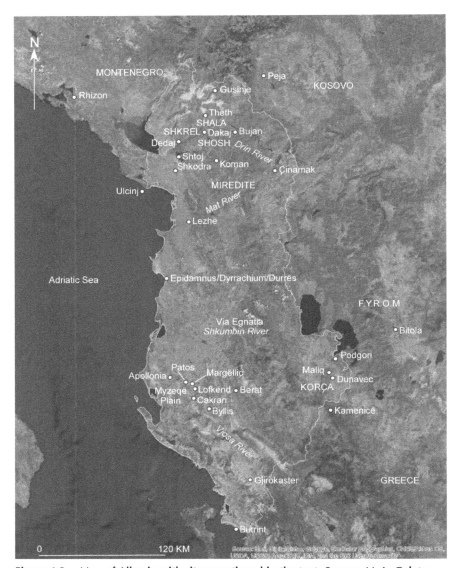

Figure 4.2. Map of Albania with sites mentioned in the text. *Source:* M. L. Galaty.

large and elaborate, and are comparable to figurines from Middle Neolithic Vinča sites located to the north, in Kosova and Serbia. Given the careful detail with which these figurines were made, including individualized facial features, sculpted items of dress, and, perhaps, indications of personalized tattoos or scarification, they may have represented real people, as opposed to deities. Moreover, figurines are often accompanied by so-called cult objects, including small tables or "altars," which may have been used, along with figurines, to create displays, as described for northern Greece by Marangou (1996). That being the case, figurines may have served as memory cues in Albanian Neolithic communities, triggering collective memory engrams related to deceased members of families and clans, and their former roles in village life.

The seeming lack of interest in complex mortuary rites in Neolithic Albania (and other parts of the Balkans) may be correlated with a resistance to—and lack of evidence for—social inequalities, of the kinds that preceded the rise of Mycenaean states in southern Greece (and the unification of Upper and Lower Egypt). As described in chapter 3, the border between the Roman provinces of Achaia and Epirus, which roughly marked the northern extent of the Greek poleis, may have been just as meaningful in prehistory, spanning the Mycenaean frontier, separating the palace societies of Greece from the largely trans-egalitarian societies of Illyria and the rest of the Balkans.

From Neolithic to Iron Age

The first formal, extramural burials appear in Albania at the beginning of the Bronze Age, *circa* 3100 BC. Unlike Greece, there are no flat cemeteries; rather—with the exception of six intramural pit graves from Early Bronze Age (EBA) Maliq (Prendi and Bunguri 2008: 26)—EBA tombs are found exclusively in tumuli. Mound burial appears to have spread from north to south through Albania, arriving in Mainland Greece via the Ionian Islands early in the Middle Bronze Age (see chapter 3). Of the 24 known Albanian EBA tumuli, a majority (n = 18) have been identified in northern Albania (Prendi and Bunguri 2008: 26). EBA tumuli typically contain a single, sunken central grave, or, more rarely, two central graves, surrounded by rings of stones (so-called mound architecture), and capped by a cairn. Cremation burial was sometimes practiced, as in the case of the tumuli of Dedaj in Shkrel in northern Albania, ten of which (out of an estimated 40) were excavated by Jubani (1995). There is also one urn burial, from Tumulus 10 at Çinamak (Jubani 1971). Two tumuli from Bujan (VII and VIII) were found to be cenotaphs (Prendi and Bunguri 2008: 220–21); obviously constructed, though empty, prehistoric mounds are an under-reported, though probably common, phenomenon. Most EBA graves contain few or no grave goods. One exception is Shtoj Tumulus 6, excavated near Shkodra in northern Albania by Koka (2012). It contained two central graves: an earlier pit grave of "local" type (Grave 15), and a subsequent cist grave of "Cetina" type (Grave 14). Grave 14 contained one "Cetina"-style pot. Grave 15 contained two pots, a small cup and a small bowl. Six violin-shaped figurines of a type found elsewhere in Albania (e.g., at Maliq), but typically associated with the spread of Cetina culture (2200–2000 BC, with origins in southern Croatia), were deposited atop the grave fill, together with an animal burial/sacrifice (Koka 2012: 100–102). A similar situation obtained in Tumulus 10 at Apollonia in central Albania, where a violin-shaped figurine was found in fill, with an animal burial, above the EBA central grave, which contained no grave goods and was AMS radiocarbon dated to *circa* 2500 BC calibrated (Amore 2010: 254, 329). In both cases, Shtoj and Apollonia, earlier mounds containing a single central grave were reused later, by Cetina or Cetina-affiliated peoples. Thus begins a long, complex tradition in Albania of reusing burial mounds. This can be contrasted with Greece, where mound burial went out of fashion during the early Late Bronze Age (LBA; *circa* 1500 BC), never to return (with a few prominent, later exceptions, like the tumulus at Marathon).

Many EBA mounds were reused in the later Bronze and Iron Ages. Tumulus 6 at Shtoj, for example, contained an additional 13 graves dating to the Late Bronze and Early Iron Age, many of which contained grave goods, including items of dress, such as jewelry and fibulae, pottery, and weapons (Koka 2012: 90–97). Tumulus 10 at Apollonia contained an additional 47 prehistoric graves, most of which could not be precisely dated due to a lack of associated grave goods, but are probably Late Bronze and Early Iron Age (Amore 2010: 91, 324). EBA tumuli were often expanded to accommodate later burials, and additional mounds were built through time, adding to the tumulus field. For instance, in the late 1980s Koka (2012: 19) estimated that there were 160 mounds total at Shtoj. More recent, systematic surveys have counted half that number; either Koka overestimated, or 50 percent of the original tumuli have since been destroyed (Galaty et al. n.d.). Nevertheless, the Shtoj tumulus field is impressively large. Other large, multi-component tumulus fields, also located in northern Albania, include those at Mat, where 53 tumuli were excavated, and Çinamak, where 28 were excavated (Bejko 2014: 518). There is thus a marked difference between northern Albania and southern Albania: as one moves south, the fields get smaller, but the tumuli, many of them singletons, get larger and produce larger numbers of graves with more grave goods. The Lofkënd tumulus, mentioned above, contained 85 prehistoric tombs and 154 individuals (Schepartz 2014: 141–42). Kamenicë in Korçë, a massive tumulus partially excavated in the early 2000s, produced 395 graves and 420 individuals; most graves contained one or more objects (Bejko et al. 2006: 316).

These patterns may be a result of chronology—larger fields are found in the north because tumulus burial was adopted there first—or demography, but a social explanation is also possible. As described by Papadopoulos (2006), and discussed briefly above, prehistoric burial mounds may have served as *lieux de mémoire*, memory monuments that tied local communities to the past and to a particular landscape. They may have marked territories exploited by different, rival social units. One major problem in prehistoric Albanian archaeology, however, is that very few prehistoric settlement sites, including those clearly connected to tumuli and tumulus fields, have been excavated, and those that have were often found to be either very lightly occupied, very disturbed (by later settlement), or both (Papadopoulos et al. 2014a: 8–10). In Albania, during the Bronze and Iron Ages, beginning in the EBA (or perhaps earlier; Galaty et al. n.d.), people appear to have moved from flat sites to hill forts, as was also the case in much of the rest of Europe (Parkinson and Duffy 2007). This shift probably signals competition, and therefore a need for defense (as further indicated by the presence of weapons in the graves of males) (Bejko et al. 2006: 311), but can also be linked to changes in social inequality and organization. As the Albanian Bronze and Iron Ages progress, there is increasing evidence for both ascribed status (cf. the extremely large number of child/adolescent, mostly female burials, with grave goods, including several diadems, from Lofkënd; Stapleton 2014) and differential displays of wealth in tumulus burials. This trend is apparent at Kamenicë and comes to a climax in the seventh century BC (during the Late Iron Age), when numerous "monumental grave structures" were appended to the main mound (Bejko et al. 2006: 313). It seems apparent that, during the Bronze and Iron Ages, Albania, southern Albania in particular, like southern Greece, was on a path to greater social and political complexity, which culminated in "chiefly" societies, probably at the start of the LBA (*circa* 1600 BC). However, whereas in Greece this process gave way to proto-states, which in the Argolid in particular were individualizing, networked, and extremely competitive, in Albania, state formation was either truncated (in the south) or never really began (in the north). The sociopolitical inertia evident in prehistoric Albania is dramatically symbolized by the stubborn preference for mound building and tumulus burial. In this way, Albania is superficially similar to Messenia in southwest Greece, which, like Albania, also experienced the impacts of the Cetina expansion (see chapter 3) and also displays a preference for mound burial (as compared to other parts of Greece), and is a lot like the Mani, which similarly clung to, and revisited, earlier forms of mortuary practice (*viz*. the Mycenaean ossuary at Ksagounaki). I contend that the primary reason why states did not form in Albania, as compared to both Greece and Egypt, is that collective memories and memory systems were structured differently there. As early as the Neolithic, Albanian collective memory systems followed a very different trajectory, marked by widely distributed collective memory stores, which could not be easily co-opted by aspiring elites. The exception that proves this rule is the fascinating site of Apollonia, introduced already above.

Apollonia was colonized by Greeks from Corinth, perhaps by way of Corcyra (Corfu), during the Greek Archaic period. The city's traditional founding date is 588 BC, but literary and archaeological evidence points to an earlier, late-seventh century foundation (Stocker 2009; Stocker and Davis 2006). Apollonia sits on top of a ridge overlooking a coastal plain, the Myzeqë Plain, which, before being drained by the Communists, was a vast marsh. The Vjosa River (the ancient Aous), which today runs well to the south, provided a river port, with navigable access to the Adriatic. To the west, in the Kryegjata Valley, there is a large tumulus field, which also served as the city's pre-Roman necropolis. Currently there exists no good evidence for an earlier, "Illyrian" settlement at Apollonia (Amore 2010: 23), but there is, of course, as described above, evidence that the city's necropolis formed around a prehistoric core, one with EBA roots.

The Apollonia necropolis consists of *circa* 100 mounds (Davis et al. 2002–2003: 311–13; 2007: 19–20) and, therefore, does not fit the north-south pattern described above; it is far larger than it should be. To date, 11 mounds have been excavated (see review in Amore 2010: 24–41) and, with the striking exception of Tumulus 10, they *only* contain graves from the Archaic to Hellenistic period (i.e., from the sixth to the fourth century BC, *after* the foundation of the colony), *all* of which emulate "Greek" grave types. Both inhumation and cremation burials are present, with the former preferred over the latter. The Archaic-Hellenistic graves are of various kinds, all common in Greece: 1) simple pits; 2) *enchytrismoi* (i.e., burials in large pots); 3) tile graves; 4) brick graves; 5) urn burials; 6) rock-lined graves; and 5) stone sarcophagi, cut from single limestone blocks (a typical Corinthian custom) (Amore 2010: 96–102). The Apollonia necropolis is thus unlike any other contemporary Greek necropolis known: composed of Greek-style graves placed in Illyrian-style burial mounds, special-built for the purpose (i.e., with the important exception of Tumulus 10, they were not reused prehistoric tumuli).

Explaining this phenomenon—Greek-style graves in Illyrian-style mounds—is particularly difficult, since the demographic composition of the colony is unknown. We can assume that mostly Greeks lived there, though comparative biometric analysis of skeletal remains—from Lofkënd (pre-colonization), Apollonia (pre- and post-colonization), and Corinth (the Greek mother-city)—points to a mixed population of Greeks and Illyrians (McIlvaine et al. 2013). Only one individual (from the entire necropolis), an Archaic female from Tumulus 9, Grave 45, is clearly a Greek-acculturated Illyrian (Amore 2010: 154). She was buried in a pit with 13 grave goods, including two Corinthian *kotylai* (two-handled bowls/cups) and two bronze bracelets typical of the local Developed Iron

Age culture (Ibid.). Given these data, it seems very likely that Greeks and acculturated Illyrians living together at Apollonia adopted (or co-opted) local Illyrian mortuary customs and, therefore, I would assert, their collective memory systems as well. Stocker and Davis (2006) have drawn a similar conclusion. They argue that having arrived at Apollonia, colonists discovered at least one unused tumulus (Tumulus 10), which confirmed for them a particular foundation myth: that the vicinity of Apollonia had originally been settled by wandering Trojans, who, of course, were known to bury their dead in mounds. In reopening the tumulus, the colonists visibly linked themselves to the region's constructed heroic past. As described in chapter 3, this is very typical Greek collective memory behavior. All Greek poleis and all Greek colonies regularly constructed fictive foundation myths, which bent collective memory, and supported a particular group's territorial claims. Adopting tumulus burial as their own allowed colonial Greeks to lay claim to Apollonia and its hinterland, by appropriating Illyrian mortuary customs, dislodging Illyrian *lieux de mémoire*, and undercutting Illyrian collective memory systems. Thus, in Albania it took processes of Greek colonization, which emanated from the outside, to disrupt stable, Illyrian memory systems and thence drag (some) Illyrians into state-level systems of sociopolitical organization. Interestingly, though, these disruptive processes, which were most active along the coast in the vicinity of the colonies, appear to have had little or no impact on the wider Illyrian world, just as earlier contact with the Mycenaeans likewise had little or no impact (Galaty 2016). Illyrians, for their part, appear to have reacted *not* by creating counter-memories, as might be expected, but rather by assimilating certain Greek practices and ignoring others, thereby generating hybrid, syncretic cultural systems. Illyrian reaction to Greek colonization thus sets a precedent that is repeated again and again throughout Albanian history: accommodation, adaptation, and survival, against all odds.

We can now put prehistoric Albania through the memory model constructed in chapter 1. Compared to those of Egypt and Greece, prehistoric Albanian collective memory systems were decentralized and seemingly not dependent on highly elaborated mortuary rites, particularly in northern Albania, and everywhere prior to the Late (Developed) Iron Age (*circa* 700 BC). Collective memories were made in other ways, using other (more portable) media. There is some evidence that bodies were brought to tumuli on wooden supports—traces of them have been found in some graves in Tumulus 10 at Apollonia (Amore 2010: 97)—in rituals that were perhaps similar to the Greek practice of *ekphora*, the carrying of the body to the grave site, but beyond that, it may be that the most important ritual activity was in fact the construction and maintenance of the mound itself. The fill used to build Albanian tumuli typically contains numerous stray artifacts, such as pottery sherds, animal bone, chipped stone tools, and daub, often from periods that predate tumulus construction. This was certainly the case at Lofkënd, for example, where all tumulus fill was screened and all such artifacts were collected and carefully documented, leading Papadopoulos et al. (2014b: 27–29) to conclude that a prehistoric settlement somewhere in the vicinity of the mound had been mined for the soil used to make it, and that this had been done repeatedly through time, as tombs were opened and closed. This practice—of building tumuli using fill from earlier settlements—represents a striking example of communal, collective memory behavior, which continued for (literally) millennia, from the EBA through the historic period, at Apollonia in particular. Indeed, Albania's prehistoric mounds remained foci for ritual and burial through Roman and medieval times, and into the modern era, as will be discussed at length below. As for the singing of laments, so prominent in Egypt and Greece, we have no evidence from prehistoric Albania (though see the Japodian burial chest from Bosnia, *circa* 450–400 BC, incised with scenes of funeral dancers; Wilkes 1992: 199), but such behavior was absolutely critical to later Albanian mortuary customs, as will also be discussed below.

With reference to figures 1.2 and 1.3, prehistoric Albania remained trans-egalitarian up to and through Greek colonization. Even then, most Illyrians appear to have been only minimally affected by contact with Greeks, and any impacts were greater to the south and along the coast. Prehistoric states never formed. Collective memory systems were conservative yet flexible, situated firmly within the domestic sphere, as they had been since the Neolithic. Individual loyalties were to family first, followed by tribe. Collective memory behaviors were "simple" and resilient, and strongly tied to local landscapes, primarily through the construction and curation of tumuli (Martin-McAuliffe 2014). Institutionalized forms of political control were non-existent, given the absence of states, and consequently, memory systems were relatively open, albeit slow to change. When change did finally come, in the form of Roman conquest, the Illyrians appear to have retreated or, in some cases, assimilated, but never to the extent that an Illyrian (i.e., proto-Albanian) identity was completely lost.

Classical, Roman, and Byzantine Albania

Ancient writers make scarce mention of the Illyrians and their way of life. While we do know the names of many of the southern Illyrian tribes—the Parthini, Atintanae, Ardiaiae, Bylliones, Labeates, and others—we do not know the exact sizes and locations of their territories. Illyrians are typically described as fierce fighters and intrepid pirates, sailing to sea in hide boats, called *lembi*, attacking merchant ships. By the late fifth century BC, Illyrian "kings" begin to appear in Greek accounts, leaders of so-called tribal states. Illyrian societies may well have been tribal, but they most certainly were not states. There is no evidence for state-level institutions, complex, diversified economies, or regional administration, and the Illyrians did not write. While some Illyrian settlements have been described as urbanized, particularly those in south Albania, most Illyrians were farmers and herders, who likely lived in small villages, and practiced small-scale, short-distance vertical transhumance (Galaty 2002). During this period, most urbanized Illyrians were buried in flat cemeteries, sometimes with Greek and, later, Roman grave goods. In the north (e.g., in Cetina, Croatia), some Illyrians continued to bury their dead in mounds, down to the second century AD (Wilkes 1992: 242–43), but elsewhere, with some exceptions (see below), the practice faded away.

Discerning Classical and Roman Illyrian memory systems is difficult. Given the rural, perhaps transhumant lifestyle of most Illyrians, we might expect that other *lieux de mémoire* replaced tumuli. The history of the landscape and built environments surrounding Apollonia, beyond the city and necropolis, are thus pertinent to discussions regarding Albanian collective memory systems during Classical and Roman times, and can be compared to other parts of Albania, with illuminating results. The Mallakastra Regional Archaeological Project (MRAP), which I co-directed from 1998–2003, surveyed the *chora* (hinterland) of Apollonia, the catchment of a nearby Illyrian hillfort, called Margelliç, and spaces in between (totaling 35 sq km). Results indicate that for several hundred years after the foundation of the colony (i.e., through the beginning of the third century BC), there was little or no settlement outside the city walls (Davis et al. 2007: 18–19). A defensive posture obtained, despite evidence for Greek-Illyrian trade. Imported Archaic and Classical pots, including Corinthian A amphorae, were, for example, retrieved from Margelliç (Ceka 1986, 1987). The situation changed dramatically at the start of the Hellenistic period (323 BC), when settlement throughout the region exploded. MRAP identified 61 sites total, nearly all of which were occupied or at least used during the Hellenistic period (Stocker 2009: 866–77). Whereas MRAP surveyors collected 54 Archaic pot sherds and 92 Classical pot sherds (an additional 71 were Archaic-Classical), they collected 5,908 Hellenistic pot sherds (an additional 14,332 were Hellenistic bricks and tiles) (Stocker 2009: 835, 848, 866). One of these Hellenistic sites, Site 034, was test excavated and appears to have been a small farmstead (Galaty et al. 2004). It is perhaps no accident that this settlement shift should have occurred during the Hellenistic period, which began when Alexander the Great invaded Asia, spreading Greek culture and language across the known world, including to Egypt. For their part, the Greeks, as described in chapter 3, did not consider Alexander to be Greek—whereas the Egyptians welcomed him as a Son of God—perhaps because he did not speak Greek as his first language. Indeed, his father, Philip, was Macedonian and his mother, Olympias, was Mollossian, from Epirus. Alexander himself knew the Illyrians well enough that before departing for Asia, he subdued them, securing his rear flank (Arrian 1971: 42–54). Macedonian occupation and subsequent Hellenization may have encouraged (or allowed) Greek colonial settlement to expand in Albania, at sites like Apollonia, for the first time, changing landscapes, further destabilizing Illyrian memory systems.

The structure at Site 034 appears to have burned down *circa* 237 BC, based on two AMS radiocarbon dates from destruction deposits (Galaty et al. 2004: 301). This date is remarkably close to the date of the first Illyrian War, 229 BC, during which various Illyrian tribes joined together under their queen, Teuta, who hailed from the north—her capital was at Rhizon in Montenegro—to attack the "Greek" cities of south Albania (i.e., "Illyris"), including Apollonia and Epidamnus, and lay siege to Corcyra (Wilkes 1992: 160). In response, Apollonia, Epidamnus, and many of the other Hellenized cities of south Albania, became "friends of Rome" and were placed under Roman protection (Ibid.: 161). Most of the Illyrian tribes on the interior surrendered and pledged fealty to Rome (Ibid.: 161). All of Illyria was finally conquered by the Roman Republic in 167 BC, when Gentius, then king of Illyris and an ally of Macedonia, was defeated by the Roman praetor Gallus (Ibid.: 173). During the winter of 168 BC, the countryside had been ravaged by avenging Romans and 150,000 Illyrians were sold into slavery (Ibid.: 208). Indeed, archaeological survey indicates that settlement in many regions contracted (e.g., at Apollonia [only 519 Roman pot sherds and 302 Roman tiles were found by MRAP; Stocker 2009: 878], around Shkodra, and in the Albanian Alps; Galaty et al. 2013). According to Wilkes (1992: 207–8), "No Illyrian resistance is known to Roman rule after AD 9, less an indication of native compliance than of the state of human exhaustion to which the Illyrian lands had been reduced."

Given the above, we might expect the Illyrians to have been absorbed by the Roman Empire, and to have disappeared. But that did not happen. What collective memory behaviors, if any, helped close the 1,000-year gap between Illyrians and Albanoi? Generally speaking, Romanized Illyrians adopted many Roman traits, as had their ancestors adopted Greek traits. The coastal cities were Romanized and Roman colonization occurred at various Illyrian sites, including Scodra (Shkodër), Byllis, and Buthrotum (Butrint) (Shpuza 2006). Colonization was part of a larger Roman plan to control the eastern Adriatic Sea lanes (Royal 2012), and to connect Rome to Thessaloniki along a new road system, called the Via Egnatia (Amore et al. 2001; Fasolo 2003). The Via Egnatia had two starting points, at Apollonia and Dyrrachium (modern Durrës), and ran along the Shkumbin River (Ibid.). A similar, though less developed, road was built in the north along the Drin River, connecting Lissus (Lezhë) and Scodra to Naissus (Niš) in modern-day Serbia via Kosovo, with access to the Danube (Wilkes 2006: 170). These roads encouraged trade and travel, but also allowed the Roman army to move quickly through Illyricum to Macedonia and Thrace. They also served as vehicles for Illyrian pacification and Romanization, and remnant Illyrian populations were likely drawn to the roads and road stations (Shpuza 2006: 166), accelerating processes of abandonment that had begun immediately following Roman conquest. For example, intensive survey of the Shkodra region by the Projekti Arkeologjik i Shkodrës (PASH; the Shkodra Archaeological Project), which I co-directed from 2010–2014, identified a possible settlement hiatus immediately following Roman conquest, and then slow but steady population expansion, which peaked in the Medieval period. Environmental data collected from Lake Shkodra (Mazzini et al. 2016) and along its riverine fringes (Galicki et al. n.d.) support this conclusion.

And yet, even given Illyrian depopulation and Roman colonization, Illyrian memory practices survived. PASH also conducted excavations at various sites in Shkodra, including several burial mounds. One mound (Tumulus 88) was found to be a cenotaph (i.e., there was no central grave), and was composed of layers upon layers of archaeological material from different periods, beginning at the bottom with prehistoric pottery, through Roman times (including Roman glass and coins), and capped by hundreds of medieval tile fragments, some of which were engraved (Galaty et al. n.d.). Analysis of faunal remains indicates a preference for cattle over sheep/goat, which reverses the patterns identified for prehistoric tumuli and settlement sites (Ibid.). Tumulus 88 appears to have been some kind of long-term ritual installation, used (probably discontinuously) over thousands of years, a true "mound of memory" (cf. Papadopoulos 2006). It points to a continuing interest in mounds, as places of commemoration, touch points to an Illyrian past. Similar behaviors are known from other parts of Albania. At Lofkënd, several painted Corinthian potsherds were found broken and scattered along the mound's crest, two or more centuries after the last prehistoric burial took place (Morris 2014). Medieval and later graves were often inserted into tumuli, for example at Lofkënd (Morris and Papadopoulos 2014: 577–78), Apollonia (Amore 2010), Patos (Korkuti 1981), and many others (Andrea 2005: 359). In prehistory, building and maintaining a mound was memory work, since they often incorporated fill from earlier settlements. This memory work continued well after Greek and Roman colonization, buttressing Illyrian identity, building a bridge to Albanian ethnogenesis.

In the third century AD, after generations of Roman military service, a resurgent northern Illyrian aristocracy, based at Sirmium in northern Serbia, took control of the Empire, placing no fewer than ten emperors on the throne (Wilkes 1992: 259–63), culminating in the reign of Diocletian (AD 284–305), who was from Salona, Dalmatia. Diocletian divided the empire into four administrative units, led by four tetrarchs, including himself. Following his retirement, the empire descended into civil war, which was eventually won, at the Milvian Bridge, by Constantine, who hailed from Naissus. It was, of course, Constantine who converted to Christianity and moved the capital to Byzantium, setting in train a series of historical events that connect Illyria to Greece to Egypt, via Rome. The last Illyrian emperor was Justinian (AD 527–65), also from Dalmatia, who set about refortifying the lands of Illyricum, reportedly building 43 new forts and repairing 50 existing ones in the region of modern-day Albania (Wilkes 1992: 268). To no avail: the southern Balkans were invaded first by Avars and Huns, and later by Slavs, who occupied much of Albania (as indicated by numerous Slavic place names), with the exception of the coastal towns, such as Dyrrachium, which remained under Byzantine control.

Illyrian continuity through the Slavic invasions is, however, displayed by the remarkable Koman culture sites and cemeteries, which date to the seventh–ninth centuries AD (Wilkes 1992: 273–78; see Nallbani 2008, Nallbani et al. 2012, and Nallbani et al. 2013 for reports on recent excavations at the Koman type site at Dalmace). Most such sites are located at high altitude, which may indicate that the Illyrians survived to become Albanians by retreating to the mountains. The argument for Illyrian-Albanian continuity via the Koman culture is made based on similarities between Illyrian and Koman material culture, jewelry in particular, as well as burial practices, such as the renewed interest in mound burial, mentioned above (Korkuti 2003; see also Ceka 2014). Koman sites are often located in close proximity to churches, suggesting that the Koman people were Christians. Christianity may have served, therefore, to mark Komani versus Slavic identity, since the Slavs did not convert to Christianity until the late ninth century. That said, Koman burials are distinctive, as compared to typical Byzantine burials, in that they are lavishly furnished with grave goods, including small ceramic jugs, perhaps used for libations (Korkuti 2003). Dzino (2010: 86–87; see also Buchet et al. 2008), however, argues that Komani mortuary practices can be generally associated with a similar shift in Early Medieval burial practices seen throughout the western Balkans, including Dalmatia, and need not necessarily be attributed to a new "Arbër" culture, as argued by many Albanian archaeologists. Nevertheless, the similarity between Komani material culture, dress in particular, and that of the earlier Illyrians is striking (compare Wilkes 1992: figures 27 [Late Iron Age "Illyrian"] and 38 [Koman]).

As described above, Christianity came early to Albania and spread first among the urbanized Greek and Roman populations of the coast. Fifty paleo-Christian churches have been discovered in Albania, signaling the spread of Christianity among the Illyrians, with full conversion by *circa* AD 600 (Korkuti 2010: 109). By this time, Apollonia was in steep decline, its harbor silted up, and malaria in the marshes. Nevertheless, sometime after AD 900 a large monastery was constructed there, dedicated to Saint Mary. The monastery buildings, most of which date to the 13th century, including a refectory, the lower portions of a tower, living quarters, and a very large church, make copious use of Roman bricks and spolia, apparently scavenged from the ancient city (Dimo et al. 2007). As was also the case in Greece (see chapter 3), Albanian Christian churches were frequently built at sites of Classical antiquity, often using spolia, symbolically appropriating earlier, non-Christian *lieux de mémoire*. This was not simply a matter of convenience. It was memory work. Large numbers of early churches were also built at former Illyrian tribal centers, thereby linking Christianization to processes of Illyrian-Albanian ethnogenesis (Muçaj 2010). For example, at least five basilicas were built, beginning in the late fourth century AD, at Byllis, capital of the Bylliones tribe (Muçaj 1993). By then, the Illyrians had already experienced a millennium's worth of Hellenization and Romanization, and yet they continued to bury (at least some of) their dead in tumuli and, in the case of Koman culture, with grave goods that, while Byzantine in form, were fully Illyrian in their contexts of consumption and final deposition. As was also true in late prehistory at the close of the Iron Age, the southern Illyrians of Late Antiquity persisted by forming a hybrid culture, which emulated Christian/Byzantine practice, but which, at its core, preserved Illyrian language and memory systems. The outcome was a "new" Albanian identity, which flowered in the Middle Ages, sustaining the egalitarian ethos that had characterized Albanian prehistory (in contradistinction to the Mycenaeans), and generating a "society against the state" (Clastres 1989). Even if the *doket* did not yet exist, the preconditions for their formulation had certainly been created.

We can now apply chapter 1's memory model to ancient Albania. Generally speaking, ancient Albanian memory systems appear quite similar to prehistoric Albanian memory systems, being characterized by wide distribution across numerous, relatively non-competitive memory communities, overall resilience, and long-term stability. Throughout the course of the early historic period, from Classical to Byzantine times, the Illyrians and their ancestors experienced almost continuous crisis, leaving no time for nostalgia; rather, collective memory making was approached creatively and Illyrian ethnic identities were reimagined, in real-time. No sense of Illyrian nationhood formed. The tribal "states" described in historical accounts were non-institutionalized and revolved around larger-than-life personalities, such as Teuta and Gentius, who, while charismatic, possessed very little real power over Illyrian people. Their large armies, so terrifying to the Romans, dissolved upon their deaths. The later Illyrian royalty were in reality chiefs, not far removed from the "big men" of the Early Bronze Age, those buried at the centers of the first tumuli. Ancient Albania thus falls squarely alongside Bronze Age Albania on figure 1.3: political control was low and situated within families and clans, and memory systems were relatively open, but conservative. As such, the Arbër societies that formed during the Late Byzantine period were cut from Illyrian cloth. And while the Albanian culture that coalesced during medieval times represents a hybrid amalgam of various influences—Hellenistic urbanism, Roman rule of law, Byzantine Christianity, perhaps even the Slavic *zadruga*—at its core, it, too, was Illyrian, through and through. Albanian memory systems were, it seems, relatively impervious to change, even following Ottoman conquest. But they could not withstand the impact of the dictator, Enver Hoxha. Under Hoxha, Albanian traditional collective memory systems, landscapes, and memory workers were absolutely and utterly consumed. The *Kanun* was outlawed, 98 percent of the country's churches and mosques were destroyed, and the practice of religion was made punishable by death.

MEMORY AND THE MAKING OF THE MODERN ALBANIAN STATE

Egyptian memory systems were inexorably changed, primarily through the spread of Islam, and finally by Mehmed Ali, who was himself Albanian. Greek memory systems generated almost constant competition, between different memory communities, right up to and through Greek independence. Albanian memory systems experienced "dynamic stability" and were "emergent" (Galaty et al. 2013: 244): there was permanency in change. As the Middle Ages unfold, Albanians make more, and more regular, appearances in historical records. They served as mercenaries, fighting as far north as England (Millar 1976). The Vatican took extraordinary steps to "missionize" them, even though they had been Christian for hundreds of years (Lee et al. 2013: 64–65). And Albanians are found at merchant towns throughout the region, Ragusa (Dubrovnik) in particular, looking to buy all manner of goods, salt especially (Thalloczy et al. 2002). Following the decline of the Eastern Roman Empire, Albania was subjected to a series of invasions, and administered by numerous small principalities. The country was incorporated into the Bulgarian state in the 10th century, with a regional capital at Beligrad (Berat), in southern

Albania (Martin 1992: 53). The Bulgarians were expelled from Albania by the Byzantine Emperor Basil ("Bulgaroctonus") the Bulgar-slayer in 1018, followed by decades of revolts by Albanians against Byzantine rule, prompting Michael Atalliates' 1080 reference to Albanoi, cited above (Ibid.). Over the course of the next two centuries, Albania was variously ruled by Venetians and Normans. A semi-autonomous principality of "Arbanon" controlled most of the country, including the mountains, from 1190 to 1216 (Ibid.: 54). Byzantine activity ended in Albania in 1341, and the region fell under Serb control, which was only broken following the Ottoman invasion of 1385 (Ibid.: 55).

Ottoman and Modern Albania

In the decades prior to and following the Ottoman occupation, Albania was partitioned into several spheres of influence, each dominated by a single "baronial" family—Thopia, Balsha, Dukagjin, Kastriot, Muzaki, Shpata, Araniti, Span, Dushmani—many of which were intermarried with the extended Serb royal family (Martin 1992: 67). Despite their noble pretensions, in reality the leaders of these "great" families were war lords, regional chiefs who ruled by the sword. They are analogous to the Illyrian "kings" of the Hellenistic and Roman period, and to the nameless Bronze and Iron Age strong men who came before them. They brokered shifting alliances with Venice and the Ottoman Porte, playing one off the other, and switched religions, from Christianity to Islam, and back again, as needed. They were colorful characters, prodigious drinkers, quick to anger, treacherous, and prone to violence (Winnifrith 1992: 76). It was within this Late Medieval sociopolitical context that the modern Albanian tribes and the *doket* formed.

From 2004 to 2008, I co-directed the Shala Valley Project (SVP; Galaty et al. 2013). The main goal of the SVP was to study the northern Albanian tribes and explain their origins, with a particular focus on the Shala *fis* (tribe). Most scholars, both Albanian and foreign, were of the opinion that the northern Albanian tribes had survived, isolated, high in the Accursed Mountains, since prehistoric times (see, e.g., Durham 2000 [1909]). Archaeological, historical, and ethnographic data collected by the SVP, however, indicate that while there may have been "indigenous" groups living in Shala prior to the Late Medieval period, so-called *anas* (Lee et al. 2013: 58–59), the modern Shala tribe, which is 100 percent Catholic, stems from a founding population that arrived sometime during the early 1400s, perhaps fleeing Ottoman conversion. Shala had been settled earlier, as well, during the Late Bronze–Early Iron Ages, followed by a hiatus that matches the depopulation of Illyrian lands generally, in the aftermath of the Roman conquest, as described above. During this time, movement through the mountains was likely channeled by the Romans along the Lissus-Naissus/Drin River road and away from tributary valleys, like Shala.

While the people of Shala did not have an identifiable, direct-historical connection to the Illyrians, they nonetheless undertook various memory practices that are distinctly "Illyrian" in character. Many such practices are described in the *Kanun*, which I have already discussed at some length above. Shala is one of the three primary Dukagjin tribes (along with Shosh and Mirdita), and so the *Kanuni i Lekë Dukagjinit* was strictly applied. The *Kanun* is a memory machine. Many of the rituals it prescribes are specifically designed to create and maintain a tribal collective memory and anchor it in the landscape. These include the laying of boundary stones and the building of *muranë*, as described above, but also directions for building, expanding, and destroying houses, and dividing a family's material goods. Houses were constructed following very specific rules, all of which have clear connections to "pagan" practices: blood and ashes were used to mark out the foundation, under the light of the moon, for example (Tafilica 2013: 154–55). Catholic priests stationed in Shala and nearby communities describe these practices in letters to their Vatican superiors, and sought to eliminate them (Lee et al. 2013: 64–65). Likewise, houses were carved with numerous symbols, drawn largely from the natural world, such as sun disks, stars, moons, caves, etc. (Tafilica 2013). A cross was carved on the door of a house once the household had been freed from feud, and the adze used to cut the carving was tossed over the roof (Book Ten: The Law Regarding Crimes, chapter 22: Murder, CXXXIX "The Cross on the Door," Gjeçov 1989: 184). Upon the death of a patriarch, household items were split among his sons following explicit rules related to the "separation of brothers" (Lee 2013: 129–30). Whereas the house went to the youngest son (though his older brothers might continue to live in it), the armaments always went to the first-born (Book Four: Marriage, chapter 7: Division of Property, Gjeçov 1989: 46–51). Houses were only purposefully destroyed when the sole male heir had died (Kondi 2012: 94), or in response to serious offenses, by burning, and the family of the perpetrator was expelled from the tribe (Book Eleven: Judicial Law, CLVII "Fire, Destruction, and Execution," Gjeçov 1989: 210–12). Once burned, the house was left standing, as a reminder of the transgression, a powerful memory cue.

Through these, and many other, mnemonic behaviors, a history of the tribe was inscribed in the landscape. The comings and goings of ancestors, the good and the bad, things done and left undone: all were recorded in the built environment, and could be read by tribal members, elders in particular. Shala's landscape of memory was underpinned by oral histories, including complex genealogies. Shala elders interviewed by SVP ethnographers could, in some cases, recite male ancestors back 15 generations to the founding father (Lee et al. 2013: 57). Another important element in collective memory making was the singing of epic songs, like the *Songs of the Frontier Warriors*, referenced above. The musicologist Albert Lord (1948: 43), a student of Milman Parry, collected over 100 recordings of epic verse in Shala. Generally speaking, they document the heroic deeds of tribal warriors; but they are instructive, as well, reminding tribal members of their rights and responsibilities, and the importance of honor. The epic songs of northern Albania are distantly related to the *mirologia* of Epirus—which are similar in form and function to the mirologia of the Mani, described in chapter 3, but are sung by men and accompanied by violin, clarinet, and other instruments—and to the polyphonic tradition of southern Albania and northern Greece. Polyphony, in particular, is thought to have ancient roots, perhaps stretching back to Classical times. According to Sugarman (1997: chapter 6), the singing of polyphony, at weddings for instance, creates "communities of honor" and reinforces the egalitarian nature of village life.

Throughout Albania, therefore, speech and singing were (and are) used to make memories and reinforce social norms in the absence of the written word. This was especially true during funerals (figure 4.3). The basic steps in a traditional, Albanian funeral are outlined in the *Kanun*, with reference to feud:

> If the family of the victim has agreed to a truce with the murderer, the latter, even though he is the one responsible for the death, must go to the funeral, participate in *gjamë*, accompany the body to the cemetery and share in the funeral meal.
>
> (Book Ten: The Law Regarding Crimes, chapter 22: Murder, CXXII "The Truce," Gjeçov 1989: 166; see also Gjeçov 1989: 218–20, Kondi 2012: 79)

The *gjamë* is a ritualized men's lament. Men gather in a circle around the body of the deceased, kneel, bow their heads to the ground, strike the earth, scratch their cheeks, and shout "like thunder," to express the unbearable pain, grief, and anger that comes with death (Kondi 2012: 208–10). Additionally, the *gjamë* dramatically fixed the dead individual in collective memory, and was meant to take place outside, so that the deceased might receive "the proper honor of his tribe . . . on the land of his forefathers" (Kondi 2012: 214). Moreover, as mourners approached the funeral, coming from other tribes, they made stops at the borders of the village, neighborhood, and the family's compound, reaffirming the spatial, and therefore kinship, affiliations of the deceased (Kondi 2012: 217). If the *gjamë* was for the last male in a patriline, it must be especially

Figure 4.3. Ceremoni Vorrimi ne Dukagjin [Funeral Ceremony in the Dukagjin], by Shan Pici, 1929. *Source:* Used by permission of the Fototekës Kombëtare 'Marubi,' Shkodër.

powerful, since the "hearth of the house was to be extinguished" (i.e., the house would be destroyed) (Ibid.). According to Kondi (2012: 218):

> Patriarchal prestige finds the highest and most meaningful expression in the noble group of the "elders upon the elders" (*pleq e ma pleq*), who perform in the face of the expectant, eager world of the living and the dead. Societal mourning is permanently fired by the epic past: "woe is me o my brother" "woe is me o my arm [i.e. gun]" "woe is me o my friend."

This final lament, shouted at the conclusion of the ceremony, had the ultimate effect of unifying the community, by actively creating collective memory, under the guidance of memory workers, the elders, reconstructing social solidarity in the face of loss. It is not a stretch to imagine ancient Illyrians, gathered around a tumulus, doing the same thing, or something similar.

In addition to *gjamë*, various forms of call and response and so-called free lamentation (*vaj*)—improvised, sometimes incomprehensible crying—were undertaken by women (Kondi 2012: 131–32). These were sometimes led by a professional mourner (*vajtore*), an older woman who made a living traveling to funerals and wailing (figure 4.4). Together, women gathered around the body and undertook the *vaj i madh* (the great wailing), during which most were rendered senseless with grief, throwing themselves onto the dead body, washing it with their tears (Kondi 2012: 265). Next, two groups of women from two associated neighborhoods, or in divided villages, from the two different religions, Christian and Muslim, traded laments, back and forth (Kondi 2012: 266). Finally, individual women recounted the characteristics and exploits of the deceased, placing him or her into proper oral-historical context:

> The most painful individual laments of the family members are often carved into social memory and became commemorative complaints, songs of longing, lyrical sighs and faint echoes from a far-distant past. (Kondi 2012: 279)

Recounting laments were particularly expressive and of the greatest social (and mnemonic) importance, in particular when addressed to a man who had died in a feud, whose murder must be remembered and avenged at all costs:

> O I, your sister, want to see your blood,
> O but your blood rises like a fortress
>   O my brother, *ooœ moo!*
> O I, your sister, want to kiss your eye,
> O but your gaze is fixed forever on the gun,
>   O my brother, *ooœ moo!*
> O I, your sister, want to touch your finger,
> O but your trigger finger has fired thunderbolts
>   O my brother, *ooœ moo!*
> O I, your sister, have come to sit near you
> O right over the cairn (muranë) in the high place
>   O my brother, *ooœ moo!*
>
> —(Kondi 2012: 279)

In this particular lament, from the Lura region of the northeastern mountains, a direct reference is made to the cairn, built over the dead body, which, like the blood of the dead man, rises like a fortress. In pursuing feud, young men protected and reproduced the body politic, in reality and in memory. To not pursue vengeance—to forget, or be afraid—brought dishonor—the blackening of one's face, in the language of the *Kanun*—shunning of the family, and weakness in the tribe.

As was also the case in Mani, Greece, Albanian women sometimes used laments to express their own displeasure with men and their actions, a form of counter-narrative, counter-memorial behavior. However, unlike Greece, where mourning was a female activity held in a "female" space, in Albania, mourning was done by both sexes, together, outside

Figure 4.4. Zoje Mustafa–Vajtojce nga Dukagjini [Lady Mustafa–Wailer from Dukagjin], by Shan Pici, 1938. *Source:* Used by permission of the Fototekës Kombëtare 'Marubi,' Shkodër.

and in public view. Thus, if men did not like what a particular woman was singing, they could disrupt her lament (Kondi 2012: 219), exercising control over the memory-making process, which was ultimately a function of patrilocality.

This give and take between men and women within the mortuary context betrays a general flexibility in Albanian medieval and modern memory systems, as also revealed in the *Kanun*, which likewise extended into the realm of religion. Following the Ottoman invasion, and with the dissolution of the resistance under Skanderbeg, most Albanians converted to Islam (Winnifrith 1992: 77–78). Tribes like Shala, which preserved an exclusive adherence to Christianity, are exceptional. As described in chapter 3, an estimated 60 percent of Albanians are Muslim (Census-AL 2011), as compared to 1 percent of Greeks (United States Department of State 2006). I have already attributed these differences to dissimilar memory systems in operation in both countries, each of which responded to Ottoman occupation very differently. Because Greeks had experienced strongly hierarchical state systems, by Mycenaean times at least, and because Greek identity and collective memory had been completely subsumed by the Orthodox Church during the Byzantine period, on a micro-regional scale, Greeks did not convert. Had they done so, they would have incapacitated their primary source of resistance to Ottoman domination. By contrast, Albanians never formed states of their own and only loosely depended on Christianity when it came to identity formation and collective memory making. Their *modus operandi* in the face of conquest had always been to transmogrify and, after years of historical absence, to magically reappear. The practice of crypto-Christianity was, for example, common under the Ottomans (and later, under Communism; see below) (Winnifrith 1992: 77). Albanians who had converted to Islam practiced Christianity in secret, hiding their faith, baptizing their children, keeping secret Christian names, and, when it suited them, reasserting their Christian identities. This practice does not betray a burning commitment to Christianity; rather, it displays ambivalence on the part of Albanians toward religion generally. As asserted by the famous Albanian nationalist poet Pashko Vasa (1825–1892), "The faith of the Albanian is Albanianism" (*Feja e shqyptarit asht shqyptarija*). This ambivalence is further indicated by the prevalence of Bogomilism in Albania (as noted above) and the Albanian preference for Bektashism, a Muslim dervish sect that allowed its adherence to consume alcohol (Winnifrith 1992: 77–78). So well did Albanians play the part of Muslim adherents that the Turks pressed tens of thousands of them into service, throughout the empire. Several Grand Viziers were Albanian, most notably those of the Köprülü dynasty (Winnifrith 1992: 75), and, of course, Mehmed Ali, the Ottoman governor of Egypt, was an Albanian from Kavala, in northern Greece. It is an ironic, or perhaps tragic, twist of fate that it was an Albanian governor of Egypt who attacked Greece and was repulsed by the Maniate women. So strong was the historical connection between Albania and Egypt via the Ottomans that the word for maize in Albanian is *misr* (i.e., Egyptian corn). And *mSr* is the Classical Egyptian word for Egypt.

The relationship between the Albanians and Ottomans was not without conflict, of course. Between 1550 and 1750 the Albanians were in almost continuous revolt, often in response to burdensome tax rates (Winnifrith 1992: 78). Many of these revolts began in the northern mountains, which the Ottomans sought, unsuccessfully, to administer (Lee et al. 2013: 49–51). When military action did not work, the Ottomans pursued other means of controlling the mountaineers. For example, beginning in the mid-18th century, they instituted the *bajrak* system, which was designed to divide and destabilize the tribes (Lee et al. 2013: 49). Tribal leaders were presented the opportunity to pledge their allegiance to the Porte, for which they were given, in return, a banner, a *bajrak*, and the title of *bajraktar*, banner chief. These banners became powerful symbols, passed down from father to son in a system of hereditary leadership that bore little resemblance to tribal governance as dictated in the *Kanun*. *Bajraktars* administered tribal zones that often overlapped and combined disparate tribal segments and villages, cross-cutting tribal boundaries and politics. They agreed to raise military levies as needed, and were granted free passage through the mountains. They often obtained privileged access to Ottoman trade goods, like ammunition, that other chiefs did not have. In Shala, the northern village of Theth was granted a single banner, whereas in the south, in Shala proper, no fewer than four *bajraks* were created (Mustafa et al. 2013: 88). This divide and conquer policy was almost certainly intended by the Ottomans to sow discord and it did, to some extent. As a result, SVP interviews in Shala reflect almost no lingering respect for *bajraktars*, but an abiding allegiance to one's *fis*, well before nation and religion (Mustafa et al. 2013: 85). I contend that this is because the *bajrak* system struck at the heart of Albanian collective memory practices, and was therefore perceived, ultimately, as a threat. Bajraks did not respect boundaries, both physical and social (e.g., they were based on hereditary leadership, whereas the *Kanun* emphasized equality), which, as we have seen, were of paramount importance to the customary law codes and, therefore, the proper functioning of the tribal ideological system, based on honor. In the end, the Porte never did manage to incorporate the northern tribes. They remained free and unconquered, as did the Maniates in Greece, who have traditionally employed remarkably similar language to describe their history of resistance, against the Turks and vis à vis other Greeks.

Ironically, it was not the Ottomans who finally destroyed the tribal system and with it, millennia-old traditional Albanian memory structures. The leaders of the new Albanian nation began that process, and the Communists completed it. Albania gained its independence from the Ottoman Empire in 1912, prior to the onset of World War I (Hutchings 1992). The key figure in interwar Albanian politics was Ahmed Zogu, who became King Zog in 1928 and ruled until the Italian invasion of 1939 (Ibid.: 115). Zog was himself a mountaineer, from Mat, and so understood well how the tribal system worked, and how to disrupt it (Vickers 1999: 118). First, he sought to disarm the tribesmen (Ibid.: 117), who needed guns to pursue feud, and therefore honor, but might also turn them on the new government (figure 4.5). Second, he built roads, which decreased tribal isolation, but also allowed for speedier troop movements (Ibid.: 119). The road to Theth in Shala, for example, was built in 1934 (Lee et al. 2013: 72). Finally, the border with Montenegro was closed, which was particularly devastating for the people of Shala, who traveled to markets in Gusinje and Peja (in Kosovo), as opposed to Shkodra, to acquire much-needed goods, like felt, flour, coffee, sugar, tobacco, matches, and, of course, guns and bullets (Lee et al. 2013: 72–73). Closing the border caused general pain and suffering, but also undercut systems of customary law by rendering scarce those items needed to fulfill hospitality obligations and prosecute feuds. As a result of these various strategies, by the time Hoxha came to power, the stage had been set for a full-fledged assault on the tribes, and dismemberment of Albanian memory systems, in general.

Enver Hoxha (1908–1985) hailed from Gjirokastër in south Albania. He fought during World War II as a partisan, and, after Albania had been liberated from the Germans, he was elected First Secretary of the People's Republic of Albania. When Hoxha came to power, Albania possessed a limited state apparatus—few schools, no industry, and little infrastructure—and no unifying national imagery (Anderson 1983). To create an Albanian nation-state, when one had never before existed, Hoxha and his government had to encourage, or force, the Albanian people to accept centralized rule, from Tirana. This was difficult for several reasons: as described above, most Albanians owed allegiance to their tribe (*fis*) first, and religion (a far distant) second, and there continued to exist considerable distrust between Ghegs in the north and Tosks in the south (Vickers 1999: 164–65). Ghegs viewed Tosks as Ottoman collaborators and Hoxha was a Tosk. A crucial step to consolidating control was, therefore, to undermine local traditional memory and religious systems. As I have already argued at length above, *all* states must appropriate traditional memory systems, a necessary step in the nation-building process. Whereas this first happened for Egyptians and Greeks during prehistory, Albanians, and Illyrians before them, did not experience state formation prior to the 20th century. Even under the Ottomans, many Albanians operated well outside the state's administrative system. Hoxha had no choice but to build an Albanian nation from the ground up, which entailed crafting a new national identity, one which all Albanians, regardless of their regional, linguistic, ethnic, or religious affiliation, would recognize and support. Philology, archaeology, and history, not collective memory, became the keys to constructing Albania's new national identity.

Hoxha first sought to establish the Illyrian origins of the modern Albanians, and therefore their autochthony. However, in the absence of Illyrian written sources (i.e., documents written in an Illyrian language), this proved difficult. Albanian philologists were able to identify small numbers of ancient Illyrian names within longer Greek and Roman inscriptions, on tombstones, for instance (Wilkes 1992: 67–87). These names, it was argued, connected the Illyrian to the Albanian languages. Next, it was necessary to define, using archaeology, an "Illyrian" material culture (to go along with the names) that was distinct from Greek and Roman material culture. The sources for Illyrian art, ways of life, economy, architecture, and belief systems were traced to the Bronze-Iron Age tumulus cultures, and, via Koman culture, from ancient Illyris/Illyricum down to

Figure 4.5. Dorezimi Armeve (Kaipten Mark Raka dhe Bajraktari i Shales) [Surrendering Arms (Captain Mark Rapa and the Bajraktar of Shala)], by P. Marubi, 1922. The last barakktar of Shala hands in his gun to state authorities. He receives a copy of the new constitution in return. *Source:* Used by permission of the Fototekës Kombëtare 'Marubi,' Shkodër.

the present (i.e., from Parailirët to Ilirët to Arbërit) (Korkuti 2003). Finally, a history of Illyrian resistance was written, through Marxist interpretation of ancient texts. The ultimate conclusion was that Albanians had fought for their ethnic survival over the course of thousands of years, and must keep fighting, under the leadership of the Communist party. Hoxha thereby acknowledged Albania's turbulent past, and embraced it, using it to support an isolationist policy of non-engagement with the outside world (Galaty and Watkinson 2004: 8–9).

> Through all the centuries of their history, the Albanian people have always striven and fought to be united in the face of any invasion which threatened their freedom and the motherland. This tradition was handed down from generation to generation as a great lesson and legacy, and precisely herein must be sought one of the sources of the vitality of our people, of their ability to withstand the most ferocious and powerful enemies and occupiers and to avoid assimilation by them. (Hoxha 1984: 11)

With this new nationalist narrative in place, the Hoxha government embarked on an unprecedented effort to root out all possible sources of counter-memorial/-historical activity.

Hoxha drew inspiration from both Stalin and Mao, but in the end, decided that neither had gone far enough in efforts to advance Communism (Bland 1992; O'Donnell 1999; Vickers 1999). He ruthlessly attacked and destroyed, or co-opted, all forms of traditional collective memory making. Memory workers, such as tribal elders, were assassinated or imprisoned (Pearson 2006; Vickers 1999: 189–90). The *Kanun* was denounced and rendered anathema (O'Donnell 1999: 97–108). Traditional memory practices were outlawed or severely curtailed. *Gjama* were prohibited outright, while limited forms of female mourning were encouraged, so long as they espoused socialist principles (Kondi 2012: 46). Age-old laments were adapted, and made to extol the virtues of dead revolutionary heroes, closing with a final chant of "May our Party have a long life!" (Ibid.: 48). When Hoxha died in 1985, a *vaj i madh* was held in the streets of Gjirokastër, involving all the old women of the city (Ibid.: 18). Those *lieux de mémoire* that did not fit the new nationalist narrative of unity, defiance, and self-sufficiency were torn down, and new ones were built, such as hundreds of commemorative historical lapidars (689 still remain, as counted by the Albanian Lapidar Survey; see Van Gerven Oei 2015). This orgy of destruction reached a climax in the 1960s, when Albania endeavored to become the world's first fully atheist state. Religious leaders across the country, those who remained, were imprisoned or executed (O'Donnell 1999: 142; Pearson 2006). All of the country's 2,169 churches and mosques were destroyed or repurposed (Elsie 2001: 17–18; O'Donnell 1999: 142). Albanian Christians once again went underground, as they had under the Ottomans (Elsie 2001: 61–62).

In the end, the Hoxha government's attempts to dislodge Albania's memory systems, by completely re-engineering landscapes (Rugg 1994), failed, but not before severe mnemonic trauma had been visited upon the Albanian people (Galaty et al. 2009). The Church of St. Mary at Apollonia, which was too historically important to demolish, became a movie theater. The Church of St. Ilias, one valley over, in Shtyllas, did not fare as well. When MRAP surveyors visited it in 1998, it had been reduced to a pile of rubble. But one block caught our attention (figure 4.6). It was clearly *spolia*, probably brought to Shtyllas from Apollonia and built into the church. It sat upright, covered in candles and flowers, surrounded by small piles of potsherds. When we asked locals about it, they told us that the occupants of Shtyllas were mostly political exiles. During Communism, they came secretly to the ruined church and left offerings on the block. These small acts of resistance, by both Christians and Muslims, gave people hope in hopeless times. But they also tapped much deeper collective memories, of a time when the Albanian people had been free from persecution, free to chart their own course, free to worship at a mound or a church, as it happened to suit them, free to practice the "art of not being governed" (Scott 2009).

Figure 4.6. Carved Hellenistic block from the destroyed Church of St. Ilias, Shtyllas, Albania. *Source:* M. L. Galaty.

In addition to tearing down religious monuments and reconstructing and reinterpreting archaeological sites, as sources of Illyrian and Albanian ethnogenesis, Hoxha's government pursued other means of dominating Albanian landscapes. Perhaps the most infamous of these was the bunkerization program, which began as early as 1967 and continued through 1986 (Galaty et al. 1999). Over the course of nearly 20 years, between 400,000 and 800,000 small pillbox bunkers were constructed throughout Albania. In theory, bunkerization was a logical outgrowth of the isolationist policies of Hoxha, meant to help the Albanian people defend themselves in the event of an invasion. In reality, bunkers represented an extreme form of social control. Bunkers were omnipresent. Visible along every ridgetop, found around every corner, they acted as powerful reminders that Hoxha and his government were all-powerful. Each bunker was maintained by a family, which was required to keep it clean and supplied (Galaty et al. 1999: 203). Bunker construction accounted for an estimated 2 percent of the Albanian "net material product" (Ibid.: 202). Ironically, when the Albanian Communist government fell in 1991, small soapstone bunker ashtrays became the country's most popular souvenir. Every tourist who came to Albania wanted to see bunkers. Now, 26 years later, bunkers, along with many other Communist monuments, are disappearing from the landscape (Eaton and Roshi

2014). Whatever collective memories of Communism might be developed and cued by such monuments are fading fast, to be replaced by a new, forward-facing nationalist narrative, one that embraces democracy, capitalism, and Western Europe. This new narrative, like the old one, also encourages selective forgetting, of those aspects of Albanian history that do not fit comfortably the new political-economic agendas.

With the fall of Communism, many formerly tribal Albanians living in the high mountains of the north began to "retribalize" and rededicated themselves to interpretation and application of the *Kanun* (Schwandner-Sievers 1998, 2001, 2003, 2004). Feuds that had lain dormant and "forgotten" for 50 years reignited (Mustafa et al. 2013: 103–6). Tribal councils were reconstituted and, in the absence of state authority, often took legal matters into their own hands (Ibid.). Throughout the rest of the country, however, most Albanians, especially urbanized Tosks, continued to view the *Kanun* as archaic and at odds with emerging notions of civil society and rule of law. In actuality, retribalization represented a primary form of heterodox, counter-memory production, employed by the relatively impoverished, northern mountaineers, eager to stake their claim to an Albanian future from which they had generally been excluded. The new Albanian national narrative, which was being crafted by the educated urban elite, emphasized, however, the "European" character of the Albanian people. It did not require Illyrian-Albanian autochthony; in fact, Illyrian-Greek-Roman miscegenation made for a far better story. This new narrative also tended to devalue Albanian diversity in favor of a monolithic Albanian racial history, which did not include Roma, Albanian Egyptians (more about them in chapter 5), Jews, Vlachs, and Slavs. In this way, recent Albanian collective memory making is very much like modern Egyptian and Greek memory making. In all three nations, powerful political agents seek to stamp out any form of dissent by enforcing mnemonic orthodoxies that have no real historical basis: pan-Islamic for Egypt, pan-Hellenic/Orthodox Christian for Greece, and pan-Albanian cum European for Albania.

In conclusion, we can now apply chapter 1's memory model to Ottoman and modern Albania. Ottoman strategies of occupation and administration were quite similar throughout the empire. For example, a policy of religious tolerance held, whether in Egypt, Greece, or Albania. And yet, in all three places the response to Islam was very different. Egyptians were introduced to Islam well prior to the Ottoman conquest, which resulted in almost universal conversion. Any echoes of Classical Egyptian collective memory and identity scarcely survived and were filtered through the Coptic Church. Greeks, on the other hand, maintained traditional memory systems into and through Ottoman occupation. If anything, the Greek sense of identity was strengthened during the Turkokratia, as (most, but not all) differences were set aside in pursuit of independence. For their part, the Albanians, and the Illyrians before them, had always avoided being pulled into state systems of governance. Under the Ottomans, they meta-morphed, or simply slipped away. It is interesting to note that unlike Egypt and Greece, where sizable Turkish-speaking minorities persisted after independence, in Albania the Turkish minority is almost non-existent, scarcely 2,000 individuals (Census-AL 2011). With reference to figure 1.3, then, Ottoman Albania can be situated alongside Ottoman Egypt and Ottoman Greece: memory systems were relatively open and of little concern to the Sublime Porte, and political control was on the high side. By contrast, modern Albania was ruled by one of the most repressive totalitarian dictatorships ever created. Communist Albania was characterized by the very highest levels of political control and collective memory systems that were almost completely closed. Countermemorial activity scarcely registers in the historical record; all those who undertook such activity were eliminated.

With reference to figure 1.2, modern Albania experienced relatively low levels of crisis, as compared to earlier eras. As a result, nostalgia for the "Golden Age" of Albanian history flourished. Periods of unification, such as under Gentius and Skanderbeg, became touchstones. Post-Ottoman collective memories, which had been completely constructed, were treated as orthodox and inviolate. There was no room for imagination or identity formation. Nationalism ran high. Whereas Hoxha and members of his party likely believed they were building a new society, one which would last forever, that society imploded not long after Hoxha died. Post-Communist Albania, like post-war Bosnia, is now experiencing a period of wild, imaginative collective memory making, one in which individuals and groups seek to reclaim lost identities. At Apollonia, most of the movie seats have been removed from the Church of St. Mary and regular services are now held. The Church of St. Ilias in Shtyllas has been rebuilt and the Hellenistic block—a rare symbol of anti-Hoxha, counter-memorial resistance—has been cemented into one of its walls, just above the main entrance. And in Shala, blood feuds still simmer, boundary stones are raised, and every once in a while, a *gjama* echoes like thunder through the mountains.

5

Conclusion

All These Memories Have Gone

He smiled. Whatever he did, he could not escape its definitions. It was no use deceiving himself. The *Kanun* was stronger than it seemed. Its power reached everywhere, covering lands, the boundaries of fields. It made its way into the foundations of houses, into tombs, to churches, to roads, to markets, to weddings. It climbed up to mountain pastures, and even higher still, to the very skies, whence it fell in the form of rain to fill the watercourses, which were the cause of a good third of all murders.

When for the first time he had convinced himself that he had to kill a man, Gjorg had called to mind all that part of the Code that dealt with the rules of the blood feud. If only I don't forget to say the right words before I fire, he thought. That's the main thing. If I don't forget to turn him the right way up and put his weapon by his head. That's the other main point. All the rest is easy, child's play.

However, the rules of the blood feud were only a small part of the Code, just a chapter. As weeks and months went by, Gjorg came to understand that the other part, which was concerned with everyday living and was not drenched with blood, was inextricably bound to the bloody part, so much so that no one could really tell where one part left off and the other began. The whole was so conceived that one begat the other, the stainless giving birth to the bloody, and the second to the first, and so on forever, from generation to generation.

—Ismail Kadare, *Broken April*, 1990: 27

Ismail Kadare (b. 1936) is Albania's most famous living writer. Ironically, he was also born in Gjiorkastër, the same southern Albanian city as the dictator Enver Hoxha. As a young man, he cultivated interests in languages and literature, and history, not unlike Hoxha himself. Beginning in 1960, when he published his first short story, through the death of Hoxha in 1985, he was a thorn in the dictator's side. Most of his novels include thinly veiled references to totalitarianism, both its inhumanity and its absurdity. *The Pyramid*, for example, was written as the Albanian Labour Party's hold on power crumbled, and it was published in 1992. It is set in ancient Egypt in 2600 BC and describes efforts on the part of "Cheops" to construct a great stone pyramid, to the detriment of the state and the state's economy. The character of Cheops clearly represents Hoxha, and dictators in general, and the pyramid symbolizes his desire to be remembered after his death, to be memorialized. (Hoxha's life was in fact memorialized in a "pyramid," a museum building designed by his architect daughter, located in downtown Tirana.) Timur the Lame also makes a cameo appearance in the book. His "pyramids" are giant piles of skulls that must be replenished from time to time, not unlike an Albanian tumulus, marking the landscape, activating and reinvigorating collective memories, reminding all who look of the great warrior's power. As I argued in chapter 4, for Hoxha, bunkers served a similar purpose, and indeed in the epilogue to *The Pyramid*, Kadare writes:

> In the land that had previously belonged to the Illyrians and been handed down to their descendants under the name of Albania . . . the old pyramid spawned not thousands, but hundreds of thousands of little ones. They were called bunkers, and each of them, however tiny it may have been in comparison, transmitted all of the terror that the mother of all pyramids had inspired, and all the madness too.

What Kadare so skillfully demonstrates in all of his novels is that history provides the bricks and mortar from which nations are created, but hidden inside, immured within like a body in a bridge, is memory. Memory is the lifeblood of cultures, the fuel that fires the Albanian *Kanun*, the running dog of dictators and presidents alike.

In chapters 2 through 4, I made the case that collective memory was essential to creating states and resisting them, in Egypt, Greece, and Albania. In all three, collective memory was employed over the *longue durée*, first to support traditional systems of social organization, and later, having been co-opted, in support of the state (though at very different times in each). In this chapter, I will demonstrate, using the framework developed in chapter 1, how collective memory continues to resonate in our modern world, with sometimes devastating consequences. I focus on Egyptian,

Greek, and Albanian efforts to manage "heritage" systems, manufacture homogenous national imaginaries, and undercut counter-narratives of resistance, many of which are promulgated by minority populations. I end with a discussion of the Islamic State (IS), which provides a dramatic, often brutal, example of collective memory making and forgetting.

EGYPTIAN NUBIANS

More than perhaps any other country in the world, Egypt depends on so-called heritage tourism. As of 2010, 12 percent of Egyptians were employed in the tourism sector, generating $12.5 billion in revenue (Smith 2014). Tourism is so important to the Egyptian people that during the Arab Spring revolution, on January 28, 2011, individuals, including guides, rushed to the National Museum in Cairo and formed a human shield around it, preventing it from being looted. In the years following the revolution, though, the tourism industry suffered. Total revenue from tourism contracted 47 percent from $12.5 billion in 2010 to $5.9 billion in 2013 (Smith 2014). Now, in 2018, tourism appears to be rebounding, but revenue remains well below that of the peak year of 2010 (Magdy 2017). The slow pace of recovery is a direct result of well-publicized terrorist attacks in Egypt, such as the downing of a Russian plane in Sinai in October 2015, for which the Islamic State claimed responsibility.

This very short description of tourism in Egypt allows several, additional key points to be made regarding the continuing importance of collective memory to the nation-state in the 21st century. First, use of the term "heritage," as in heritage management, which is now *de rigeur* the world over, is really code for memory (see Anheier and Raj Isar 2011). In most nation-states, heritage is managed such that collective memory systems and workers can be made to support historical orthodoxies that are not easily challenged. Memory work is big business, but also remains necessary to the proper, stable functioning of nations themselves: nostalgia and nationalism are encouraged, imagination and identity formation are repressed, and political crises rarely bloom. In modern Egypt, the decision was made to promote the Pharaonic period and harness Pharaonic ideals. This could not occur, of course, until Pharaonic Egypt itself had been rediscovered, a project that began in the early 19th century during the French occupation (Reid 2003, 2015). The classical Egyptian memory tropes of unity, stability, and harmony, which depended upon a homogenized Egyptian identity, were particularly attractive to the generals, who ruled post–World War II Egypt like latter-day Ramessids.

As described in chapter 2, Egyptian unity was constructed against external threats, both real and perceived. One of the pharaoh's primary tasks was to maintain stability and encourage social harmony by ensuring that Upper and Lower Egypt remained integrated, as they had been since the Early Dynastic period. The primordial danger to Egyptian unity emanated from Asia, and was most fully realized in the form of the Hyksos domination, the collective memory of which was a traumatic one. Later pharaohs who did not protect Egypt's borders fully, or were thought to be too accommodating, like Hatshepsut, were stricken from the record. Akhenaten's sin was to attack Egyptian religious and memory systems directly; he was subsequently erased in full from Egyptian collective memory. While it is true that "Asia" and "Asiatics" represented the primary, stereotypical sources of foreign peril, other regions and peoples were likewise targeted by the Egyptian state, in both Old and New Kingdoms, as threats requiring mitigation. One of these was Nubia, home to the so-called Nubian peoples, who lived in the border zone separating Egypt from Kush, between the first and sixth cataracts. As described in chapter 2, as early as the first dynasty, a fortress was built on the island of Elephantine, and by the Middle Kingdom, areas encompassing Lower Nubia, from the first to the second cataract, had been fortified and militarized. The Third Intermediate Period (1080–644 BC) marked the collapse of the New Kingdom and ended with Egypt under Kushite rule. Control of Lower Nubia was demonstrated by Egypt and Kush in different periods through the building of temples (Ashby 2016: 35–36), such as at Philae.

The earliest cult facilities at Philae date to the New Kingdom, during which Egypt held sway over Nubia, and were dedicated to Amun and Horus of Kubban (Ashby 2016: 36). Kubban stood at the mouth of the Wadi Allaqi, along the route to the Nubian gold mines (Ibid.). Thus, in addition to their military efforts in Nubia, Egyptians also sought to pacify the Nubians by co-opting their religious pantheon, which appears to have worked exceedingly well. Over the course of the New Kingdom, numerous temples were built by the Egyptians throughout Lower Nubia, including the fantastic, unique monuments at Abu Simbel, completed by Rameses II in 1244 BC to commemorate his victory at the Battle of Qadesh. So enamored were the Nubians when it came to the Egyptian gods, that in the Greco-Roman period, they adopted Philae and Isis as their own and, over the course of several centuries (in three phases, from 10 BC to AD 456), left numerous dedicatory graffiti at the temple complex (analyzed in detail by Ashby 2016) (figure 5.1). These inscriptions (*proskynema*—i.e., prayers, sometimes accompanied by a report citing who made the inscription and why) chart Nubian efforts to preserve access to Philae, and other temples, in Lower Nubia during the time when Christianity was spreading through the Roman Empire, including Egypt. While we do not know precisely the ethnic identity of the individuals who wrote the inscriptions, we do know that they were most certainly not Egyptian; rather they were local officials and priests who served the Meroitic and Blemmye kings, all of whom wrote using a "Meroitic" script (or the Demotic script to write Meroitic) and, later, in Greek (Ashby 2016: 16). These inscriptions thereby preserve a remarkable example of counter-memory production, vis-á-vis the Egyptian state, by peoples operating at the edge of state institutions. Eventually, a bishop was assigned to Philae (*circa* AD 330) and pagan worship was banned (by Justinian in AD 537), at which point the Nubians (the Noubadae, as they were then known) converted to Christianity. This, however, followed 200 years of Christian and traditional Egyptian worship, undertaken by Egyptians and Nubians, side by side, at Philae. The Nubians thus provided an important, though underappreciated, bridge connecting classical Egyptian memory and belief systems to those of later, Coptic Egypt. And yet, even though in some ways they acted more Egyptian than Egyptians, the Nubians continued to be marginalized by the Egyptian state, and, despite their conversion to Islam in the Late Medieval period (under the Mamluks, between the 13th and 16th centuries AD; Fernea 1973: 9), were never assimilated. For most Egyptians, Nubians triggered age-old, deeply held, xenophobic fears about the foreign Other. Much like the Libyans and Bedouins of the western and eastern deserts, the Nubians represented a problematic, liminal population, positioned in a buffer zone.

The Nubian "problem" was addressed by Mehmed Ali, who established garrisons in Nubia, but was not solved until the completion of the Aswan High Dam in 1970. The dam, which is located at the first cataract, flooded 5,250 square kilometers of land (i.e., all of Nubia) and required relocation of the entire population of 50,000 Egyptian Nubians to refugee towns built for them in the vicinity of Kom Ombo, north of Aswan (Dafalla 1975). All of the traditional Nubian villages now rest under the waters of Lake Nasser, which stretches well past the second cataract. In advance of the flood, the Egyptian government, working with UNESCO, arranged to move archaeological sites throughout Nubia to high ground, or in some cases to other countries (the Temple of Dendur was, for example, moved to the Metropolitan Museum in New York City). Abu Simbel was moved, as was Philae (Dafalla 1975: chapter 25). None of the *circa* 560 traditional Nubian villages was moved; rather, a five-year ethnological survey, under the direction of American anthropologist Robert A. Fernea, was commissioned (Hopkins and Mehanna 2010). The Nubian Ethnological Survey (NES) collected much valuable information about Nubian beliefs and practices, and in the aftermath of the moves, an attempt was made to assess the effects of relocation.

According to the Egyptian government, the main justification for building the Aswan High Dam was economic, to control the annual Nile floods. An unspoken corollary result, however, was political: an end to

Figure 5.1. Philae temple. Note the Christian altar and various graffiti. *Source:* M. L. Galaty.

Nubian independence. The results of the NES make clear that the move to "New Nubia" was a painful experience for most, if not all, of the Egyptian Nubians. In general terms, we can characterize the Nubian relocation, which meant a complete loss of access to the Nubian homeland (i.e., the *balad el-aman,* the "place of safety/security") and landscape, as an attack on their collective memory systems. Nubians placed great emphasis on their homes as key memory spaces, with high walls, plastered, painted interiors, and a *mastaba*, a platform on which guests and family members sat together, drank tea, ate, and socialized (Fahim 1983: 20–21). The small, concrete block structures built for them by the Egyptian government as replacements did not conform to these basic architectural principles, and therefore were ill-suited to traditional Nubian domestic life. Loss of access to ancestors dealt another significant blow to Nubian memory systems. Villages were typically built in close proximity to cemeteries, and before the first relocation boat left for Aswan, "the women rose at dawn to sadly and silently visit their dead, spraying the graves with water expressing compassion and sanctification" (Fahim 1983: 43). Finally, the Nubian ritual cycle was built around the *moulid,* joyous festivals that celebrated the lives of local saints (*shaykhs*), each of whom was buried in his own shrine (al-Messiri 1978; Wahab 2010: 231). None of these shrines was moved and the bones of the saints were left behind. At the time of the relocation, villagers planned to continue to hold the *moulid*, despite the absence of shrines. In practice and over time, however, most Nubian communities have become more orthodox in their religious beliefs and "pagan" or "popular" rituals, like the *moulid*, have been abandoned, or greatly curtailed (Fahim 2010: 219–21; see also Kennedy 1978). This trend—toward Islamic orthodoxy—matches the wider Egyptian trend, which, as discussed in chapter 2, involves memory-system closure. Closure serves modern Egypt's current political needs, encouraging stability and allowing crisis management in a time of intense change. As Nubian memory systems disintegrate or transform, to match those of the wider Egyptian population, the Nubian people are being slowly assimilated, further homogenizing Egyptian national identity. Given the current situation, counter-memory production has become particularly difficult, even for the powerful Coptic community, let alone the Nubians.

Scholars with the NES, who continue to study the relocated Nubians, report that they, and their offspring, suffer high rates of various illnesses, both physical and mental, including severe depression (Fahim 1983: 116–19). In fact, sociologists who work with relocated populations have identified a cross-cultural condition, called "loss of home," which prompts intense grief, severe distress, and, in some cases, suicide. Fried (1963: 156), for example, conducted research in Boston's West End, from which large numbers of Italian-Americans had been relocated in the 1950s. He describes their loss of home, and with it, loss of "a sense of spatial identity," which is "fundamental to human functioning." A similar condition may afflict the Nubians, who have likewise experienced a loss of home and spatial identity. As I have argued above, following Alcock (2002) and others, collective memory systems depend strongly on a sense of place, linked to a particular landscape, and its associated *lieux de mémoire*. When a memory community loses access to a landscape of memory, or that landscape is destroyed, its members can expect to experience turmoil and cultural disintegration as a result. Depending on the situation, loss of collective memory can amount to ethnocide, but often, a memory community will fight back.

In recent years, small numbers of Nubian activists have begun to agitate for a "right to return" (see, for example, Islam 2017). A right to return to Nubia was enshrined in the new 2014 Egyptian constitution, but has since been rescinded and Nubia declared a "military zone" (Janmyr 2016). Of course, Nubians have been denied a right to return not for security reasons *per se*, but because the underlying reasons for their relocation were political all along, linked to underlying, primal Egyptian memory systems and tropes. The Nubian issue is in a broad sense a "heritage" issue, not simply because archaeological sites were moved to safety, but also because it is fundamentally linked to collective memory: who shapes Egyptian collective memory, in what ways, and to what ends. The Nubians have been forcibly and finally locked out of that process as a result of being dispossessed of their memory systems and workers. Countermemory production is difficult or impossible given their total separation from Nubia itself. In fact, many of the sociologists involved in the NES wondered why the Nubians were having such difficulty adjusting to life in "New Nubia," given the supposedly better economic and social conditions afforded them by the move (see Geiser 1973, who referred to the Nubian propensity to blame the dam for all of their problems as a "myth"). Unless or until Nubians return to Nubia, they cannot and will not form new, viable memory communities, and they will continue to suffer the effects of the "loss of home" syndrome.

Over time, and in recent years, the Egyptian government has used "heritage" as a means of punishing certain populations and promoting others. The Nubian case is extreme, but not unique. For example, a thriving community built in and among the pharaonic tombs near Thebes, called Qurna (the so-called looters' village), was bulldozed, from 2006 to 2009, and its inhabitants were relocated, like the Nubians, to planned villages (figure 5.2; see Schwartzstein 2017; van der Spek 2012). The official reason

Figure 5.2.   Destroyed village of Qurna, near Valley of the Kings, Egypt. *Source:* M. L. Galaty.

Figure 5.3. Luxor, Egypt. Looking south toward Karnak. Avenue of the Sphinxes in foreground, Coptic Cathedral in background. *Source:* M. L. Galaty.

given for the relocations was that the homes built there were illegal and unsightly, and that they impeded tourist access. Residents, however, told me that they had been targeted due to their political affiliations. Similarly, houses built above the so-called Avenue of the Sphinxes, which in ancient times connected the Luxor and Karnak temples, were demolished so that it could be rebuilt, thus creating a broad pedestrian mall. Those who lived in the destroyed neighborhood—the Muslim owners of the so-called *hantoors*, the horse-drawn carriages used to carry tourists back and forth between the temples—were relocated to a planned community far outside of the city, which would, according to government officials, be better for their "ill-treated" horses. *Hantoor* drivers, however, described to me the hardships that relocation had caused for them and their families (and their horses) and focused their anger on the Coptic Cathedral that also stood above the avenue, but had been spared (figure 5.3). Instead, an artificial jog around the cathedral had been added to the avenue.

These brief examples can be best explained not simply as "heritage" decisions but rather as contestations over collective memory. In fact, the whole Egyptian heritage enterprise represents the culmination of a centuries-long experiment in collective memory work that began with

Mehmed Ali. The primary aim was to manufacture orthodox systems of collective memory, and to suppress imagination and identity formation, in favor of a scrubbed version of Egyptian history and nationalism. Certain historical periods served these needs better than others. The strong, militaristic pharaohs of the New Kingdom, who unified Egypt in the aftermath of the Second Intermediate Period and solidified its borders, were presented as analogues for the generals who ruled modern Egypt. Periods of foreign domination (e.g., Greek, Roman, Persian, and Ottoman) were acknowledged but generally dismissed as anomalous. The liberalizing tendencies of Mehmed Ali and his efforts to modernize the Egyptian economy were strongly endorsed, while, at the same time, a particular brand of humanistic, but doctrinal, Islam, associated with the Al-Azhar mosque and university, was officially promoted. There were clearly winners and losers in this process. Ethnic minorities, such as the Nubians, were encouraged or forced to assimilate. Coptic and Orthodox Christians were tolerated, so long as they supported the generals' neoliberal agenda. The Jewish community disappeared. Moderate Muslims flourished. Wahhabism and Salafism, puritanical Islamic movements that emanated from the Arabian Peninsula and had long been thorns in Egypt's side (going back to Mehmed Ali), were strongly discouraged, as was membership in the Muslim Brotherhood, and, now, the Islamic State in Egypt and the Sinai. These latter groups seek to push Egyptian collective memory systems even further toward closure and thereby secure full social and political control over Egypt and the Egyptian people. We can therefore see many of the activities of the Islamic State and other terrorist organizations, in Egypt and elsewhere, as extreme memory work, as will be discussed further below.

GREEK ALBANIANS

After Egypt, perhaps no other country in the world depends on heritage tourism more than Greece. Since the turn of the century, the number of tourists visiting Greece has steadily increased, from 12.4 million international arrivals in 2000 to 24.8 million in 2016 (Greek Tourism Confederation 2017). In 2016, tourism accounted for 18.6 percent of Greece's GDP (Ibid.). Like Egypt, Greece has carefully cultivated its "heritage" image, focusing on certain periods at the expense of others. Since the revolution, Greece's heritage—and, therefore, memory—touchstone has been, and continues to be, the Classical age, which is strongly associated, of course, with numerous emblematic monuments, like the Athenian Acropolis (see, for example, Hamilakis 2007). Prehistoric periods, like the Minoan and Mycenaean Bronze Ages, act as interesting, romanticized backdrops

(Duke 2016). The Ottoman period, and, to a far lesser extent, the Byzantine period are largely ignored, but for the Greek longing for and desire to re-establish the Byzantine Empire (see various discussions in Baram and Carroll 2002). The Greek meta-history, presented to tourists, identifies Greece, writ large, as the ultimate source of Western civilization, but this narrative elides the underlying collective memory tropes of regionalization and competition, and obscures considerable diversity.

As described in chapter 3, ancient Greece was characterized by numerous, competitive memory communities, which coalesced in prehistory, and laid the foundations for the formation of the Classical city-states. Generally speaking, Greek memory systems were highly distributed, and yet certain identifiable memory engrams bound them together, generating a shared sense of Greek identity. Those peoples who did not speak Greek, for instance, were, by definition, barbarians, and could not become citizens of a Greek city-state. In later times, Greek identity, and citizenship, was linked to membership in the Greek Orthodox Church (Clogg 2002: ix). Connecting Greek identity to religion helped sustain Greek memory communities through the years of the Tourkokratia. Despite these limits, Greek memory systems were relatively open, allowing great latitude when it came to the composition of regional, mythic imaginaries—city-state by city-state, citizen by citizen—and so nationalism was curtailed, even following liberation from the Turks. In recent times, strong, centralized governments operating out of Athens have forced Greeks into confederation, begun the process of breaking down regional boundaries, and moved Greece into the European Union and onto the Euro. Open borders have led to very high levels of immigration, and net increases in ethnic and racial diversity, especially in urban centers, like Athens. The response from the Greek right wing has been particularly vicious. Greek nationalist parties, such as Golden Dawn, call for a return to the days when "only Greeks lived in Greece," prompting violent attacks on minority Greek citizens.

This idea, that Greece has always been a homogenous place, home to Greeks and Greeks alone, is a myth (Gogonas 2010: chapter 1). On the contrary, multiple minority groups have called Greece home, beginning in prehistory, up to and through the modern day. Greek collective memory workers, and Greek nationalist movements, have, however, since independence, constructed a powerful memory engram, drawing on Greek heritage efforts, centered on Greek autochthony, recidivism (to Byzantine borders, thus including much of the Eastern Mediterranean), and racial purity, which reinforces the idea of a non-diverse Greek past. For example, Golden Dawn has used (and misinterpreted) recent ancient genetic evidence to argue for Greek primacy among Balkan peoples (see Laziridis et al. 2017 and the response by Golden Dawn 2017; see also blog posts by

Hamilakis 2017 and Nakassis 2017). Given the recent wars in the Balkans, this brand of counter-memory production, operating around the edges of Greek historical orthodoxies, is particularly alarming. The example of the Greek Albanians, the so-called Arvanites, can help make this point.

Among the numerous minority populations living in Greece in the aftermath of the War of Rebellion were Muslims, Slavs, Turks, Vlachs, Roma, Armenians, and Jews (Clogg 2002), and large numbers of Albanians. Most scholars agree that these "Arvanite" communities arrived in Greece from the region of Albania during the Middle Ages, perhaps in the aftermath of Skanderbeg's defeat, perhaps somewhat earlier at the invitation of various Byzantine rulers (Bintliff 2003; Gogonas 2010: 3). They were largely but not exclusively Orthodox Christian and are most plentiful in Attica and Boeotia (Bintliff 2003). Most Arvanites continue to speak their language, Arvanitika, a dialect of Albanian, though language fluency is waning as young people move from natal villages to cities (Gogonas 2010). Generally speaking, the Arvanites have nearly fully assimilated, to the extent that they are rarely recognized as being of non-Greek origin. Bintliff (2003: 140) refers to them as a "passive" ethnicity, as opposed to an "assertive" ethnicity, which is more commonly deployed by other Greek minority communities, such as the Slavs and Muslims of northern Greece. For example, non-Greek nick- and surnames sometimes identify Arvanites, but naming conventions have changed such that more often than not, given names are Greek. Arvanite names thereby serve as tools of conformity rather than resistance (Maglvieras 2013).

The history and "Greekness" of the Arvanites has in recent years been questioned, despite the fact that they fought on the side of ethnic Greeks in the War of Independence, often against Albanians (both Muslim and Christian), who fought with the Turks. In fact, many famous Greek military commanders have been Arvanites (e.g., Andreas Vokos Miaoulis, an admiral; Laskarina Bouboulina, the only female member of Filiki Etaireia [mentioned above]; Georgios Koundouriotis, admiral and briefly president of the Greek Republic [Clogg 2002: xvi]; and Dimitris Plapoutas, a general from Epirus). The suddenly rocky social position of the Arvanites is to some degree a result of Albanian immigration to Greece in the aftermath of the collapse of Communism in 1991, some of it legal, much of it illegal. Hart (1999) describes the cultural heterogeneity of the Greek-Albanian border, where bilingual Greeks and Albanians live and work together, and have done, presumably, for centuries, if not millennia. This heterogeneity does not fit well the nation-state models promoted now by both the Greek and Albanian governments, in particular in the aftermath of the Balkan Wars of the 1990s. For their part, Arvanites were quick to distance themselves from the thousands of Albanians who poured into Greece in the early 1990s, were branded criminals by Greeks, and were generally marginalized, exploited, and often deported. Some Greeks (and some Arvanites) have responded by reimagining the origins of the Albanians, arguing that despite language differences, Albanians were in reality historically and racially Greek, and they should be assimilated as such (Hart 1999: 211–12). Albanians have responded to this rhetoric by arguing that they are "Pelasgian" and, therefore, of earlier, autochthonous stock, as compared to Greeks. In this model, Arvanites become the more authentic occupants of Greece, because their language is closer to the original "Pelasgic" language of the peninsula (De Rapper 2009: 11).

The Arvanite experience of life in Greece is of course strongly conditioned by collective memory, both theirs and that of Greeks. Arvanites, like Albanians generally, deploy memory systems that are extremely flexible, encouraging cultural, linguistic, and religious code shifting. These systems are not strongly bound to a particular, primal memory engram, and this allows Arvanites to act Greek as needed. The Arvanite tendency has been to assimilate, whereas most other minority groups in Greece fiercely defend their identity and with it, their autonomy (various examples in Clogg 2002). Each Arvanite village traces its ancestry to a particular founding ancestor (Bintliff 2003: 133), the leader of a small military band called a *fara* (Athanassopoulou 2005: 269). The Arvanite *fara* is quite similar in many respects to the Albanian *fis*, described in chapter 4, but each *fara* is more firmly linked to a village, named after its eponymous founder (Bintliff 2003: 133). Traditionally, these Arvanite villages formed symbiotic relationships with the fewer, larger Greek villages, providing various pastoral products, like cheese (Ibid.). Through time, as Arvanites adopted modern, more fully sedentary lifestyles that mimicked those of Greeks, Arvanite memory communities came into conflict with Greek memory communities, over ancestral access to land, for example. One Greek response to these conflicts was to change the names of Arvanite villages, thereby undercutting the *fara* system. For example, the name of one of the villages in Bintliff's (2003: 138) study region was officially changed from Zogra Kobili to Leondarion, a name with Classical overtones.

Nevertheless, despite Greek attacks on their memory systems, the Arvanite story is one of persistence and transmogrification, quite similar to that of the Albanians in Albania under Ottoman rule. It is quite unlike the Nubian story, which involved wholesale mnemocide. Greek memory systems were designed to stretch and envelope heterodox memory communities. Egyptian memory systems were inelastic and could not easily accommodate independent counter-memory communities within the Egyptian state, a condition exacerbated by nationalism and growing Islamic extremism. The case of the Albanian Egyptians is different once again, marked by change, instability, and recent, intensive counter-memory production and conflict.

ALBANIAN EGYPTIANS

The Albanian heritage tourism industry is still in its infancy, having appeared only recently, following the end of isolation and the reopening of the country. Since 2000, the total number of annual foreign visitors has grown steadily, from 317,149 in 2000 to 4,735,411 in 2016 (Republika e Shqiperisë Instituti i Statistikave [INSTAT] 2017). The majority (e.g., 3,855,617 in 2016, or 81 percent of the annual total) hailed from other, nearby southern European nations and likely accessed Albania by bus for short visits, to places like Shkodër. Most of the rest, including Western Europeans and Americans, probably visited the large, coastal Classical sites, like Butrint, Apollonia, and Durrës, which are accessible to tourists by land transport from cruise ships. Interestingly, unlike Egypt and Greece, Albania's official heritage narrative is still very much influx, and often runs counter to the heterodox memory tropes of interest to, and promulgated by, Albanian citizens. For example, many of the books concerning the purported "Pelasgian" origin of the Albanians, compiled by De Rapper (2009), have been written by amateur historians for an Albanian popular audience, and are rife with mistakes and misinterpretations. Barring a few prominent exceptions (e.g., Ceka 2005; Korkuti 2003), modern Albanian archaeologists, including those who control the country's heritage management system, have rejected the Pelasgian origin theory altogether. While many Albanian archaeological sites and museums posit Albanian descent from the Illyrians, to the best of my knowledge none cite the Pelasgians. In fact, telling an Illyrian origin story at Classical sites like Butrint and Apollonia itself proves difficult, given the general absence at these sites of "Illyrian" material culture. And while the Albanian National Museum in Tirana certainly displays various prehistoric artifacts, including some that are Illyrian, the clear focus of the museum is on the medieval period, when the Albanians first appeared on the world stage, and on Skanderbeg's defense of the country.

As described in chapter 4, through time Albanian memory systems have remained extremely flexible, which is one source of their remarkable resilience. Ancient "Illyrian" collective memory was deeply invested in a vibrant mortuary landscape, composed of burial mounds. Unlike most other Balkan nations, mound use in Albania continued through ancient times and right down to the present, in the form of *muranë*, as described in the *Kanun*. The "emergent" properties of Albanian culture and memory systems, and their "dynamic stability," sustained trans-egalitarian social systems that were not easily incorporated into the Ottoman Empire (see Galaty et al. 2013: 237–40). Albanians never experienced statehood, as was the case, as early as the Bronze Age, for the Egyptians and Greeks. The first indigenous Albanian state, declared in 1912, set about disrupting and/or appropriating local memory systems, something the Ottomans had never managed to do. This process reached a tragic crescendo in the aftermath of World War II, when Albanian society, including the northern tribes, was fully subsumed by the Communist dictatorship of Enver Hoxha and Albania's open memory systems were closed. Albanian collective memory systems became tightly hitched to the totalitarian political system, including memory workers of all kinds, and Hoxha embarked on a massive nation-building effort, which involved creating a national imaginary essentially from scratch.

After 1912, the Albanian government sought to construct a sanitized national history, one in which Albanian minority groups played little or no role. The presence in Albania of some national minority groups, like the Greeks of southern Albania, the Vlachs, and various Slavic populations, including Montenegrins and Macedonians, was acknowledged, but their identities were often challenged and they were encouraged to assimilate (see, again, Hart 1999). Unlike "white" minority groups, most Roma were categorized in racial terms, based on the color of their skin, making assimilation more difficult (the Roma in Albania are referred to as *dorë e zezë*, i.e., "black hand/side"; see Ohueri 2016). After the fall of the Communist government in 1991, different minority groups in Albania responded differently to freedom. Some Albanian Greeks migrated to Greece, while those who stayed have formed a surprisingly powerful minority political party, called Omonoia. Most of the Albanian Jews left for Israel, which is ironic, given that Albania is the only country in Europe where not a single Jew was killed or deported during the German occupation, primarily due to the strict hospitality laws outlined in the *Kanun* (Fischer 1999: 187). Montenegrins, such as those living in Vraka near Shkodër, emigrated en masse to Montenegro. Some have since returned, but, generally speaking, their presence in the region is quickly being erased from local collective memory, as their Orthodox churches and cemeteries fall into ruin and disappear from the local landscape (Deskaj 2017). The Aromanian Vlachs of Albania, based out of the so-called Vlach capital of Moskopole (Albanian Voskopoja), have since 1991 continuously reaffirmed their minority status and rights, with financial support from the Romanian government (Schwandner-Seivers 1999).

One interesting phenomenon of the post-Communist period has been the emergence in Albania, and in Kosovo and Macedonia, of a "new" minority group, the so-called Albanian Egyptians (De Soto et al. 2005). Given their dark skin, they are often confused with Roma people, but do not speak the Romani language. They are mostly Muslim, speak Albanian, and refer to themselves as Jevgs (Ohueri 2016: 117–21), and whereas the Roma assert Indian origins, they claim to have arrived in the Balkans from Egypt at some point in the past. There is, however, scant historical evidence to support their Egyptian roots, and their ethnic authenticity has been questioned. Whether or not to acknowledge the Jevgs and grant them some kind of minority status and protection—which have yet to be extended to the Roma—has become a controversial political issue, which hinges on the question of whether they are truly Egyptian, as opposed to being, for example, a covert Roma splinter group (Marushiakova and Popov 2013).

Recently, some scholars have addressed Jevg origins, but as of yet there is little consensus regarding whether or not they might, in truth, be Egyptian. It does in fact appear to be the case that Jevg communities existed in Albania well prior to the present day: British linguist Stuart Mann (1933: 2–3) described meeting Egyptians in Albania in the early 1930s, and Ohueri (2016: 118–19) recently uncovered in the Albanian National Archives a 1930 letter to the Albanian government from a Jevg village in Korçë. There are, of course, ancient references to Egyptians in the Balkans, such as those in Herodotus (reviewed by Jevg activist Rubin Zemon 2001), which form the basis for Bernal's "Black Athena" hypothesis (Bernal 1987, 1991, 2006), but these have yet to be substantiated archaeologically and most scholars question their veracity (Trubeta 2005). There is also, however, good evidence that Africans, including Egyptians, came to Europe in Roman times, as merchants, soldiers, pirates, and, in large numbers, as slaves (see Scheidel 2011 regarding the origins and final disposition of Roman slaves through time). Likewise, there was an active slave trade under the Ottomans, which would have moved Africans, including Egyptians, to Anatolia and the Balkans (Hunwick and Powell 2002), including Albania (Muhaj 2017). Small communities of African origin, the descendants of Ottoman slaves, are found in Istanbul (the so-called Afro Turks) and in the Balkans. For example, there is an Albanian-speaking African diaspora community in Ulcinj, Montenegro (Canka 2013). Indeed, given the strong ties forged between Egypt and Albania during late Ottoman times, particularly under Mehmed Ali, founder of Egypt's Albanian dynasty, it is entirely possible that Albanian individuals returning to Albania from Egypt, or elsewhere in the Ottoman Empire, brought African slaves with them, to serve in their households or for resale in slave ports, like Ulcinj. As such, Jevg descent from Egyptian slaves, brought to Albania in Roman or post-Roman times, seems entirely plausible.

That said, the issue of Jevg identity is less a question of historical origins *per se*, and is more aptly framed in terms of collective memory. In post-Communist Albania, political control is very low and collective memory systems remain relatively open. Crises—both economic and political—have kept nostalgia—for any particular period of the past—and nationalism low as well, while imagination and identity-making operate at breakneck pace, accelerated by recent, almost universal access to the

Internet. In this context, various interest groups jockey for seats at the national table, including the Jevgs, who, like the Greeks of southern Albania, comprise an "active" ethnic group (Bintliff 2003: 140). Actively engaging ethno-religious identity politics runs counter to the typical Albanian mode of "passive" resistance and assimilation, characterized by the Arvanites of Greece, but also through time by Albanians, in general. As a result, Jevg counter-memories, which in some cases (e.g., Zemon 2001) posit a Jevg presence in Albania as old as or older than the Albanian presence, have come into conflict with emerging Albanian memory orthodoxies that revolve around autochthony, especially vis-à-vis the Serbs. The collective-memory conflicts pitting Albanians against Serbs mostly concern Kosovo's independence, which Serbs reject. Failed Jevg recognition efforts in Albania and Kosovo are thus a casualty of Albanian-Serb nationalism and national contests. This was certainly the case in the aftermath of the Kosovo War, when many Egyptians in Kosovo sided with the Serbs against the Albanians, and were subsequently expelled from their homes, along with most of the Serb population (Marushiakova and Popov 2013).

To summarize, each of these modern case studies demonstrates the important roles played by collective memory in nation-building efforts. In Egypt, Greece, and Albania, efforts were made to restrict memory systems and thereby facilitate political control. Doing so required crafting official, orthodox national imaginaries, built on small numbers of shared collective-memory engrams, and supported by cadres of professional "heritage" (i.e., memory) workers. The nationalistic imaginaries thus created left no room for counter-memory production and the promotion of alternate national identities, whether Nubian, Arvanite, or Jevg. Importantly, while in all three cases the goal was the same—harnessing collective memories in support of nation-building projects—the means varied. The Arab Republic of Egypt is the latest, most successful expression of Egypt's primary collective memory trope, that of unity in the face of countervailing, centrifugal forces. Egyptian unity depends on strict adherence to national codes that are today firmly rooted in one-party, military rule and an increasingly restrictive brand of Islam. Indeed, Egypt's generals and the Ulama (the Egyptian religious elite) may succeed where Akhenaten failed. Likewise, the Hellenic Republic aims to unify Greece by integrating age-old, highly-dispersed, competitive memory communities and constructing a modern, centralized national bureaucracy, based in Athens, where nearly 40 percent of the Greek population now lives. This Modern Greek nation is expressly dedicated to Classical Greek ideals, as enshrined in the constitution, and is officially committed to promoting the Greek Orthodox faith, preserving the Greek language, and realizing *omoinia* (i.e., concord). Greece's bureaucrats and priests may succeed where Alexander failed. Finally, the Albanians survived as a people by deploying and maintaining extremely flexible, highly stable collective memory systems. These systems were almost completely destroyed under Enver Hoxha. Today, a new generation of Albanian politicians, committed to full integration with the European Union, seeks to build an Albanian nation from the ground up. Unlike Egypt and Greece, in Albania religion does not serve as a national organizing principle; rather, as was also true during the *rilindja*, the Albanian National Awakening (from 1870 to 1912), the religion of Albanians remains Albanianism. This form of gut-level nationalism leaves no room for alternative identities, and we can therefore expect significant collective-memory competition and conflict in Albania in the near future, as different minority populations contest the emerging national imaginary. The new Albanian technocrats may well succeed where Hoxha (and Skanderbeg) failed, but it will not be easy.

THE ISLAMIC STATE

> A cafe owner from Palmyra who generally supports the government lamented the destruction [of the Temple of Baalshamin], speaking by telephone as he prepared to leave for Turkey by boat, perhaps for good.
> It was a local tradition, he said, to hold weddings at the temple. A nut tree grew inside its walls, residents said, where men sometimes played the oud. "They used to bring the bride and groom inside," he said, speaking on the condition of anonymity because he feared for his safety. "People used to go there to drink tea, coffee and barbecue. *All these memories have gone.*" —Barnard 2015 [italics added]

We now come to the penultimate section of this book. It will not be long; I am not an expert on terrorism and terrorist organizations. Rather, I use the Islamic State (IS, so named in 2014; also known as ISIL, the Islamic State in Iraq and the Levant, ISIS, the Islamic State in Iraq and al-Sham, and DAESH, the Arabic acronym) as an extreme example of contemporary nation building. I apply to IS the same collective memory model already used to address nation-building strategies in both ancient and modern states. Ultimately, I determine that there is little difference between the methods employed by IS and those employed by formative states through time, the world over, beginning as early as the Late Neolithic, in places like Egypt. Some might argue that there are differences in scale that separate the activities of ancient from modern states, and IS from other national actors. I think scale does matter, but would counter that differences in scale do not necessarily point to differences in kind and intent. For example, IS has access to technologies that the early Egyptian pharaohs did not—that can cause destruction quickly, from afar, with terrifying consequences—but their goals and strategies as regards collective memory and political control are similar, if not identical. Moreover, as a specifically Islamic nation-building enterprise, IS sits at the current end of a social-evolutionary process that began in the seventh century, with the Prophet himself. As I have already described, what accounts for some of the similarities in Egyptian, Greek, and Albanian history is their common experience of Islamic, specifically Ottoman, conquest and incorporation. The differences between the three in terms of their specific, idiosyncratic historical trajectories, however, relate directly to very different collective memory systems, communities, and counter-memory behaviors. An analysis of IS throws these differences into even sharper relief.

We can begin with the obvious: IS has made destroying *lieux de mémoire* in its territory, of all periods of the past, a top priority (see monthly reports at the ASOR-Cultural Heritage Initiatives website: http://www.asor-syrianheritage.org/). But destruction of cultural heritage is not and has never been, to the best of my knowledge, a stated, primary IS goal (see the 19-point list of IS fundamentals, released by IS in 2007, and reproduced in Bunzel 2015: 38–41). The Islamic State's antecedents were various terrorist organizations (e.g., beginning in 1999, JTWJ, followed by al-Qaeda in Iraq, MSM, and, by 2006, the Islamic State in Iraq, or ISI) that sought first, to undermine "apostate" Middle Eastern governments, such as that of Jordan, and second, following the 9-11 attacks in 2001, to expel American forces from Iraq (Lister 2015: 5–7). In 2003, they also began targeting the Iraqi Shia community, which was believed to constitute a direct obstacle and threat to the reestablishment of Sunni dominance in the region (Lister 2015: 7). On June 29, 2014, ISIS announced the restoration of a caliphate, with a capital at Raqqa in northern Syria (Lister 2015: 2). Given these practical, rather direct political and military objectives, it is difficult to explain the IS obsession with archaeological and historical sites and museums. What might destroying cultural heritage have to do with challenging Middle Eastern governments, fighting U.S. troops, killing Shia Muslims, and, most importantly, establishing a caliphate?

Some individuals, mostly journalists, have argued that the destruction of prominent archaeological monuments, like the Temple of Baalshamin at Palmyra, distracts from and masks industrial-scale looting at numerous, other, less famous archaeological sites and that the sale of looted artifacts helps fund IS activities. But there are multiple problems with this utilitarian explanation: among them, the profits gained from black-market sale of artifacts pales in comparison to the profits gained from (the easier) black-market sale of oil, and therefore seems counterproductive; obscure historical sites, such as mosques and churches, are not looting targets, but have been similarly destroyed; and artifacts from museums typically have been vandalized, often on film, not stolen and sold. As such, it is more likely that there exists an ideological, rather than an overtly economic, explanation for the Islamic State's devastation of cultural heritage sites.

IS ideology, including its religious ideology, is poorly understood (Bunzel 2015). At its most basic level, IS is a "Jihadi-Salafist" organization, which promotes an extreme, "pre-modern" brand of Islam (Lav 2012). It is Jihadi in its desire, like the Egyptian Muslim Brotherhood, to reestablish the caliphate (Bunzel 2015: 7–8). It is Salafist in its commitment to a sanitized practice of Islam, from which all potential idolatry has been scrubbed (Bunzel 2015: 8–9). In this, it has links to Saudi Wahhabism, which, like IS, is particularly antagonistic to Shia Islam, and encourages the destruction of Shia tombs and shrines, primarily because they are foci for idolatrous behaviors, such as the "worship" of various saints (Bunzel 2015: 9; see also Rentz 2004). This last bit provides a possible motivation for IS destruction of some tombs and mosques: those that are Shia and, more specifically, those that allow or encourage idolatry. But it does not help explain the destruction of non-Islamic heritage sites, archaeological sites in particular, by IS, except insofar as they are venues for idolatrous behavior, whether in the past or the present. To the best of my knowledge, Saudi Arabia, the most staunchly Wahhabist nation on the planet, has not destroyed pre-Islamic archaeological sites in its territory, and has supported regional archaeological survey and excavation projects, such as at ancient Jurash. The Taliban's 2001 dynamiting of Afghanistan's Bamiyan Buddhas may provide a rare, even singular, example of the complete destruction of a pre-Islamic heritage site by Muslim extremists for purely religious reasons. Even so, the reasons why Mullah Omar, the Taliban's leader, ordered the Buddhas destroyed remain unclear, and he is now dead (Falser 2011). In brief, an ideological explanation for the IS destruction of archaeological (and historic) sites based solely on religion falls short. Something else is going on.

I have already asserted, following Connerton (1989), that of all major religions, Islam is the most historical (i.e., historicizing) and least ritualized (i.e., ritualizing) in terms of practice and outlook. It therefore possesses, when coupled with state-level systems of administration, great potential for memory system closure and political control. Pushed to a Salafist extreme, Islam allows only very strict, highly circumscribed interpretations of the Koran, by a small number of specialists. Access to venues for collective memory production, including heritage sites, is restricted. As such, traditional memory workers become obsolete, or constitute threats, and are eliminated. Counter-memory behaviors that might generate viable, heterodox collective memory engrams, and thus threaten the status quo, are thereby also eliminated, or made difficult to pursue. The Islamic State fits this pattern perfectly and has endeavored, over the course of its short existence, to stamp out collective memory systems of all kinds. Applying my collective memory model to IS reaffirms this conclusion.

Most, if not all, traditional collective memory systems are rooted in highly distributed, domestic memory practices, including disposal and commemoration of the dead. It is therefore no surprise that Salafist governments, including IS, seek to modify family dynamics and disrupt mortuary systems. Throughout territories under its control, IS has killed male members of families, of all faiths and ethnicities, and wed (or enslaved) surviving wives and daughters to IS fighters, creating strict patriarchies (Alexander and Alexander 2015: 70–71, 187–88; Atwan 2015: 144–45). Women in the Islamic State are not allowed to leave, or work outside, the home and when they do, they must be fully covered and chaperoned by a male family member (Alexander and Alexander 2015: 155). Furthermore, in many IS cities, marking of graves is no longer allowed (Ibid.). Because women in many traditional societies are primary memory workers, and because they often operate within and through mortuary systems (e.g., in the composition and singing of laments), it makes sense that formative nation-states, like IS, should seek to control both, by concurrently limiting female agency and prohibiting commemoration of the dead.

At a slightly wider spatial scale, IS has disrupted the education of adults and children by replacing local public schools and places of worship with fundamentalist madrasas and Salafist mosques (Alexander and Alexander 2015: 68, 71; Atwan 2015: 145). In many cities, schools of any sort do not function at all and children are recruited as fighters (Alexander and Alexander 2015: 71–72). A nation's schools and places of worship generally support its orthodox memory systems. In the case of IS, schools and diverse religious institutions had to be closed or repurposed, and, in the case of the latter, often destroyed, if new mnemonic systems, or as I have argued above, amnemonic systems, were to be built. IS nation-building efforts are based not on collective memories but rather on very narrow, heterodox religious cum historical ideologies, justifying and enabling very high levels of political (and social) control.

In trying to build its caliphate, IS also sought means to consolidate regional political control. A key challenge has been managing many, very different, non-Sunni and, in some cases, non-Muslim populations, including Shia, Christians, Yazidis, and Kurds. The IS response to these populations has invariably involved forms of ethnic cleansing, including involuntary conversions, executions, and forced migrations (Alexander and Alexander 2015: 59–60). However, to be clear, integrating diverse ethnic communities is *always* a primary goal of nation-states and empires, whether modern or ancient, established or in formation. The Islamic State is no different. Moreover, the generally violent, genocidal approaches taken by IS to these communities are *not* unique, or even rare; they are common. Anyone who doubts this need only read ancient Babylonian poetry (George 2013) or descriptions of the conquest of the Americas by Europeans (Todorov 1999). In fact, diverse ethnic groups constitute profound threats to new nations precisely because they are fertile sources of counter-memories, which may be used to question and resist new national imaginaries. In the case of IS, the new national imaginary had been so narrowly and inflexibly conceived and drawn, with so little room for accommodation and expansion, that *all* competing collective memory communities in IS territory had to be exterminated, whether presently constituted or already dead. It was not enough to wipe out functioning memory communities and their *lieux de mémoire*. Ancient memory communities and their *lieux de mémoire* were targeted, too, in a process described by Alexander and Alexander (2015: 145) as "cultural annihilation." Throughout IS territory, archaeological sites have been bulldozed, including famous places like Nimrud and Palmyra, and memory workers, including archaeologists, have been murdered. In destroying these sites, the main goal was not to loot them: the looting and sale of artifacts was a lucrative collateral benefit. Rather, the main goal was to erase from the caliphate any potential source of collective counter-memories. By removing the mnemonic infrastructure from the landscape in full, IS rendered impotent any competing memory systems. When the archaeology went, so too did all the memories.

One interesting characteristic of the Islamic State is its sophisticated use of social media, both for recruiting purposes, but also as branding and marketing tools, leading Atwan (2015) to refer to IS as the "digital" caliphate. But social media cut both ways, of course. For example, they helped facilitate and encourage Arab Spring movements across the Middle East (Howard and Hussain 2013), producing a maelstrom of memory and counter-memory conflicts. Generally speaking, social media sites can act as cyber *lieux de mémoire*, helping disenfranchised memory communities share and preserve collective memory engrams, in particular when landscapes of memory have been disrupted (Birkner and Donk 2018). Digital, or "prosthetic" (Landsberg 2004), memory systems have appeared, for example, in response to the destruction of archaeological sites in IS territory, documenting and commemorating them via digital photo archives, satellite imagery, and, in some cases, laser scanning (Casana and Laugier 2017). For their part, IS leaders realize social media's potential for generating and promoting counter-memories and so they have sought to disrupt communications systems within their territory. All that said, nothing can ever replace intact, ancestral collective memory landscapes, as demonstrated by the Nubian example. Without them, cultures wither and die. Consequently, the wholesale destruction of memory landscapes is one very effective means of implementing genocide, and is generally cheaper and easier than mass murder. It is thus essential that we continue to study and understand how and why nations construct particular collective memory systems, and then promote or suppress them through time.

CONCLUSION

With reference to figure 1.2, there is little room in the Islamic State for imagination and identity formation. Opinions cannot be formulated and the realm of doxa is kept closed, based on a small number of narrowly defined, fundamental historical truths. IS leaders promote their ability to manage crisis (glossed as "savagery" and "barbarism"), based on Salafist principles, as a means to encourage stability (Atwan 2015: 156–64), which sets up a nostalgic desire for the peace and order of the original, medieval caliphate. Nationalism rides high, as witnessed in the numerous, online IS propaganda videos, and national histories are meant to span generations, having been promulgated in Salafist mosques. With reference to figure 1.3, political control in the Islamic State is very high and memory systems are tightly constrained. Ironically, IS political strategies are much like those of Communist Albania. However, whereas the former uses religion as a political weapon, the latter deployed state systems of atheism.

Ultimately, nations at either end of the political-mnemonic spectrum are characterized by volatility and have shorter life spans than those clustered at the center (figure 5.4). Of course, most of the nations at the "open" end of the spectrum, such as post-Communist Albania, Modern Bosnia, and post-Mubarak Egypt, are still in the process of forming; we have no way of knowing how long their life spans might ultimately be. Those on the other, "closed" end of the spectrum, such as Communist Albania, Communist Yugoslavia, Amarna Egypt, and the Islamic State, all had very short life spans (30 years, on average). Interestingly, those polities, such as the United States and the Ottoman Empire, that clump together at the center of figure 1.3 have life-spans of between 200 and 500 years. Moderate levels of political control coupled with relatively open, but not wide-open, memory systems would appear to generate relative stability. Democracy does not seem to be a shared, defining feature of these polities; rather, their willingness to accommodate various, interacting memory communities and to appropriate counter-memories, when necessary, would appear to be significant factors. Leaving aside very long, artificial archaeological periods, such as the Bronze Ages in Albania and Greece and Pre- and Early Dynastic Egypt, two long-lived empires, Byzantine and Arab, seem to buck these trends, and for different reasons.

Byzantine political control over conquered territories, including Greece, which emanated from Constantinople, was generally weak, backed by the

156   Chapter 5

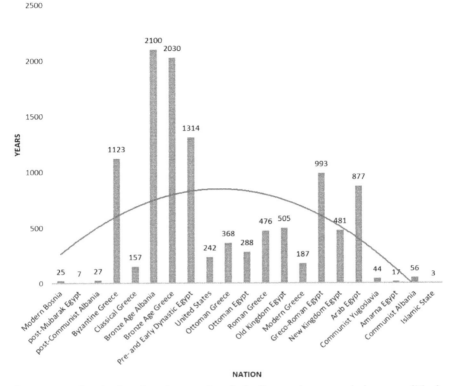

Figure 5.4. Graph of nation-states and periods discussed, arranged along a political-mnemonic scale from weak to strong, depicting varying life spans, created with reference to figure 1.3, producing a "normal" distribution. *Source:* M. L. Galaty.

military, and focused on tax collection. Paradoxically, rather than unifying the empire, Christianity divided it, particularly in Greece, where it was grafted onto remnants of the diverse memory communities of the Classical period. Because Byzantine imperial structures were flaccid and relatively ineffectual—they waxed and waned through time—memory systems remained open and flexible, reinforcing rather than closing Greece's age-old divisions. The Byzantine memory engine thus somehow managed to chug along in Greece for well over a millennium, demonstrating that nations composed of many, small, competing memory communities, and little overt political control, can be highly successful.

By contrast, Arab political control over conquered territories, like Egypt, was overt and unchecked, linked to religious, linguistic, and cultural domination of subject peoples. Arab Egypt provides a glimpse of what life under the Islamic State might have been like had it retained its regional integrity. Arab imperial strategies were linked to a strongly evangelizing religion, a primary goal of which was to build a global caliphate, a world community of believers, all of whom lived under Islamic principles of governance and law. The basis for this agenda was a single holy book, the Koran, leaving little or no room for counter-memory behaviors. Such a system is extremely difficult to create and maintain—it may prompt armed resistance, for example, since attacks on memory systems are, as I have noted, genocidal in intent and outcome—but once assembled, can be very stable and effective.

In many ways, the Ottoman Empire, as an extension of the Arab Empire, realized greater potential by moving toward the middle of the political-mnemonic spectrum, and had the advantage of also occupying former Byzantine territories. The Ottomans thereby wedded Islamic ideologies to Byzantine imperial infrastructure, creating a hybrid system of government. Different conquered peoples reacted differently to Ottoman occupation. The Greeks, who had not experienced Arab conquest, doubled-down on diversity, allowing Greek memory systems, which were highly distributed, to survive. The Albanians did as they had always done: they assimilated, forming syncretic memory systems that were, nevertheless, firmly grounded in a prehistoric, "Illyrian" past. Finally, the Egyptians, who had experienced several millennia of foreign domination, largely lost their collective memories and memory systems, and thus their identity as Egyptians. An Egyptian identity was only reconstructed after Ottoman conquest, under Mehmed Ali, forming the basis for a modern Egyptian nation.

These data, based on the analyses presented in chapters 2 through 4 and interpreted through the memory model outlined in chapter 1, present object lessons for today's world. First and foremost, archaeologists are necessary to the study of nations and nation building, both past and present, through their ability to reconstruct collective memories and memory systems. Ours is not a peripheral academic pursuit; rather, it is absolutely necessary if we are to make sense of world history, which is largely viewed, by most people, through the prism of memory. As I have endeavored to demonstrate in this book, memory is at the root of what it means to be human and human cognition would be impossible without it. Likewise, collective memory constitutes the foundation for all complex social formations, including states, and the modern world, as we know it, would be impossible without it. In order to form and function, nations must access and control, to some degree, the collective memory systems of their citizens. This often entails manipulating, or destroying, landscapes of memory, including mortuary monuments. Controlling collective memories facilitates political control, and vice versa. However, when leaders of nations, like Akhenaten, Hoxha, and

Baghdadi, close memory systems fully, stifling imagination and identity formation, unhealthy forms of nationalism and nostalgia bloom, leading to instability and, eventually, collapse. As a result, the best way to grow freedom and stability in the world is to support diverse, vibrant, non-competitive memory communities, from which new, powerful counter-memories may stem.

Epilogue
Alabama

Birmingham, Alabama. March 8, 2015. 10:00 a.m. Destination: Starkville, Mississippi. 65 degrees F. Memory: sun. The last game of the tournament ended and we hit the road. Liam was happy, having scored several goals. Georgia, our rescue beagle, was nervous. She hated car trips. Sylvia was seven months pregnant with Danny, large and uncomfortable. I was content.

Yesterday we had visited the 16th Street Baptist Church. An important stop on the Civil Rights trail, a National Historic Landmark, and a World Heritage site. Four young girls had been murdered there in 1963, killed by a coward's bomb. Somewhere, from across the street, in the park, a voice drifted, singing songs of resistance. Liam bows his head, then looks up and snaps a photo. He is only twelve years old. Old enough to understand, I think. Memory: dark brown hair, freckles, a camera, and light, glinting on stained glass.

The country roads from Birmingham to Selma are empty. It is Sunday in the South, after all. Folks are at church. Small farms dot the horizon, floating above the neon green, early spring grass. We stop for gas and a drink. Liam wants candy. Skittles. He loves Skittles. The station attendant smiles and nods. He is old and Black, face creased and care worn. *Where ya headed?* Selma. He smiles again, a knowing smile. Fifty years. What has changed?

Fifty years ago, Alabama was on fire. It began with a bus boycott. Followed by freedom rides, sit-ins, and Martin Luther King Jr.'s Letter from Birmingham City Jail: "We know through painful experience that freedom is never voluntarily given by the oppressor; it must be demanded by the oppressed." Then, the march, from Selma to Montgomery, seeking voting rights. The first attempt, on March 7, 1965, ended in chaos. "Sunday Bloody Sunday." Police, many of them on horseback, met the marchers as they crossed the Edmund Pettus Bridge, and beat them back. Fifty-nine were hospitalized. The second attempt, on March 9, was again thwarted, though this time by the courts, without violence. Finally, on March 21, the protesters, led by MLK himself, crossed the Alabama River. Four days later they arrived at the state capitol in Montgomery, 25,000 strong.

Selma, Alabama. March 8, 2015. 12:00 p.m. Destination: Starkville. 69 degrees F. Still sunny. We pull into Selma, escorted by Black motorcycle gangs and church buses. President Obama had been here the day before. The sun is hot, despite the moderate temperature. We find a shady street near downtown and park the car. Leave Georgia with some water.

The streets are eerily quiet. Many buildings stand abandoned, windows cracked, doors boarded up. Testament to an American South that continues to suffer, years after the Great Recession. Memory: red brick, graffiti, weeds.

We turn a corner onto Broad Street and the world opens up. Music thumps me in the chest. It is a carnival. We laugh in delight. The baby kicks. Smoke from BBQ grills and deep-fat fryers fills the air, billowing about. Thousands move slowly toward a distant destination, a shim-

Image 1.

mering hill, a giant metal gate: the bridge. We join the throng, pushed inexorably forward, caught in a human stream. People smile, swept along as well, incapable of resisting. Mostly Black faces, some White, all smiling.

We see aged veterans of the Civil Rights struggle. They wear T-shirts and carry posters, reading: I WAS HERE! An aged priest from Boston waves to the crowd. *I was here fifty years ago*! An old woman, unable to walk, is pushed by her granddaughter toward the bridge in a wheelchair. *I was here. I bled on Bloody Sunday*. Liam looks to me in confusion. He does not understand the significance. Tears (of gratitude? joy? sadness?) run down my face.

Members of various African American service organizations, segregated by sex, wait patiently in ranks for their turn to cross the bridge. Fraternities and sororities. Men, old and young, in tuxedos. Women, old and young, in their Sunday best, wearing giant, colorful hats. They wait,

Image 2.

quietly. Honoring their ancestors. Honoring those who came before. It is the 50th anniversary of the march.

We reach the base of the bridge and are lifted up onto it, pushed from behind by the muttering crowd. Teenagers snap selfies. A drum crew from South Africa bangs out a steady beat. Bit by bit we near the bridge's crest, headed towards the river's far bank. There, White troopers had met the (mostly) Black marchers with tear gas, dogs, and clubs. Congressman John Lewis, who was only 25 at the time, led the march. His skull was fractured. He almost died.

As we reach the other side of the bridge, I am shocked to see that the road is blocked by police, some on horseback. They greet us, not with anger and violence, but with hugs and bottles of water. Memory: a badge, a gloved hand, a sweaty embrace. I cannot help but think that some of these men must be the children of those same troopers who beat marchers, many almost to death, way back when, on Sunday Bloody Sunday. Fifty years. What has changed?

Sylvia is exhausted. We waste no time heading back across the bridge, against the tide, toward our car. Liam eats a funnel cake as we walk. Georgia is relieved to see us.

I reflect on the day as I drive. How can we explain the change in attitude, in behavior, that marked today's march versus that of 50 years ago?

Image 3.

Epilogue

Image 4.

Did Blacks in fact demand and receive their freedom? Or, did Whites (in the words of Lauryn Hill) get "right" within?

Starkville, Mississippi. March 8, 2015. 8:00 p.m. 60 degrees F. Stormy. We passed through Tuscaloosa just as the sun set. The sky glowed red and dark clouds gathered in the west. Lightning flashed. It is difficult to square the idea of racial reconciliation with reality. Edmund Pettus was a Confederate general and a grand dragon of the KKK. There are nearly 1,500 Confederate monuments in the United States. In most surveys, a majority of Americans prefer that the monuments not be removed, despite their overtly racist symbolism. Why?

Most scholars explain the existence of Confederate monuments in historical terms. But when a Southerner defends a Confederate monument, only rarely does he make an historical argument. Something deeper is at work. Something much more visceral than history. Something primeval.

Memory.

His Daddy told him to remember his Confederate ancestors. And his Daddy before him. The last Confederate soldier died in 1951. Scarcely three generations ago. Removing monuments is a direct attack on collective memory—whether "right" or "wrong"—and is perceived as such. One more step in the American nation-building effort, at the heart of which have always been conflicts over memory.

Image 5.

Now, in 2018, as I write these words, Danny has been born and Liam has died. Like anthropologist Renato Rosaldo, who could not understand the grief and rage that drove Ilongot men to head hunt until his wife, Michelle, had died, I, too, could not really appreciate the force with which death confronts memory until my son died. When a Neolithic father buried his child under the floor of his house, alongside his grandparents, a new link in a collective memory chain was forged. Such chains of memory connect us, today, across time, across the generations, to our ancestors, to the recent and deeper past. Memory echoes across the ages in ways obvious and imperceptible. Without this understanding, the task of archaeology, as memory work, will remain incomplete. Without this understanding, the task of building a "more perfect union" will continue to elude us.

Bibliography

Adler, Michael A., and Richard H. Wilshussen
  1990 Large-Scale Integrative Facilities in Tribal Societies: Cross-Cultural and Southwestern U.S. Examples. *World Archaeology* 22: 133–45.

Alcock, Susan E.
  1993 *Graecia Capta: The Landscapes of Roman Greece*. Cambridge: Cambridge University Press.

Alcock, Susan E.
  2002 *Archaeologies of the Greek Past: Landscape, Monuments, and Memories*. Cambridge: Cambridge University Press.

Alexander, Yonah, and Dean Alexander
  2015 *The Islamic State: Combating the Caliphate without Borders*. London: Lexington Books.

Al-Messiri, Nawal
  1978 The Sheikh Cult in Dahmit. In *Nubian Ceremonial Life: Studies in Islamic Syncretism and Cultural Change*, edited by John Kennedy, pp. 61–103. Los Angeles: University of California Press.

Amore, Maria Grazia
  2010 *The Complex of Tumuli 9, 10, and 11 in the Necropolis of Apollonia (Albania)*. Volumes I and II. BAR International Series 2059(I and II). Oxford: British Archaeological Reports/Archaeopress.

Amore, Maria Grazia, Lorenc Bejko, Ylli Cerova, and Ilir Gjipali
  2001 The Via Egnatia (Albania) Project and the Bridge at Topcias. *Journal of Roman Archaeology* 14: 381–89.

Anderson, Benedict
1983 *Imagined Communities: Reflections on the Origin and Spread of Nationalism.* London: Verso.

Andrea, Zhaneta
2005 Varrë të Periudhës Antike të Vonë dhe Asaj Mesjatre në Varrezat tumulare të Pellgut të Korcës dhe në Varrezën e Sheshtë të Gërmenjit. *Candavia* 2: 349–60.

Anheier, Helmut, and Yudhishthir Raj Isar (eds.)
2011 *Heritage, Memory, and Identity.* The Cultures and Globalization Series 4. Los Angeles: Sage.

Appadurai, Arjun
1996 *Modernity at Large: Cultural Dimensions of Globalization.* Minneapolis: University of Minnesota Press.

Arrian
1971 *The Campaigns of Alexander.* Translated by Aubrey de Sélincourt. New York: Penguin Books.

Ashby, Solange
2016 *Calling out to Isis: The Enduring Nubian Presence at Philae.* Unpublished Ph.D. dissertation. University of Chicago, Department of Near Eastern languages and Civilizations.

Assmann, Jan
1992 *Das kulturelleGedächtnis: Schrift, Erinnerung und politische Identität in frühen Hochkulturen.* Munich: Beck.

Assmann, Jan
1997 *Moses the Egyptian: The Memory of Egypt in Western Monotheism.* Cambridge: Harvard University Press.

Assmann, Jan
2002 *The Mind of Egypt: History and Meaning in the Time of the Pharoahs.* Translated by Andrew Jenkins. New York: Henry Holt and Company.

Assmann, Jan
2008 Communicative and Cultural Memory. In *Cultural Memory Studies: An International and Interdisciplinary Handbook,* edited by Astrid Erll and Ansgar Nünning, pp. 109–18. New York: de Gruyter.

Athanassopoulou, Angélique
2005 Nos Albanais à nous: Travailleurs émigrés dans une communauté arvanite du Péloponnèse. *Ethnologie française* 35: 267–78.

Atwan, Abdel Bari
2015 *Islamic State: The Digital Caliphate.* London: Saqi Books.

Bahloul, Joell
1996 *The Architecture of Memory: A Jewish-Muslim Household in Colonial Algeria, 1937-1962.* Cambridge: Cambridge University Press.

Bailey, Douglass
  2005   *Prehistoric Figurines: Representation and Corporeality in the Neolithic.* London: Routledge.

Bal, Mieke
  1999   Introduction. In *Acts of Memory: Cultural Recall in the Present*, edited by M. Bal, J. Crew, and L. Spitzer, vii–xvii. Hanover: University Press of New England.

Baram, Uzi, and Lynda Carroll
  2002   *A Historical Archaeology of the Ottoman Empire: Breaking New Ground.* New York: Kluwer Academic Publishers.

Barnard, Anne
  2015   ISIS Speeds Up Destruction of Antiquities in Syria. Available at: https://www.nytimes.com/2015/08/25/world/isis-accelerates-destruction-of-antiquities-in-syria.html. Accessed: October 17, 2017.

Bartlett, Frederic C.
  1932   *Remembering: An Experimental and Social Study.* Cambridge: Cambridge University Press.

Basso, Keith H.
  1996   *Wisdom Sits in Places: Landscape and Language Among the Western Apache.* Albuquerque: University of New Mexico Press.

Bastide, Roger
  1970   Mémoire collective et sociologie du bricolage. *L'Année sociologique* XXI: 65–108.

Beaton, Roderick
  2003   *George Seferis: Waiting for the Angel, a Biography.* New Haven: Yale University Press.

Bejko, Lorenc
  2014   Research on Tumuli in Albanian Archaeology. In *The Excavation of the Prehistoric Burial Tumulus at Lofkënd, Albania*, edited by John K. Papadopoulos, Sarah P. Morris, Lorenc Bejko, and Lynne A. Schepartz, pp. 517–24. Monumenta Archaeologica 34. Los Angeles: UCLA Cotsen Institute of Archaeology Press.

Bejko, Lorenc, Todd Fenton, and David Foran
  2006   Recent Advances in Albanian Mortuary Archaeology, Human Osteology, and Ancient DNA. In *New Directions in Albanian Archaeology: Studies Presented to Muzafer Korkuti*, edited by Lorenc Bejko and Richard Hodges, pp. 309–22. International Center for Albanian Archaeology Monograph Series No. 1. Tirana: ICAA.

Bendall, Lisa M.
  2004   Fit for a King? Exclusion, Hierarchy, Aspiration and Desire in the Social Structure of Mycenaean Banqueting. In *Food, Cuisine and Society in Prehistoric Greece. Proceedings of the 10th Aegean Round Table, University of*

Sheffield, January 19–21, 2001, edited by Paul Halstead and John Barrett, pp. 105–35. Sheffield Studies in Aegean Archaeology 5. Oxford: Oxbow.

Bennet, John
  1995 Space Through Time: Diachronic Perspectives on the Spatial Organization of the Pylian State. In *POLITEIA. Society and State in the Aegean Bronze Age*, edited by W.D. Neimeier and R. Laffineur, pp. 587–602. Austin: University of Texas at Austin Program in Aegean Scripts and Prehistory.

Benton, Tim (ed.)
  2010 *Understanding Heritage and Memory*. Manchester: Manchester University Press.

Ben-Yehuda, Nachman
  1995 *The Masada Myth: Collective Memory and Mythmaking in Israel*. Madison: University of Wisconsin Press.

Bergson, Henri
  2004 *Matter and Memory*. Republication of the 1912 Macmillan edition. Translated by N. Margaret Paul and W. Scott Palmer. Mineola, NY: Dover Publications.

Bernal, Martin
  1987 *Black Athena: Afroasiatic Roots of Classical Civilization, Volume I: The Fabrication of Ancient Greece, 1785–1985*. New Brunswick: Rutgers University Press.

Bernal, Martin
  1991 *Black Athena: Afroasiatic Roots of Classical Civilization, Volume II: The Archaeological and Documentary Evidence*. New Brunswick: Rutgers University Press.

Bernal, Martin
  2006 *Black Athena: The Afroasiatic Roots of Classical Civilization, Volume III: The Linguistic Evidence*. New Brunswick: Rutgers University Press.

Bialor, Peter
  2008 Chapter 2, Greek Ethnic Survival Under Ottoman Domination. Amherst Research Report 09: The Limits of Integration: Ethnicity and Nationalism in Modern Europe. University of Massachusetts—Amherst ScholarWorks@UMass. Available at: http://scholarworks.umass.edu/cgi/viewcontent.cgi?article=1002&context=anthro_res_rpt9. Accessed: December 28, 2016.

Bintliff, John
  2003 The Ethnoarchaeology of a "Passive" Ethnicity: The Arvanites of Central Greece. In The Usable Past: Greek Metahistories, edited by K.S. Brown and Yannis Hamilakis, pp. 129–44. Lanham, MD: Lexington Books.

Birkner, Thomas, and André Donk
  2018 Collective Memory and Social Media: Fostering a New Historical Consciousness in the Digital Age? *Memory Studies* 1: 1–17.

Black, David W., Donald Kunze, and John Pickles (eds.)
  1989 *Commonplaces: Essays on the Nature of Place*. Lanham, MD: University Press of America.

Bland, William
  1992 Albania after the Second World War. In *Perspectives on Albania*, edited by Tom Winnifrith, pp. 123–36. London: Palgrave Macmillan.

Blanton, Richard E., Gary M. Feinman, Stephen A. Kowalewski, and Peter N. Peregrine
  1996 A Dual-Processual Theory for the Evolution of Mesoamerican Civilization. *Current Anthropology* 37: 1–14.

Bodnar, John
  1992 *Remaking America: Public Memory, Commemoration, and Patriotism in the Twentieth Century*. Princeton: Princeton University Press.

Bonanno Anthony, Tancred Gouder, Caroline Malone, and Simon Stoddart
  1990 Monuments in an Island Society: The Maltese Context. *World Archaeology* 22: 190–205.

Boozer, Anna
  2010 Memory and Microhistory of an Empire: Domestic Contexts in Roman Amheida, Egypt. In *Archaeology and Memory*, edited by D. Borić, pp. 138–57. Oxford: Oxbow Books.

Borg, Alan
  1991 *War Memorials: From Antiquity to the Present*. London: Leo Cooper.

Bourdieu, Pierre
  1977 *Outline of a Theory of Practice*. Cambridge: Cambridge University Press.

Bradley, Richard
  2003 Time in Translation. In *Archaeologies of Memory*, edited by Susan Alcock and Ruth Van Dyke, pp. 221–27. Oxford: Blackwell.

Bradley, Richard
  1990 Monuments and the Monumental. *World Archaeology* 22: 119–243.

Braudel, Fernand
  1972 *The Mediterranean and the Mediterranean World in the Age of Philip II, Vol. 1*. Translated by S. Reynolds. New York: Harper & Row.

Breasted, James Henry
  1906 *Ancient Records of Egypt*. Chicago: University of Chicago Press.

Brewer, David
  2011 *The Greek War of Independence*. London: Overlook Duckworth.

Buchet, Luc, Elvana Metalla, and Etleva Nallbani
  2008 Lissos, Alessio (Albania). Espace des Morts et Organisation de l'Habitat Médiéval. In *Les Destinées de l'Illyricum Meridional Pendant le haut Moyen Age*. MEFRM 120-22: 438–443.

Bunzel, Cole
    2015   *From Paper State to Caliphate: The Ideology of the Islamic State*. The Brookings Project on U.S. Relations with the Islamic World, Analysis Paper No. 19. Center for Middle East Policy, the Brookings Institution.

Camaj, Martin
    1989   Foreward. *Kanuni i Lekë Dukagjinit* [The Code of Lekë Dukagjini], pp. xiii–xv. Translated by Leonard Fox. New York: Gjonlekaj Publishing Company.

Canka, Mustafa
    2013   Only Memories and Emptiness Remain: The History of Ulcinj's Afro-Albanian Community in Montenegro. Available at: http://www.criticatac.ro/lefteast/only-memories-and-emptiness-remain-the-history-of-ulcinjs-afro-albanian-community-in-montenegro/. Accessed: October 16, 2017.

Carruthers, Mary
    1990   *The Book of Memory: A Study of Memory in Medieval Culture*. Cambridge: Cambridge University Press.

Casana, Jesse, and Elise Jakoby Laugier
    2017   Satellite Imagery-based Monitoring of Archaeological Site Damage in the Syrian Civil War. *PLoS ONE* 12(11): e0188589. https://doi.org/10.1371/journal.pone.0188589.

Casey, Edward S.
    1996   How to Get from Space to Place in a Fairly Short Stretch of Time: Phenomenological Prolegomena. In *Senses of Place*, edited by Steven Feld and Keith H. Basso, pp. 13–52. Santa Fe: School for Advanced Research Press.

Casey, Edward S.
    1987   *Remembering: A Phenomenological Study*. Bloomington: Indiana University Press.

Cavafy, C.P.
    1992   *Collected Poems*. Translated by Edmund Keeley and Philip Sherrard, edited by George Savidis. Revised Edition. Princeton: Princeton University Press.

Cavanagh, William
    2008   Death and the Mycenaeans. In *The Cambridge Companion to Aegean Bronze Age*, edited by Cynthia W. Shelmerdine, pp. 327–41. Cambridge: Cambridge University Press.

Cavanagh, William, Joost Crouwel, R. W. V. Catling, and Graham Shipley (eds.)
    2002   *Continuity and Change in a Greek Rural Landscape: The Laconia Survey, Volume I: Methodology and Interpretation*. London: British School at Athens.

Ceka, Neritan
    1986   Amfora Antike nga Margëlliçit. *Iliria* 16(2): 71–98.

Ceka, Neritan
 1987 Arkitektura e qytezës së Margëlliçi. *Monumentet* 33: 5–25.

Ceka, Neritan
 2005 *The Illyrians to the Albanians*. Tirana: Migjeni.

Ceka, Neritan
 2014 The Time and Place of the Formation of the Albanians in the Middle Ages. In *International Congress of Albanian Archaeological Studies*, edited by L. Përzhita, I. Gjipali, G. Hoxha, and B. Muka, pp. 527–46. Tirana: Albanian Institute of Archaeology.

Census-AL
 2011 Population and Housing Census of Albania, 2011. Republic of Albania, Institute of Statistics. Available at: http://www.instat.gov.al/media/177354/main_results__population_and_housing_census_2011.pdf. Accessed: December 29, 2016.

Cherry, John F.
 1986 Palaces and Polities: Some Problems in Minoan State Formation. In *Peer Polity Interaction and Sociopolitical Change*, edited by Colin Renfrew and John F. Cherry, pp. 19–45. Cambridge: Cambridge University Press.

Cherry, John F.
 2001 Travel, Nostalgia, and Pausanias's Giant. In *Pausanias: Travel and Imagination in Roman Greece*, edited by Susan E. Alcock, John F. Cherry, and Jaś Elsner, pp. 247–55. New York: Oxford University Press.

CIA World Factbook
 2016 Egypt. Available at: https://www.cia.gov/library/publications/the-world-factbook/geos/eg.html. Accessed: December 28, 2016.

Clastres, Pierre
 1989 *Society Against the State: Essays in Political Anthropology*. Translated by R. Hurley and A. Stein. New York: Zone Books.

Clogg, David
 1976 *The Movement for Greek Independence, 1770–1821: A Collection of Documents*. London: Macmillan.

Clogg, David (ed.)
 2002 *Minorities in Greece: Aspects of a Plural Society*. London: Hurst and Company.

Cohen, Anthony P.
 1985 *The Symbolic Construction of Community*. London: Routledge.

Coleman, Janet
 1992 *Ancient and Medieval Memories: Studies in the Reconstruction of the Past*. Cambridge: Cambridge University Press.

Comaroff, Jean, and John Comaroff
 1991 *Of Revelation and Revolution: Christianity, Colonialism, and Consciousness in South Africa*. Volume 1. Chicago: University of Chicago Press.

Connerton, Paul
    1989   *How Societies Remember*. Cambridge: Cambridge University Press.

Cooney, Kathlyn M.
    2012   Coffin Re-use in the Twenty-First Dynasty: The Demands of Ritual Transformation. *Backdirt: Annual Review of the Cotsen Institute of Archaeology at UCLA* 2012: 22–33.

Coser, Lewis A.
    1992   Introduction: Maurice Halbwachs 1877–1945. In *On Collective Memory*, by Maurice Halbwachs, pp. 1–36. Chicago: University of Chicago Press.

Crawford, Harriet (ed.)
    2007   *Regime Change in the Ancient Near East and Egypt: From Sargon of Agade to Saddam Hussein*. Oxford: Oxford University Press.

Dafalla, Hassan
    1975   *The Nubian Exodus*. London: C. Hurst & Company.

Danforth, Loring
    1982   *The Death Rituals of Rural Greece*. Princeton: Princeton University Press.

Davis, Jack L., Muzafer Korkuti, Lorenc Bejko, Michael L. Galaty, Skendër Muçaj, and Sharon R. Stocker
    2002–2003   The Hinterlands of Apollonia. *Iliria* 31(1–2): 305–22.

Davis, Jack L., Muzafer Korkuti, Lorenc Bejko, Michael L. Galaty, Skendër Muçaj, and Sharon R. Stocker
    2007   The Hinterlands of Apollonia. In *Apollonia d'Illyrie. 1. Atlas Archéologique et Historique*, edited by V. Dhimo, P. Lenhardt, and F. Quantin, pp. 13–23. Collection de l'École Française de Rome – 391. Rome.

De Rapper, Giles
    2009   Pelasgic Encounters in the Greek-Albanian Borderland. Border Dynamics and Reversion to Ancient Past in Southern Albania. *Anthropological Journal of European Cultures* 18(1): 50–68.

Deskaj, Sylvia
    2017   Living Among the Dead: Establishing and Maintaining Community in Northern Albania. *Archaeological Papers of the American Anthropological Association* 28(1): 82–90.

De Soto, Hermine G., Sabine Beddies, and Ilir Gedeshi
    2005   *Roma and Egyptians in Albania: From Social Exclusion to Social Inclusion*. World Bank Working Paper No. 53. Washington, D.C.: The World Bank.

Dillehay, Tom D.
    1990   Mapuche Ceremonial Landscape, Social Recruitment and Resource Rights. *World Archaeology* 22(2): 223–41.

Dimo, Vangjel, Phillipe Lenhardt, and François Quantin
    2007   Le Monastère Sainte-Marie et Ses Environs. In *Apollonia d'Illyrie. 1. Atlas Archéologique et Historique*, edited by V. Dhimo, P. Lenhardt, and F. Quantin, pp. 275–90. Collection de l'École Française de Rome – 391. Rome.

Drews, Robert
   1993   *The End of the Bronze Age: Changes in Warfare and the Catastrophe ca. 1200 BC*. Princeton: Princeton University Press.

Duke, Phillip
   2016   *The Tourists Gaze, The Cretans Glance: Archaeology and Tourism on a Greek Island*. London: Routledge.

Durham, M. Edith
   2000 [1909]   *High Albania: A Victorian Traveller's Balkan Odyssey*. Edward Arnold, London. 2000 reprint ed. Phoenix Press, London.

Dykstra, Darrell
   1998   The French Occupation of Egypt, 1798–1801. In *The Cambridge History of Egypt, Vol. 2. Modern Egypt, from 1517 to the End of the Twentieth Century*, edited by M. W. Daly, pp. 113–38. Cambridge: Cambridge University Press.

Dzino, Daniel
   2010   *Becoming Slav, Becoming Croat: Identity Transformations in Post-Roman and Early Medieval Dalmatia*. Leiden: Brill.

Eaton, Jonathan, and Elenita Roshi
   2014   Chiseling Away at a Concrete Legacy: Engaging with Communist-era Heritage and Memory in Albania. *Journal of Field Archaeology* 39(3): 312–19.

Ebbinghaus, Hermann
   1885   *Memory: A Contribution to Experimental Psychology*. New York: Dover.

Eber, Dena Elisabeth, and Arthur G. Neal
   2001   The Individual and Collective Search for Identity. In *Memory and Representation: Constructed Truths and Competing Realities*, edited by Dena E. Eber and Arthur G. Neal, pp. 169–82. Bowling Green: Bowling Green State University Popular Press.

Elsie, Robert
   2000   The Christian Saints of Albania. *Balkanistica* 13: 35–57.

Elsie, Robert
   2001   *A Dictionary of Albanian Religion, Mythology, and Folk Culture*. London: Hurst and Company.

Elsie, Robert, and Janice Mathie-Heck
   2004   *Songs of the Frontier Warriors*. Wauconda, IL: Bolchazy-Carducci Publishers, Inc.

Erll, Astrid
   2011   *Memory in Culture*. Translated by Sara B. Young. New York: Palgrave Macmillan.

Fahim, Hussein M.
   1983   *Egyptian Nubians: Resettlement and Years of Coping*. Salt Lake City: University of Utah Press.

Fahim, Hussein M.
   2010   Change in Religion in a Resettled Nubian Community, Upper Egypt. In *Nubian Encounters: The Story of the Nubian Ethnological Survey 1961–1964*, edited by Nicholas S. Hopkins and Sohair R. Mehenna, pp. 209–26. Cairo: American University in Cairo Press.

Fahmy, Khaled
   1997   *All the Pasha's Men: Mehmed Ali, His Army and the Making of Modern Egypt*. Cambridge: Cambridge University Press.

Fahmy, Khaled
   1998   The Era of Muhammad 'Ali Pasha, 1805–1848. In *The Cambridge History of Egypt, Vol. 2. Modern Egypt, from 1517 to the End of the Twentieth Century*, edited by M. W. Daly, pp. 139–79. Cambridge: Cambridge University Press.

Falser, Michael
   2011   The Bamiyan Buddhas, Performative Iconoclasm and the "Image of Heritage." In T*he Image of Heritage: Changing Perception, Permanent Responsibilities*, edited by Andrzej Tomaszewski and Simone Giometti, pp. 157–69. Firenze: Edizioni Polistampa.

Fasolo, Michele
   2003   *La Via Egnatia I: Da Apollonia e Dyrrachium ad Herakleia Lynkestidos*. Viae Publicae Romanae I. Rome.

Feld, Steven, and Keith H. Basso (eds.)
   1996   *Senses of Place*. Santa Fe: School for Advanced Research Press.

Feldman, Marian H.
   2012   The Practical Logic of Style and Memory in Early First Millennium Levantine Ivories. In *Materiality and Social Practice: Transformative Capacities of Intercultural Encounters*, edited by Joseph Maran and Philipp W. Stockhammer, pp. 198–212. Oxford: Oxbow Books.

Fentress, James, and Chris Wickham
   1992   *Social Memory*. Oxford: Blackwell.

Fermor, Patrick Leigh
   1958   *Mani: Travels in the Southern Peloponnese*. New York: New York Review of Books.

Fernea, Robert A.
   1973   *Nubians in Egypt: Peaceful People*. Austin: University of Texas Press.

Fischer, Bernd Jürgen
   1999   *Albania at War, 1939–1945*. London: C. Hurst & Co. Publishers.

Flannery, Kent V., and Joyce Marcus
   2013   *The Creation of Inequality*. Cambridge: Harvard University Press.

Forty, Adrian
   1999   Introduction. In *Materializing Culture: The Art of Forgetting*, edited by A. Forty and S. Küchler, 1–18. Oxford: Berg.

Foucault, Michel
   1980   *Language, Counter-Memory, Practice: Selected Essays and Interviews*. Ithaca: Cornell University Press.

Fowles, Severin
   2002   From Social Type to Social Process: Placing "Tribe" in a Historical Framework. In *The Archaeology of Tribal Societies*, edited by William A. Parkinson, pp. 13–33. Ann Arbor: International Monographs in Prehistory.

Fox, Leonard
   1989   Introduction. *Kanuni i Lekë Dukagjinit* [The Code of Lekë Dukagjini], pp. xvi–xix. Translated by Leonard Fox. New York: Gjonlekaj Publishing Company.

Freud, Sigmund
   1939   *Moses and Monotheism*. Translated by Katherine Jones. New York: Vintage Books.

Fried, Marc
   1963   Grieving for a Lost Home. In *The Urban Condition: People and Policy in the Metropolis*, edited by Leonard J. Duhl, pp. 151–71. New York: Basic Books.

Friedl, Ernestine
   1962   *Vasilika: A Village in Modern Greece*. New York: Holt, Rinehart, and Winston, Inc.

Funkenstein, Amos
   1993   *Perceptions of Jewish History*. Los Angeles: University of California Press.

Galaty, Michael L.
   2002   Modeling the Formation and Evolution of an Illyrian Tribal System: Ethnographic and Archaeological Analogs. In *The Archaeology of Tribal Societies*, edited by W. Parkinson, pp. 109–22. International Monographs in Prehistory, Archaeological Series #15, Ann Arbor: International Monographs in Prehistory.

Galaty, Michael L.
   2011   Blood of Our Ancestors: Cultural Heritage Management in the Balkans. In *Contested Cultural Heritage: Religion, Nationalism, Erasure, and Exclusion in a Global World*, edited by Helaine Silverman, pp. 109–24. Springer, New York.

Galaty, Michael L.
   2016   The Mycenaeanisation Process. In *Beyond Thalassocracies. Understanding Processes of Minoanisation and Mycenaeanisation in the Aegean*, edited by E. Gorogianni, P. Pavúk, and L. Girella, pp. 207–18. Oxford: Oxbow Books.

Galaty, Michael L., Ols Lafe, Wayne E. Lee, and Zamir Tafilica
   2013   *Light and Shadow: Isolation and Interaction in the Shala Valley of Northern Albania*. Monumenta Archaeologica 28. Los Angeles: UCLA Cotsen Institute of Archaeology Press.

Galaty, Michael L., Skendër Muçaj, Sharon R. Stocker, Michael Timpson, and Jack L. Davis
  2004 Excavation of a Hellenistic Farmhouse in the Vicinity of Apollonia. In *L'Illyrie Mériondale et l'Epire dans l'Antiquité –IV. Actes du IVe colloque international de Grenoble (10–12 octobre 2002)*, edited by P. Cabanes and J.-L. Lamboley, 299–305. Paris: De Boccard.

Galaty, Michael L., William A. Parkinson, John F. Cherry, Eric H. Cline, P. Nick Kardulias, Robert Schon, Susan Sherratt, Helena Tomas, and David Wengrow
  2009 Interaction Amidst Diversity: An Introduction to the Eastern Mediterranean Bronze Age. In *Archaic State Interaction: The Eastern Mediterranean in the Bronze Age*, edited by William A. Parkinson and Michael L. Galaty, pp. 29–51. Santa Fe: School for Advanced Research Press.

Galaty, Michael L., Sharon R. Stocker, and Charles Watkinson
  1999 Beyond Bunkers: Dominance, Resistance, and Change in an Albanian Regional Landscape. *Journal of Mediterranean Archaeology* 12(2): 197–214.

Galaty, Michael L., Sharon R. Stocker, and Charles Watkinson
  2009 The Snake That Bites: The Albanian Experience of Collective Trauma as Reflected in an Evolving Landscape. In *The Trauma Controversy*, edited by K. Brown Golden and B.G. Bergo, pp. 171–88. Albany: SUNY Press.

Galaty, Michael L., and Charles Watkinson
  2004 The Practice of Archaeology under Dictatorship. In *Archaeology under Dictatorship*, edited by Michael L. Galaty and Charles Watkinson, pp. 1–18. New York: Kluwer Academic/Plenum Publishers.

Galaty, Michael L., Lorenc Bejko, Sylvia Deskaj, Richard Yerkes, Susan Allen, and Rachelann Bolus
  n.d. Landscape Archaeology in Northern Albania: Results of the 2014 Field Season of the Projekti Arkeologjik i Shkodrës (PASH). For *Landscapes of Southeastern Europe,* edited by L. Mirosevic, G. Zaro, M. Katic, and D. Birt. Lit Verlag Berlin-London-Munster-Wien-Zurich.

Galicki, Stanley, Catherine Henry, Michael L. Galaty, and Lorenc Bejko
  n.d. Medieval Anthropogenic Nonpoint Source Sediment Runoff in the Wetland Fringe of Lake Shkodra, Albania. Submitted to *Geomorphology*.

Geary, Patrick J.
  1994 *Living with the Dead in the Middle Ages*. Ithaca: Cornell University Press.

Geertz, Clifford
  1973 *The Interpretation of Cultures*. New York: Basic Books.

Geiser, Peter
  1973 The Myth of the Dam. *American Anthropologist* 75: 184–94.

George, Andrew
  2013 The Poem of Erra and Ishum: A Babylonian Poet's View of War. In *Warfare and Poetry in the Middle East*, edited by Hugh Kennedy, pp. 39–71. London: I. B. Tauris.

Giblin, Julia I.
2018 Radiogenic Strontium Isotope Results from the Burials of Alepotrypa Cave. In *Neolithic Alepotrypa Cave in the Mani, Greece*, edited by Anastasia Papathanasiou, William A. Parkinson, Daniel J. Pullen, Michael L. Galaty, and Panagiotis Karkanas, pp. 306–15. Oxford: Oxbow Books.

Gjeçov, Shtjefën
1989 *Kanuni i Lekë Dukagjinit* [The Code of Lekë Dukagjini]. Translated by Leonard Fox. New York: Gjonlekaj Publishing Company.

Gogonas, Nikos
2010 *Bilingualism and Multiculturalism in Greek Education: Investigating Native Language Maintenance among Pupils of Albanian and Egyptian Origins in Athens*. Cambridge: Cambridge Scholars Publishing.

Golden Dawn
2017 Επιβεβαιώθηκε η φυλετική συνέχεια των Ελλήνων για πάνω από 4000 χρόνια. Available at: http://www.xryshaygh.com/enimerosi/view/epibebaiwthhke-h-fuletikh-sunecheia-twn-ellhnwn-gia-panw-apo-4000-chronia/ Accessed: September 27, 2017.

Goody, Jack (ed.)
1968 *Literacy in Traditional Societies*. Cambridge: Cambridge University Press.

Goody, Jack
1977 *The Domestication of the Savage Mind*. Cambridge: Cambridge University Press.

Goody, Jack
1986 *The Logic of Writing and the Organisation of Society*. Cambridge: Cambridge University Press.

Goody, Jack
1987 *The Interface between the Written and the Oral*. Cambridge: Cambridge University Press.

Goody, Jack
1998 Memory in Oral Tradition. In *Memory*, edited by Patricia Fara and Karalyn Patterson, pp. 73–94. Cambridge: Cambridge University Press.

Green, Peter
1991 *Alexander of Macedon, 356–323 B.C.: A Historical Biography*. Berkeley: University of California Press.

Greenhalgh, Peter, and Edward Eliopoulos
1985 *Deep into Mani: Journey to the Southern Tip of Greece*. London: Faber and Faber.

Greek Tourism Confederation
2017 Greek Tourism Basic Figures Repository. Available at: http://sete.gr/en/strategy-for-tourism/basic-figures-repository/. Accessed: September 26, 2017.

Halbwachs, Maurice
 1941 *La topographie légendaire des Évangiles en Terre Sainte: étude de mémoirecollective*. Paris: Presses universitaires de France.

Halbwachs, Maurice
 1980 *The Collective Memory*. Translated by Francis J. Ditter, Jr. and Vida Yazdi Ditter. New York: Harper Colophon Books.

Halbwachs, Maurice
 1992 *On Collective Memory*. Translated by Lewis Coser. Chicago: University of Chicago Press.

Hamilakis, Yannis
 1998 Eating the Dead: Mortuary Feasting and the Politics of Memory in the Aegean Bronze Age. In *Cemetery and Society in the Aegean Bronze Age*, edited by Keith Branigan, pp. 115–32. Sheffield: Sheffield Academic Press.

Hamilakis, Yannis
 2007 *The Nation and its Ruins: Antiquity, Archaeology, and National Imagination in Greece*. Oxford: Oxford University Press.

Hamilakis, Yannis
 2017 Who Are You Calling Mycenaean? Available at: https://www.lrb.co.uk/blog/2017/08/10/yannis-hamilakis/who-are-you-calling-mycenaean/. Accessed: September 27, 2017.

Harrington, Nicola
 2013 *Living with the Dead: Ancestor Worship and Mortuary Ritual in Ancient Egypt*. Oxford: Oxbow Books.

Hart, Laurie Kain
 1999 Culture, Civilization, and Demarcation at the Northwest Borders of Greece. *American Ethnologist* 26(1): 196–220.

Hasluck, Margaret
 1954 *The Unwritten Law in Albania*. Cambridge: Cambridge University Press.

Herzfeld, Michael
 1986 *Ours Once More: Folklore, Ideology, and the Making of Modern Greece*. New York: Pella.

Hobsbawm, Eric, and Terrence Ranger (eds.)
 1983 *The Invention of Tradition*. Cambridge: Cambridge University Press.

Hodgkin, Katharine, and Susannah Radstone (eds.)
 2006 *Memory, History, Nation: Contested Pasts*. London: Routledge.

Hoffman, M. A., H. Hamroush, R. O. Allen
 1986 A Model of Urban Development for the Hierakonpolis Region from Predynastic Through Old Kingdom Times. *Journal of the American Research Center in Egypt* 23: 175–87.

Hölbl, Günter
 2001 *A History of the Ptolemaic Empire*. London: Routledge.

Hopkins, Nicholas S., and Sohair R. Mehenna (eds.)
  2010 *Nubian Encounters: The Story of the Nubian Ethnological Survey 1961–1964*. Cairo: American University in Cairo Press.

Hornung, Erik
  1999 *Akhenaten and the Religion of Light*. Translated by David Lorton. Ithaca: Cornell University Press.

Howard, Philip N., and Muzammil M. Hussain
  2013 *Democracy's Fourth Wave? Digital Media and the Arab Spring*. Oxford: Oxford University Press.

Hoxha, Enver
  1984 *Laying the Foundations of the New Albania*. Tirana: Nentori Publishing House.

Hunwick, John, and Eve Troutt Powell
  2002 *The African Diaspora in the Mediterranean Lands of Islam*. Princeton: Marcus Wiener Publishers.

Hutchings, Raymond
  1992 Albania's Inter-War History as a Forerunner to the Communist Period. In *Perspectives on Albania*, edited by Tom Winnifrith, pp. 115–23. London: Palgrave Macmillan.

Hutton, Patrick H.
  1993 *History as an Art of Memory*. Hanover: University Press of New England.

Ibrahim, Hassan Ahmed
  1998 The Egyptian Empire, 1805–1885. In *The Cambridge History of Egypt, Vol. 2. Modern Egypt, from 1517 to the End of the Twentieth Century*, edited by M. W. Daly, pp. 198–216. Cambridge: Cambridge University Press.

Islam, Salma
  2017 Egypt's Indigenous Nubians Continue Their Long Wait to Return to Ancestral Lands. Available at: https://www.pri.org/stories/2017-07-24/egypt-s-indigenous-nubians-continue-their-long-wait-return-ancestral-lands. Accessed: September 23, 2017.

Jameson, Frederic
  1989 Nostalgia for the Present. *The South Atlantic Quarterly* 88(2): 517–37.

Janmyr, Maja
  2016 Egypt's Parliament Crushes Nubian Right of Return to Ancestral Lands. Available at: https://www.opendemocracy.net/north-africa-west-asia/maja-janmyr/egypt-s-parliament-crushes-nubian-right-of-return-to-ancestral-lands. Accessed: September 23, 2017.

Jones, Andrew
  2007 *Memory and Material Culture*. Cambridge: Cambridge University Press.

Jonker, Gerdien
  1995 *The Topography of Remembrance: The Dead, Tradition and Collective Memory in Mesopotamia*. Leiden: E. J. Brill.

Joyce, Rosemary
   2003   Concrete Memories: Fragments of the Past in the Classic Maya Present (500–1000 AD). In *Archaeologies of Memory*, edited by Susan Alcock and Ruth Van Dyke, pp. 104–25. Oxford: Blackwell.

Jubani, Bep
   1971   Varreza Tumulare e Çinamakut. *Buletin Arkeologjik* 1971(3): 41–56.

Jubani, Bep
   1995   Kultura e Bronzit të Hershëm në Tumat e Shkrelit. *Iliria* 25(1–2): 53–90.

Kadare, Ismail
   1990   *Broken April*. Lanham, MD: New Amsterdam Books.

Kadare, Ismail
   1998   *The Pyramid*. New York: Vintage Press.

Karkanas, Panagiotis
   2018   Stratigraphy and Site Formation Processes of Alepotrypa Cave. In *Neolithic Alepotrypa Cave in the Mani, Greece*, edited by Anastasia Papathanasiou, William A. Parkinson, Daniel J. Pullen, Michael L. Galaty, and Panagiotis Karkanas, pp. 24–32. Oxford: Oxbow Books.

Kemp, Barry
   1989   *Ancient Egypt: Anatomy of a Civilization*. London: Routledge.

Kennedy, John (ed.)
   1978   *Nubian Ceremonial Life: Studies in Islamic Syncretism and Cultural Change*. Los Angeles: The University of California Press.

Knapp, A. Bernard
   1988   *The History and Culture of Ancient Western Asia and Egypt*. Chicago: The Dorsey Press.

Koka, Aristotel
   2012   *Kultura Ilire e Tumave të Shtojit Shkodër* [Illyrian Culture in the Tumuli of Shtoj, Shkodër]. Tirana: Albanian Institute of Archaeology.

Kondi, Bledar
   2012   *Death and Ritual Crying: An Anthropological Approach to Albanian Funeral Customs*. Berlin: Logos.

Korkuti, Muzafer
   1981   Tuma e Patosit. *Iliria* 11(1): 7–55.

Korkuti, Muzafer
   2003   *Parailirët, Ilirët, Arbërit: Histori e Shkurtër* [Protoillyrians, Illyrians, Arbers: A Short History]. Tirana: Botimet Toena.

Korkuti, Muzafer
   2010   *Qytetërimi Neolitik dhe Eneolitik në Shqipëri* [Neolithic and Eneolithic Villages in Albania]. Tirana: Albanian Academy of Science.

Korres, George S.
  1984   The Relations between Crete and Messenia in the Late Middle Helladic and Early Late Helladic Period. In *The Minoan Thalassocracy: Myth and Reality*, edited by Robin Hägg and Nanno Marinatos, pp. 141–52. Stockholm: Svenska Institutet i Athen.

Korres, George S.
  1990   Excavations in the region of Pylos. In *EUMOUSIA. Ceramic and Iconographic Studies in Honour of Alexander Cambitoglou*, edited by J.-P. Descoeudres, J.P., pp. 1–11. Mediterannean Archaeology Supplement I. Sydney: Meditarch.

Küchler, Susanne, and Walter Melion
  1991   Introduction: Memory, Cognition, and Image Production. In *Images of Memory: On Remembering and Representation*, edited by S. Küchler and W. Melion, pp. 1–46. Washington, D.C.: Smithsonian Institution.

Küchler, Susanne
  2002   *Malanggan: Art, Memory and Sacrifice.* Oxford: Berg.

Kuijt, Ian
  2008   The Regeneration of Life: Neolithic Structures of Symbolic Remembering and Forgetting. *Current Anthropology* 49(2): 171–97.

Lambertz, Maximillian
  1973   Die Mythologie der Albaner. In *Wörterburg der Mythologie*, edited by H. W. Haussig, pp. 455–509.

Landsberg, Alison
  2004   *Prosthetic Memory: The Transformation of American Remembrance in the Age of Mass Culture.* New York: Columbia University Press.

Langgut, Dafna, Israel Finkelstein, and Thomas Litt
  2013   Climate and the Late Bronze Collapse: New Evidence from the Southern Levant. *Tel Aviv* 40: 149–75.

Lav, Daniel
  2012   *Radical Islam and the Revival of Medieval Theology.* Cambridge: Cambridge University Press.

Laziridis, Iosif, et al.
  2017   Genetic Origins of the Minoans and Mycenaeans. *Nature* 548: 214–18.

Lee, Wayne E.
  2013   Modern Settlement Patterns and the Built Landscape. In *Light and Shadow: Isolation and Interaction in the Shala Valley of Northern Albania*, edited by M. L. Galaty, O. Lafe, W. E. Lee, and Z. Tafilica, pp. 129–48. Monumenta Archaeologica 28. Los Angeles: UCLA Cotsen Institute of Archaeology Press.

Lee, Wayne E., Matthew Lubin, and Eduard Ndreca
  2013   Archival Historical Research. In *Light and Shadow: Isolation and Interaction in the Shala Valley of Northern Albania*, edited by M. L. Galaty, O. Lafe,

W. E. Lee, and Z. Tafilica, pp. 45–84. Monumenta Archaeologica 28. Los Angeles: UCLA Cotsen Institute of Archaeology Press.

Le Goff, Jacques
   1992 *History and Memory*. Translated by Steven Rendall and Elizabeth Claman. New York: Columbia University Press.

Lewis, Naphtali
   1986 *Greeks in Ptolemaic Egypt: Case Studies in the Social History of the Hellenistic World*. Oxford: Clarendon Press.

Lillios, Katina T.
   2008 *Heraldry for the Dead: Memory, Identity, and the Engraved Stone Plaques of Neolithic Iberia*. Austin: University of Texas Press.

Lillios, Katina T.
   2012 Mnemonic Practices of the Iberian Neolithic: The Production and Use of the Engraved Slate Plaque-Relics. In *Material Mnemonics: Everyday Memory in Prehistoric Europe*, edited by Katina T. Lillios and Vasileios Tsamis, pp. 40–72. Oxford: Oxbow Books.

Lister, Charles R.
   2015 *The Islamic State: A Brief Introduction*. Washington, D.C.: Brookings Institution Press.

Lord, Albert B.
   1948 Homer, Parry, and Huso. *American Journal of Archaeology* 52: 34–44.

Lowenthal, David
   1985 *The Past Is a Foreign Country*. Cambridge: Cambridge University Press.

Lowenthal, David
   1999 Preface. In *Materializing Culture: The Art of Forgetting*, edited by A. Forty and S. Küchler, xi–xiii. Oxford: Berg.

Lupack, Susan
   2014 Offerings for the Wanax in the Fr Tablets: Ancestor Worship and the Maintenance of Power in Mycenaean Greece. In *KE-RA-ME-JA: Studies Presented to Cynthia W. Shelmerdine*, edited by Dimitri Nakassis, Joann Gulizio, and Sarah A. James, pp. 163–77. Philadelphia: Institute for Aegean Prehistory Academic Press.

Mackridge, Peter
   2009 *Language and National Identity in Greece, 1766–1976*. Oxford: Oxford University Press.

Maeir, Aren M.
   2015 Exodus as *Mnemo-Narrative*: An Archaeological Perspective. In *Israel's Exodus in Transdisciplinary Perspective: Text, Archaeology, Culture, and Geoscience*, edited by Thomas E. Levy, Thomas Schneider, and William H. C. Propp, pp. 409–419. New York: Springer.

Magdy, Mirette
   2017   Egypt Tourism Revenue Bounces Back After Crippling Dollar Shortage. Bloomberg. Com. Available at: https://www.bloomberg.com/news/articles/2017-08-15/egypt-quarterly-tourism-revenue-triples-as-fx-crisis-fades-away. Accessed: September, 14, 2017.

Maglvieras, Simeon
   2013   Naming People: A Reflection of Identity and Resistance in a Greek Arvanite Village. *Mediterranean Review* 6(2): 151–88.

Malkin, Irad
   1994   Inside and Outside: Colonization and the Formation of the Mother City. In Apoikia. Studi in onore di G. Buchner. *AION. Archeologia e storia antica* 16: 1–9.

Mann, Stuart
   1933   Albanian Romani. *Journal of the Gypsy Lore Society* 12(1): 1–32.

Maran, Joseph, and Philipp W. Stockhammer (eds.)
   2012   *Materiality and Social Practice: Transformative Capacities of Intercultural Encounters*. Oxford: Oxbow Books.

Marangou, Christina
   1996   Assembling, Displaying, and Dissembling Neolithic and Eneolithic Figurines and Models. *Journal of European Archaeology* 4: 177–202.

Marsot, Afaf Lutfi al-Sayyid
   2007   *A History of Egypt: From the Arab Conquest to the Present*. Second Edition. Cambridge: Cambridge University Press.

Martin, Michael E.
   1992   Conquest and Commerce: Normans and Venetians in Albania. In *Perspectives on Albania*, edited by Tom Winnifrith, pp. 58–73. London: Palgrave Macmillan.

Martin-McAuliffe, Samantha L.
   2014   Lofkënd as a Cultivated Place. In *The Excavation of the Prehistoric Burial Tumulus at Lofkënd, Albania*, edited by John K. Papadopoulos, Sarah P. Morris, Lorenc Bejko, and Lynne A. Schepartz, pp. 537–53. Monumenta Archaeologica 34. Los Angeles: UCLA Cotsen Institute of Archaeology Press.

Marushiakova, Elena, and Vesselin Popov
   2013   'Gypsy' Groups in Eastern Europe: Ethnonyms vs. Professionyms. *Romani Studies* 23(1): 61–81.

Mazzini, Ilaria, Elsa Gliozzi, Michael L. Galaty, Lorenc Bejko, Laura Sadori, Ingeborg Soulié-Märche, Rexhep Koçi, Aurelien Van Welden, and Salvatore Bushati
   2016   Holocene Evolution of Lake Shkodra: Multidisciplinary Evidence for Forgotten Landscapes in Northern Albania. *Quaternary Science Reviews* 30: 1–11.

McIlvaine, Britney Kyle, Lynne A Schepartz, Clark Spencer Larsen, and Paul W, Sciulli
   2013   Evidence for Long-Term Migration on the Balkan Peninsula Using Dental and Cranial Nonmetric Data: Early Interaction between Corinth (Greece) and its Colony at Apollonia (Albania). *American Journal of Physical Anthropology* 153(2): 236–48.

Meinardus, Otto F.A.
   1999   *Two Thousand Years of Coptic Christianity*. Cairo: American University in Cairo Press.

Meskell, Lynn
   2002   *Private Life in New Kingdom Egypt*. Princeton: Princeton University Press.

Meskell, Lynn
   2003   Memory's Materiality: Ancestral Presence, Commemorative Practice and Disjunctive Locales. In *Archaeologies of Memory*, edited by Susan E. Alcock and Ruth van Dyke, pp. 34–55. Oxford: Blackwell.

Meskell, Lynn
   2004   *Object Worlds in Ancient Egypt: Material Biographies Past and Present*. Oxford: Berg.

Mexia, Angeliki
   2016   Building Practices in the Helladic Province of Mani during the Komnenian Period: The Assimilation of the Prevailing Trends in Church Architecture. Paper presented at the conference *Against Gravity: Building Practices in the Pre-Industrial World*. University of Pennsylvania, Philadelphia, 2015.

Millar, John Gilbert
   1976   The Albanians: Sixteenth-Century Mercenaries. *History Today* 26: 468–72.

Misztal, Barbara A.
   2003   *Theories of Social Remembering*. Philadelphia: Open University Press.

Mitchell, David
   2004   *Cloud Atlas: A Novel*. New York: Random House.

Mitchell, Timothy
   1988   *Colonising Egypt*. Cambridge: Cambridge University Press.

Montserrat, Dominic
   2000   *Akhenaten: History, Fantasy, and Ancient Egypt*. London: Routledge.

Morris, Ellen F.
   2008   Sacrifice for the State: First Dynasty Royal Funerals and the Rites at Macramallah's Rectangle. In *Performing Death: Social Analyses of Funerary Traditions in the Ancient Near East and Mediterranean*, edited by Nicola Laneri, pp. 15–38. Oriental Institute Seminars, Number 3. Chicago: The Oriental Institute of Chicago.

Morris, Ian
1987 Burial and Ancient Society: The Rise of the Greek City-State. Cambridge: Cambridge University Press.

Morris, Sarah P.
2014 Illyria Capta: Corinthian Wheelmade Pottery from the Lofkënd Tumulus. In *The Excavation of the Prehistoric Burial Tumulus at Lofkënd, Albania*, edited by John K. Papadopoulos, Sarah P. Morris, Lorenc Bejko, and Lynne A. Schepartz, pp. 323–24. Monumenta Archaeologica 34. Los Angeles: UCLA Cotsen Institute of Archaeology Press.

Morris, Sarah P., and John K. Papadopoulos
2014 Epilogue. From the Stone Age to the Recent Past: The Cultural Biography of a Landscape. In *The Excavation of the Prehistoric Burial Tumulus at Lofkënd, Albania*, edited by John K. Papadopoulos, Sarah P. Morris, Lorenc Bejko, and Lynne A. Schepartz, pp. 572–79. Monumenta Archaeologica 34. Los Angeles: UCLA Cotsen Institute of Archaeology Press.

Muçaj, Skendër
1993 Les Basiliques Paléochréiennes de Byllis et leur Architecture. *XL Corso di Cultura sull'Arte Ravennate e Bizantina*. Ravena.

Muçaj, Skendër
2010 Një Panoramë e Shkurtër Arkeologjike në Territoret e Shqipërisë nga Shek. IV deri në Gjysmën e parë të Shek. VII (Vazddimësi dhe Ndërprerje?). In *Aleks Buda një Jetë për Abanologjinë. Konferencë shkenkore*. Tirana: Academy of Science.

Muhaj, Ardian
2017 Skllavëria ndër Shqiptarë Gjatë Mesjetës. *Studime Historike* LXXI (LIV), 1–2: 61–82.

Mustafa, Mentor, Antonia Young, Michael L. Galaty, and Wayne E. Lee
2013 Spatial and Temporal Patterns in Kinship Relations: Descent, Marriage, and Feud. In *Light and Shadow: Isolation and Interaction in the Shala Valley of Northern Albania*, edited by M. L. Galaty, O. Lafe, W. E. Lee, and Z. Tafilica, pp. 85–106. Monumenta Archaeologica 28. Los Angeles: UCLA Cotsen Institute of Archaeology Press.

Nakassis, Dimitri
2012 Prestige and Interest: Feasting and the King in Mycenaean Pylos. *Hesperia* 81(1): 1–30.

Nakassis, Dimitri
2017 On Genetics and the Aegean Bronze Age. Available at: https://englianos.wordpress.com/2017/08/02/on-genetics-and-the-aegean-bronze-age/. Accessed: September 27, 2017.

Nallbani, Etleva
2008 Komani (Dalmace) (Albanie). Chronique de fouilles 2008, in *Les Destinées de l'Illyricum Meridional Pendant le haut Moyen Age*. MEFRM 120-22: 427–38.

Nallbani, Etleva, Maël Julien, Elvana Metalla
   2012   Koman (Dalmace). *Iliria* 36: 463–78.

Nallbani, Etleva, Luc Buchet, and Christophe Mathevot
   2013   Komani [Dalmace] (Albanie). *Chronique des activités archéologiques de l'École française de Rome [En ligne], Balkans*, mis en ligne le 07 mai 2013, consulté le 04 octobre 2016. URL: http://cefr.revues.org/951; DOI: 10.4000/cefr.951.

Navrátilová, Hana
   2011   Intertexuality in Ancient Egyptian Visitors' Graffiti? In *Narratives of Egypt and the Near East: Literary and Linguistic Approaches*, edited by Frederik Hagen, John Johnston, Wendy Monkhouse, Kathryn Piquette, John Tait, and Martin Worthington, pp. 257–68. Orientalia Lovaniensia Analecta 189. Leuven: Uitgeverij Peeters.

Nora, Pierre
   1996   *Realms of Memory: The Construction of the French Past. Volume I: Conflicts and Divisions*. English edition, edited by Lawrence D. Kritzman, translated by Arthur Goldhammer. New York: Columbia University Press.

Nora, Pierre
   1989   Between Memory and History: Les Lieux de Mémoire. *Representations* 26: 7–24.

Norwich, John Julius
   1997   *A Short History of Byzantium*. New York: Vintage Books.

Nur, Amos
   2008   *Apocalypse: Earthquakes, Archaeology, and the Wrath of God*. Princeton: Princeton University Press.

Nur, Amos, and Eric H. Cline
   2000   Poseidon's Horses: Plate Tectonics and Earthquake Storms in the Late Bronze Age Aegean and Eastern Mediterranean. *Journal of Archaeological Science* 27: 43–63.

O'Donnell, James S.
   1999   *A Coming of Age: Albania under Enver Hoxha*. New York: Columbia University Press.

O'Grady, Desmond
   1993   *Alternative Manners: Poems of C. P. Cavafy, English Versions*. Self-published manuscript, available at the Cavafy Museum, Alexandria, Egypt.

Ohueri, Chelsi West
   2016   *Mapping Race and Belonging in the Margins of Europe: Albanian, Romani, and Egyptian Sentiments*. Ph.D. thesis, Department of Anthropology, University of Texas at Austin.

Olivier, Laurent
   2012   *The Dark Abyss of Time: Archaeology and Memory*. Translated by Arthur Greenspan. Lanham: AltaMira Press

Ostrom, Thomas M.
1989 Three Catechisms for Social Memory. In *Memory: Interdisciplinary Approaches*, edited by Paul R. Solomon, George R. Goethals, Colleen M. Kelley, and Benjamin R. Stephens, pp. 201–20. New York: Springer Verlag.

Palaima, Thomas G.
1995 The Nature of the Mycenaean Wanax: Non-Indo-European Origins and Priestly Functions. In *The Role of the Ruler in the Prehistoric Aegean*, edited by Paul Rehak, pp. 119–39. Aegaeum11. Liège.

Papachristophorou, Marilena
2013 *Myth, Representation, and Identity: An Ethnography of Memory in Lipsi, Greece*. New York: Palgrave Macmillan.

Papadopoulos, John K.
2006 Mounds of Memory: Burial Tumuli in the Illyrian Landscape. In *New Directions in Albanian Archaeology: Studies Presented to Muzafer Korkuti*, edited by Lorenc Bejko and Richard Hidges, pp. 75–84. International Center for Albanian Archaeology Monograph Series No. 1. Tirana: ICAA.

Papadopoulos, John K.,
2014 The Beginning and the End of the Lofkënd Tumulus and the Prehistory of the *Kanun*. In *The Excavation of the Prehistoric Burial Tumulus at Lofkënd, Albania*, edited by John K. Papadopoulos, Sarah P. Morris, Lorenc Bejko, and Lynne A. Schepartz, pp. 554–60. Monumenta Archaeologica 34. Los Angeles: UCLA Cotsen Institute of Archaeology Press.

Papadopoulos, John K., Sarah P. Morris, Lorenc Bejko, and Lynne A. Schepartz
2014a Introduction. Lofkënd: The Site and Archaeological Objectives. In *The Excavation of the Prehistoric Burial Tumulus at Lofkënd, Albania*, edited by John K. Papadopoulos, Sarah P. Morris, Lorenc Bejko, and Lynne A. Schepartz, pp. 3–12. Monumenta Archaeologica 34. Los Angeles: UCLA Cotsen Institute of Archaeology Press.

Papadopoulos, John K., Lorenc Bejko, and Sarah P. Morris
2014b The Excavation of the Tumulus. In *The Excavation of the Prehistoric Burial Tumulus at Lofkënd, Albania*, edited by John K. Papadopoulos, Sarah P. Morris, Lorenc Bejko, and Lynne A. Schepartz, pp. 16–41. Monumenta Archaeologica 34. Los Angeles: UCLA Cotsen Institute of Archaeology Press.

Papalexandrou, Amy
2003 Memory Tattered and Torn: Spolia in the Heartland of Byzantine Hellenism. In *Archaeologies of Memory*, edited by Ruth Van Dyke and Susan E. Alcock, pp. 56–80. Oxford: Blackwell.

Papathanasiou, Anastasia
2001 *A Bioarchaeological Analysis of Neolithic Alepotrypa Cave, Greece*. British Archaeological Report S961. Oxford: British Archaeological Reports.

Papathanasiou, Anastasia, William A. Parkinson, Daniel J. Pullen, Michael L. Galaty, and Panagiotis Karkanas (eds.)
2018 *Neolithic Alepotrypa Cave in the Mani, Greece*. Oxford: Oxbow Books.

Papathanassopoulos, George A. (ed.)
 1996 *Neolithic Culture in Greece*. Athens: N. P. Goulandris Foundation

Papoulias, Constantina
 2003 From the Agora to the Junkyard: Social Memory and Unconscious Materialities. In *Regimes of Memory*, edited by Susannah Radstone and Katherine Hodgkin, pp. 114–30. London: Routledge.

Parkinson, William A., and Paul R. Duffy
 2007 Fortifications and Enclosures in European Prehistory: A Cross-Cultural Perspective. *Journal of Archaeological Research* 15: 97–141.

Parkinson, William A., and Michael L. Galaty
 2007 Primary and Secondary States in Perspective: An Integrated Approach to State Formation in the Prehistoric Aegean. *American Anthropologist* 109: 113–29.

Parkinson, William A., Anastasia Papathanasiou, Michael L. Galaty, Daniel J. Pullen, Panagiotis Karkanas, and George A. Papathanassopoulos
 2017 "Diros in Context: Alepotrypa Cave and Ksagounaki Promontory in the Neolithic Period." In *Communities, Landscapes, and Interaction in Neolithic Greece*, edited by Apostolis Sarris, Eleni Kalogiropoulou, Tuna Kalayci, and Lia Karimali, pp. 126–36. Archaeological Series 20. Ann Arbor: International Monographs in Prehistory.

Pearson, Owen
 2006 *Albania as Dictatorship and Democracy: From Isolation to the Kosovo War, 1946–1998*. London: I.B. Tauris.

Perlès, Catherine
 2001 *The Early Neolithic in Greece: The First Farming Communities in Europe*. Cambridge: Cambridge University Press.

Pine, Frances, Deema Kaneff, and Haldis Haukanes (eds.)
 2004 *Memory, Politics, and Religion: The Past Meets the Present in Europe*. Halle Studies in Anthropology of Eurasia 4. Munich: LIT Verlag.

Popham, Mervyn R., E. Touloupa, and L. Hugh Sackett
 1982 The Hero of Lefkandi. *Antiquity* 56: 169–74.

Poulou-Papadimitriou, Natalia, Elli Tzavella, and Jeremy Ott
 2012 Burial Practices in Byzantine Greece: Archaeological Evidence and Methodological Problems for its Interpretation. In *Rome, Constantinople and Newly Converted Europe: Archaeological and Historical Evidence*, edited by Maciej Salamon, Marcin Wołoszyn, Alexander Musin, and Perica Špehar, pp. 377–428. Frühzeit Ostmitteleuropas, vol. I, Krakow-Leipzig-Rzeszów-Warszawa.

Prendi, Frano, and Adem Bunguri
 2008 *Bronzi i Hershëm në Shqipëri* [The Early Bronze Age in Albania]. Prishtinë: Albanian Institute of Archaeology.

Pullen, Daniel J., Michael L. Galaty, William A. Parkinson, Wayne E. Lee, and Rebecca M. Seifried
    2018   The Diros Project, 2011–2013: Surface Survey and Site Collection in Diros Bay. In *Neolithic Alepotrypa Cave in the Mani, Greece*, edited by Anastasia Papathanasiou, William A. Parkinson, Daniel J. Pullen, Michael L. Galaty, and Panagiotis Karkanas, pp. 407–25. Oxford: Oxbow Books.

Quibell, James E., and F.W. Green
    1902   *Hierakonpolis II*. London: Bernard Quaritch.

Redford, Donald B.
    1984   *Akhenaten: The Heretic King*. Princeton: Princeton University Press.

Reid, Donald Malcolm
    2003   *Whose Pharaohs? Archaeology, Museums, and Egyptian National Identity from Napoleon to World War I*. Los Angeles: University of California Press.

Reid, Donald Malcolm
    2015   *Contesting Antiquity in Egypt: Archaeologies, Museums, and the Struggle for Identities from World War I to Nasser*. Oxford: Oxford University Press.

Rentz, George S.
    2004   *The Birth of the Islamic Reform Movement in Saudi Arabia*. London: Arabian Publishing.

Republika e Shqiperisë Instituti i Statistikave (INSTAT)
    2017   Arrivals of Foreign Citizens According to Regions (2000–2016). Available at: http://www.instat.gov.al/en/themes/tourism.aspx. Accessed: October 12, 2017.

Rowlands, Michael
    1993   The Role of Memory in the Transmission of Culture. *World Archaeology* 25(2): 141–51.

Royal, Jeffrey
    2012   The Illyrian Coastal Exploration Program, First Interim Report (2007–9): The Roman and Late-Roman Finds. *American Journal of Archaeology* 116.3: 405–60.

Rugg, Dean S.
    1994   Communist Legacies in the Albanian Landscape. *Geographical Review* 84(1): 59–73.

Ruka, Rudenc
    2006   Prehistoric Figurines in Albania: A Review. In *New Directions in Albanian Archaeology: Studies Presented to Muzafer Korkuti*, edited by Lorenc Bejko and Richard Hodges, pp. 56–64. International Center for Albanian Archaeology Monograph Series No. 1. Tirana: ICAA.

Saitas, Yanis
    2009   The Cemeteries of the Mani in the Mediaeval and Later Periods: A First Contribution. In *Sparta and Laconia: From Prehistory to Pre-Modern*,

edited by William G. Cavanagh, C. Gallou, and M. Georgiadis, pp. 371–85. British School at Athens Studies, Vol. 16. London: British School at Athens.

Schacter, D. L.
1996 *Searching for Memory: The Brain, the Mind, and the Past.* New York: Basic Books.

Schama, Simon
1995 *Landscape and Memory.* New York: Knopf.

Scheidel, Walter
2011 The Roman Slave Supply. In T*he Cambridge World History of Slavery, 1: The Ancient Mediterranean World*, edited by K. Bradley and P. Cartledge, pp. 287–310. Cambridge: Cambridge University Press.

Schepartz, Lynne A.
2014 Bioarchaeology of the Lofkënd Tumulus. In *The Excavation of the Prehistoric Burial Tumulus at Lofkënd, Albania*, edited by John K. Papadopoulos, Sarah P. Morris, Lorenc Bejko, and Lynne A. Schepartz, pp. 139–83. Monumenta Archaeologica 34. Los Angeles: UCLA Cotsen Institute of Archaeology Press.

Schon, Robert
2010 Think Locally, Act Globally: Mycenaean Elites and the Late Bronze Age World-System. In *Archaic State Interaction*, edited by William A. Parkinson and Michael L. Galaty, pp. 213–36. Santa Fe: School for Advanced Research Press.

Schroeder, S.
2001 Secondary Disposal of the Dead: Cross-Cultural Codes. *World Cultures* 12(1):77–93.

Schwandner-Sievers, Stephanie
1998 Humiliation and Reconciliation in Northern Albania: The Logic of Feuding in Symbolic and Diachronic Perspectives. In *Dynamics of Violence: Processes of Escalation and De-Escalation in Violent Group Conflicts*, edited by Georg Elwert, Stephan Feuchtwang, and Dieter Neubert, pp. 133–52. Berlin: Duncker and Humblot.

Schwandner-Sievers, Stephanie
1999 The Albanian Aromanians' Awakening: Identity Politics and Conflicts in Post-Communist Albania. ECMI Working Paper #3. Flensburg: European Centre for Minority Issues.

Schwandner-Sievers, Stephanie
2001 The Enactment of 'Tradition': Albania Constructions of Identity, Violence, and Power in Times of Crisis. In *Anthropology of Violence and Conflict*, edited by Bettina Schmidt and Ingo W. Schröder, pp. 97–120. London: Routledge.

Schwandner-Sievers, Stephanie
  2003   Albanians, Albanianism, and the Strategic Subversion of Stereotypes. In *The Balkans and the West*, edited by Andrew Hammond, pp. 110–26. Hampshire: Ashgate.

Schwandner-Sievers, Stephanie
  2004   Times Past: References for the Construction of Local Order in Present-Day Albania. In *Balkan Identities: Nation and Memory*, edited by Maria Todorova, pp. 103–28. New York: New York University Press.

Schwartzstein, Peter
  2017   The Greatest Clash in Egyptian Archaeology May Be Fading, But Anger Lives On. *Smithsonian Magazine*. Available at: https://www.smithsonianmag.com/history/greatest-clash-egyptian-archaeology-fading-anger-lives-on-180967452/. Accessed: December 15, 2017.

Scott, James C.
  2009   *The Art of Not Being Governed: An Anarchist History of Upland Southeast Asia*. New Haven: Yale University Press.

Seferis, George, Edmund Keeley, and Philip Sherrard
  1967   *George Seferis: Collected Poems, 1924–1955*. Bilingual Edition. Princeton: Princeton University Press.

Seremetakis, C. Nadia
  1991   *The Last Word: Women, Death, and Divination in Inner Mani*. Chicago: University of Chicago Press.

Shackel, Paul
  2001   *Myth, Memory, and the Making of the American Landscape*. Gainesville: University Press of Florida.

Shipley, D. Graham J.
  1997   'The Other Lacedaimonians': The Dependent Perioikic Poleis of Laconia and Messenia. In *The Polis as an Urban Centre and as a Political Community*, edited by Mogens Herman Hansen, pp. 189–281. Acts of the Copenhagen Polis Centre 4. Copenhagen: Royal Danish Academy of Sciences and Letters.

Shipley, D. Graham J.
  2006   Sparta and Its Perioikic Neighbours: A Century of Reassessment. *Hermathena* 181: 51–82.

Shpuza, Saimir
  2006   The Roman Colonies of South Illyria: A Review. In *New Directions in Albanian Archaeology: Studies Presented to Muzafer Korkuti*, edited by Lorenc Bejko and Richard Hodges, pp. 164–68. International Center for Albanian Archaeology Monograph Series No. 1. Tirana: ICAA.

Sinopoli, Carla M.
  2003   Echoes of Empire: Vijayanagara and Historical Memory, Vijayanagara as Historical Memory. In *Archaeologies of Memory*, edited by Ruth Van Dyke and Susan E. Alcock, pp. 17–33. Oxford: Blackwell.

Smith, Matt
  2014   Egypt Tourist Numbers to Rise 5–10 Pct in 2014 –Minister. Reuters.com. Available at: https://www.reuters.com/article/egypt-tourism/egypt-tourist-numbers-to-rise-5-10-pct-in-2014-minister-idUSL5N0RC3CF20140911. Accessed: September 14, 2017.

Souvatzi, Stella
  2008   *A Social Archaeology of Households in Neolithic Greece. An Anthropological Approach.* Cambridge: Cambridge University Press.

Stapleton, Lyssa C.
  2014   The Prehistoric Burial Customs. In *The Excavation of the Prehistoric Burial Tumulus at Lofkënd, Albania*, edited by John K. Papadopoulos, Sarah P. Morris, Lorenc Bejko, and Lynne A. Schepartz, pp. 193–226. Monumenta Archaeologica 34. Los Angeles: UCLA Cotsen Institute of Archaeology Press.

Stock, Brian
  1987   *The Implications of Literacy: Written Language and Models of Interpretation in the 11th and 12th Centuries.* Princeton: Princeton University Press.

Stocker, Sharon R.
  2009   *Illyrian Apollonia: Toward a New Ktisis and Developmental History of the Colony.* Ph.D. dissertation, University of Cincinnati, Department of Classics.

Stocker, Sharon R., and Jack L. Davis
  2006   The Earliest History of Apollonia: Heroic Reflections From Beyond the Acropolis. In *New Directions in Albanian Archaeology: Studies Presented to Muzafer Korkuti*, edited by Lorenc Bejko and Richard Hodges, pp. 85–93. International Center for Albanian Archaeology Monograph Series No. 1. Tirana: ICAA.

Stratouli, Georgia, Sevi Triantaphyllou, Tasos Bekiaris, and Nikos Katsikaridis
  2010   The Manipulation of Death: A Burial Area at the Neolithic Settlement of Avgi, NW Greece. *Documenta Praehistorica* 37: 95–104.

Sugarman, Jane C.
  1997   *Engendering Song: Singing and Subjectivity at Prespa Albanian Weddings.* Chicago: University of Chicago Press.

Sutton, David E.
  1998   *Memories Cast in Stone: The Relevance of the Past in Everyday Life.* Oxford: Berg.

Tafilica, Zamir
  2013   The Sacred Landscape of Shala. In *Light and Shadow: Isolation and Interaction in the Shala Valley of Northern Albania*, edited by M. L. Galaty, O. Lafe, W. E. Lee, and Z. Tafilica, pp. 149–62. Monumenta Archaeologica 28. Los Angeles: UCLA Cotsen Institute of Archaeology Press.

Thalloczy, Ludovicus de, Cinstantius Jireček, and Emilianus de Sufflay
  2002   *Acta et Diplomata Res Albaniae Mediae Aetatis Illustrantia*. Two Volumes. Shtypi "Dukagjini"–Pejë, Tirana.

Todorov, Tzvetan
  1999   *The Conquest of America: The Question of the Other*. Norman: University of Oklahoma Press.

Triantaphyllou, Sevi
  1999   Prehistoric Makriyalos: A Story from the Fragments. In *Neolithic Society in Greece*, edited by Paul Halstead, pp. 128–35. Sheffield: Sheffield Academic Press.

Trubeta, Sevasti
  2005   Balkan Egyptians and Gypsy/Roma Discourse. *Nationalities Papers: The Journal of Nationalism and Ethnicity* 33(1): 71–95.

Tsartsidou, Georgia
  2018   Phytolith Analysis from the Sediments of Alepotrypa Cave. In *Neolithic Alepotrypa Cave in the Mani, Greece*, edited by Anastasia Papathanasiou, William A. Parkinson, Daniel J. Pullen, Michael L. Galaty, and Panagiotis Karkanas, pp. 360–72. Oxford: Oxbow Books.

Tyldesley, Joyce
  1996   *Hatchepsut: The Female Pharaoh*. London: Viking.

United States Department of State
  2006   International Religious Freedom Report. Bureau of Democracy, Human Rights, and Labor. Available at: https://www.state.gov/j/drl/rls/irf/2006/71383.htm. Accessed: December 28, 2016.

Van der Spek, Kees
  2012   *The Modern Neighbors of Tutankhamun: History, Life, and Work in the Villages of the Theban West Bank*. Cairo: American University in Cairo Press.

Van Dyke, Ruth, and Susan E. Alcock
  2003   Archaeologies of Memory: An Introduction. In *Archaeologies of Memory*, edited by Ruth Van Dyke and Susan E. Alcock, pp. 1–13. Oxford: Blackwell.

Van Gerven Oei, Vincent W.J.
  2015   *Lapidari, Volume I: Texts*. Brooklyn: Punctum Books.

Vansina, Jan M.
  1985   *Oral Tradition as History*. Madison: University of Wisconsin Press.

Vickers, Miranda
  1999   *The Albanians: A Modern History*. I.B. Tauris, London.

Von Falkenhausen, Vera
  1997   Bishops. In *The Byzantines*, edited by G. Cavallo, pp. 172–96. Chicago: University of Chicago Press.

Wachtel, Nathan, Marie-Noëlle Bourguet, and Lucette Valensi (eds.)
  1990 *Between History and Memory*. Reading: Harwood Academic Publishers.

Wahab, Mohamed Fikri Abdul
  2010 Problems of Nubian Migration. In *Nubian Encounters: The Story of the Nubian Ethnological Survey 1961–1964*, edited by Nicholas S. Hopkins and Sohair R. Mehenna, pp. 209–26. Cairo: The American University in Cairo Press.

Wengrow, David
  2006 *The Archaeology of Early Egypt: Social Transformations in North-East Africa, 10,000 to 2650 BC*. Cambridge: Cambridge University Press.

Whitehouse, Harvey
  1992 Memorable Religions: Transmission, Codification and Change in Divergent Melanesian Contexts. *Man* 27(4): 777–97.

Wickett, Elizabeth
  2010 *For the Living and the Dead: The Funerary Laments of Upper Egypt, Ancient and Modern*. London: I.B. Tauris.

Wilkes, John J.
  1992 *The Illyrians*. Oxford: Blackwell.

Wilkes, John J.
  2006 The Significance of Road-Stations for the Archaeology of Albania in the Roman Era. In *New Directions in Albanian Archaeology: Studies Presented to Muzafer Korkuti*, edited by Lorenc Bejko and Richard Hodges, pp. 169–76. International Center for Albanian Archaeology Monograph Series No. 1. Tirana: ICAA.

Wilkinson, Toby A. H.
  1993 The Identification of Tomb B1 at Abydos: Refuting the Existence of a King *Ro/*Iry-Hor. *Journal of Egyptian Archaeology* 79: 241–43.

Wilkinson, Toby A. H.
  1999 *Early Dynastic Egypt*. London: Routledge.

Williams, Howard
  2003 Introduction. In *Archaeologies of Remembrance: Death and Memory in Past Societies*, edited by Howard Williams, pp. 1–24. New York: Kluwer Academic/Plenum Publishers.

Winnifrith, Tom
  1992 Albania and the Ottoman Empire. In *Perspectives on Albania*, edited by Tom Winnifrith, pp. 74–88. London: Palgrave Macmillan.

Winter, Michael
  1998 Ottoman Egypt, 1525–1609. In *The Cambridge History of Egypt, Vol. 2. Modern Egypt, from 1517 to the End of the Twentieth Century*, edited by M. W. Daly, pp. 1–33. Cambridge: Cambridge University Press.

Wright, James C.
  2001 Factionalism and the Origins of Leadership and Identity in Mycenaean Society. Abstract, *Bulletin of the Institute of Classical Studies, University of London*. Proceedings of the Mycenaean Seminar, no. 45, p. 182.

Wright, James C. (ed.)
  2004 *The Mycenaean Feast*. Hesperia 73. Princeton: American School of Classical Studies at Athens.

Yates, Frances
  1966 *The Art of Memory*. London: Routledge and Kegan Paul.

Yoffee, Norman
  2007 Peering into the Palimpsest: An Introduction to the Volume. In *Negotiating the Past in the Past: Identity, Memory and Landscape in Archaeological Research*, edited by Norman Yoffee, pp. 1–9. Tucson: University of Arizona Press

Young, James E.
  1994 *The Texture of Memory: Holocaust Memorials and Meaning*. New Haven, CT: Yale University Press.

Zemon, Rubin
  2001 History of the Balkan Egyptians. In *Interculturalism and the Bologna Process*, Council of Europe.

Index

16th St. Baptist Church, 159
9/11, 23

Abydos, 40
Ahmose, 47
Akhenaten (Amenhotep IV), 48–50, 50–51, 64, 72, 136
Akhenaten, 36
Akhetaten (Amarna), 49–50
Alabama, 159–162
Al-Azhar University, 37, 59, 142
Alepotrypa Cave, 73–76, 91, 92, 95, 105
Alexander the Great, 34, 52–53, 86, 113–114
Alexandria, 34, 53
Amheida, 62
Annales School, 2, 22
Apollonia, 102, 108, 110–11, 113–14, 115, 117, 129
Arabic, 59
Arabs, 58, 63, 64, 90, 156–57
Avaris, 47
Areopolis, 73, 96, 97
Argolid, 77–78, 83, 109
ars memoriae, 6
Arvanites, 97, 144–45
Arvanitika, 144

Assman, Jan, xxi, xxii, 3, 7, 10, 14, 19, 35, 38, 47–50, 52
Aswan High Dam, 137
atheism, 129, 155
Athens, 96, 98
Avenue of the Sphinxes, *141*

Badarian, 38
Bajrak, 125–26
Bamiyan Buddhas, 152
Basil, 119
Battle of Actium, 87
Battle of Navarino, 62, 69
Battle of Qadesh, 50, 136
Bedouin, 58
Bektashism, 125
Bogomils, 90, 103, 125
Bosnia, xv–xviii, 26, 27, 31; pyramids, xvi–xviii, 18, 28–29
Bourdieu, Pierre, 6, 19, 21
Braudel, Fernand, 22
bunkers, 130
Byzantine Empire, 90, 91
Byzantium, 88

cadre matériel, 3, 8, 19
Cairo, 60

197

caliphate, 151, 152, 154, 155
Cape Tanairon, 73, 76, 87
Catholic priests, 120
Cavafy, C. P., 33–35
Cetina, 78, 107–8, 109
Christianity, 1, 3–4, 8, 15, 26, 37, 54–55, 83, 88, 102–3, 116, 117
churches, Greek, 89–90, 91. *See also* Greek Orthodox Church
collective imaginary (imaginaire), 21, 24, 25, 63, 135
Communism, 27, 126, 128–31
Confederate monuments, 163
Constantine the Great, 55, 88, 89, 116
Constantinople, 67, 88, 91, 93, 94
Coptic Christianity, 36, 55–59, 60, 61, 63
Coptic priests, 57, 63
Corinth, 110
corporate versus network states, 68
crisis, 17, 20–21, 23, 117
Croatia, xiii–xv, cviii
Crypto-Christianity, 125, 129

damnatio memoriae, 8, 48
Damos, 80
Dayton Accords, 27
Deir el Medina, 53
Dieser-Dieseru, 48
Diocletian, 116
Diros, 69, 73, 75, 85–86
Doxa, 19, 23, 44
Drin River, 115
Durkheim, 1, 19
dyophysites, 55, 89

Edmund Pettus Bridge, 160
Egyptian priests, 43, 48–49
Egyptian unification 36, 38–39, 40, 46
elephantine, 44, 136
engram, defined, 5, 6, 7, 8
Epidamnus, 102, 114

Fara, 145
feasting, 80
feud, 100, 102, 121, 123, 126, 127, 131
Fis, 119, 126, 127

forgetting, 3, 6, 8, 30. *See also* memory
Foucault, Michel, xxii, 16
Freud, Sigmund, 6, 35, 50, 51

genealogy, 10
Gjamë, 121–22, 129
Gjeçovi, Shtjefën, 101–2
Golden Dawn, 143
Greek Orthodox Church, 69, 94, 143
Greek priests, 90–91
Greek War of Independence, 70, 96, 97, 144
Greek War of Rebellion 69, 95

habitus, 6
Halbwachs, Maurice, 1–2, 3, 5, 9, 10, 19, 29
Hatshepsut, 36, 48, 51, 136
helots, 69, 84
heritage, xxii, 18135, 142, 146, 149
heterodoxy, 19–20, 22, 23, 44
Hierakonpolis, 39, 40, 42
history: oral history, xxi, xxii, 1, 9, 120–21; written versus oral, 9
Holocaust, 4
Homer, 68, 81, 92
Horus, 38, 44, 56
Hoxha, Enver, 31, 103, 118, 127–32, 134, 147, 150
Hyksos, 46, 47, 136

iconoclasm, 57, 89, 90
identify, defined, 25, 40
Illyria, 85, 89, 107
Illyrians, 102, 111, 112–13, 114, 127–28, 146
imagined communities, 15, 21
Isis, 44, 56
Islam, 36, 58, 59, 63, 89, 104, 152
Islamic state, 135, 142, 150–54

Jevgs, 147–49
Jews: Albanian, 147; Alexandrian, 35
Justinian, 90, 116, 137

Kadare, Ismail, 133, 134
Kalymnos, 70, 94

Kamenicë, 108, 109
Kanun, 99–102, 118, 120, 129, 131, 133, 146, 147
Kapodistrias, Ioannis 96–97
Karnak, 52
King, Martin Luther, Jr., 159, 160
kinship, 10, 12
Knossos, 79
Koman Culture, 116
Kosovo, 27, 115, 126, 149
Ksagounaki, 75–76, 78, 79
Kush, 136

Lake Nasser 58, 137
Lakonia, 84
lamentation, 44, 51, 56–57, 70, 82, 94–95, 112, 121–24, 129
landscapes, defined, 8, 10, 11, 21, 29
Lapidar, 129
Lefkandi, 83
Lekë Dukagjini, 100, 101, 119
Levant, 44
Libya, 44
lieux de mémoire, 4, 8, 37, 45, 47, 69, 80, 85, 97, 109, 113, 117, 139, 151, 154
Linear B, 68
Lipsi, 94
Lofkënd, 102, 108, 110, 112, 115
loss of home syndrome, 139, 140
Luxor, 52

Mamluks, 37, 59–60, 63, 64
Mani, 70, 73, 83, 84, 87, 88, 91, 92, 95, 96, 109
Margeliç, 113
Masada, 4
Mastaba, 43
Mavromichalis, Petrobey, 96–97
Mediterranean Sea, xxiii, 35, 67
Mehmed Ali, 35, 58, 60–62, 63, 64, 95, 118, 125, 137, 142, 157
Mehmed II, 93
memory: collective, defined, xx–xxii, 1–26; communities, defined, 3; counter, defined, xxii, 16–18, 28; cues, defined, xxi, 5–8, 41–42; cultural, defined, xxii, 3; episodic, 4–5, 6–7; individual, xx–xxi, 6; types, 4–5, 6. *See also* forgetting
memory workers, defined, 19, 29, 49
Memphis, 39, 52
Mesopotamia, 14–15
Messenia, 77, 78, 80, 83, 84
Minoans, 68, 77, 78–79, 82–83, 87
mirologia, 70, 121
monasticism, 57, 60, 63, 117
Monophysites, 55, 89
monuments, 15
mortuary practices, xxi, xxiii, 11, 38–39, 40–43, 56, 71–72, 82–83, 92
Moses, 50
Moulid, 138–139
mummification, 36, 42, 46
Muranë, 101, 102, 120, 146
Muslim Brotherhood, 142
Mycenae, 66, 70, 77, 80
Mycenaeans, 50, 68, 76, 79, 80, 82–83

Naqada, 38–39, 40, 42, 44, 45, 72
Narmer, 39
nation-building, 61, 63, 69, 85, 89, 93, 127, 149, 150
nationalism, 21, 25, 46, 62, 63
nation-states, 15, 25, 127
Nauplion, 96–97
Near East, 10–11, 72
Neolithic, 10–11, 67, 71, 104–7; figurines, 105–7
Nile River, 38, 137
Nimrud, 154
Nomes, 45
nostalgia, defined, 15, 20–21, 23–25, 46, 88
Nubia, 40, 42, 44, 58, 136–40
Nubian Ethnological Survey, 137–39, 140

opinion, 19, 23, 26, 44
orthodoxy, 19–20, 22, 23
Osiris, 44, 47, 52, 53, 56
Ottoman Empire xxiii, 1761, 63, 67, 73, 91, 93, 96, 101, 103, 119, 124–26, 131, 157

200   *Index*

Palmyra, 150, 151, 154
Papathanassopoulos, George, 73–75
parallel processing, defined, xxi, 5, 7, 9, 13
Paulicians, 90
Pelasgians, 145, 146
perioichoi, 84–85, 87
Persia, 52, 53
phenomenology, 3
Philae, 58, 136–37
place-making, 3, 8
plastered skulls, 10–11, 72
poleis, 84, 88, 92
political control, defined, xxiii, 29, 31
polyphony, 121
practice theory, 18–21
Proskynemata, 54, 136
Pylos/Palace of Nestor, 77, 78
pyramids, 43, 47; Bosnian, xvi–xviii, 18, 28–29
Pyrrichos, 86, 87

Qurna, 140–141

Ragusa, 118
Ramesid Kings, 50, 52
Ramses II (the Great), 36, 50, 136
Ramses III, 50, 68
Rayya, 151
Republika Srpska, xiii–xvi
Roma, 147
Romans, 87, 88, 90, 102, 114–16
Rome, 54–55, 116

Salafism, 142, 152, 153, 155
Saqqara, 43
Sarajevo, xvi
schemata, defined, 5, 7
Sea Peoples, 50
Sed festival, 40
Seferis, George, 67, 70
Selma, Alabama, 159–62
Seth, 44, 47, 53, 56
Shkodra, 107, 114, 126, 146

Shkumbin River, 87, 115
Shtoj, 107–8
Sinai, 44
Siwa Oasis, 52
Skanderbeg, Geroge Kastriot, 100, 103, 124, 144, 146
slavery, 148
Sparta, 69, 84, 87
Starkville, Mississippi, 163–64
states, defined, xxi–xxii, 11, 12, 113, 127

Tahrir Square, 4
Taliban, 152
temples, 14, 43, 45
Teuta, 114, 118
Tholos, 77
time, 22, 26
Tourkokratia, 69, 93, 94, 97, 131, 143
tourism, 135, 142–43, 146
tumuli (burial mounds), 76–77, 83, 102, 107–10, 115
Tuthmosis I, 48
Tuthmosis III, 48

U.S. Civil War, 17
Ulcinj, 148

Valley of the Kings, 51
Vatican, 120
Venice, 119
Venizelos, Eleftherios 62
Verga, 95
Via Egnatia, 114–15
Vlachs, 147
Voidokilia, 77, 85
Vraka, 147

Wahhabism, 62, 142, 152
Wanax, 79, 80, 81, 85

Yugoslavia, xiv, 26–27

Zalongo, 69
Zogu, Ahmed, 126

Lightning Source UK Ltd.
Milton Keynes UK
UKHW01n0744060918
328418UK00006B/207/P